D0449599

NO LONGER PROPERTY OF
ANYTHINK LIBRARIES/
RANGEVIEW LIBRARY DISTRICT

OFFBEAT BRIDE

 Create a Wedding
That's Authentically YOU

ARIEL MEADOW STALLINGS

SEAL PRESS

NEW YORK

Copyright 2019 by Ariel Meadow Stallings
Cover design by Chin-Yee Lai
Cover image by © twomeows/Getty Images; NTYS/Shutterstock.com
Cover copyright © 2019 Hachette Book Group, Inc.

Hachette Book Group supports the right to free expression and the value of copyright. The purpose of copyright is to encourage writers and artists to produce the creative works that enrich our culture.

The scanning, uploading, and distribution of this book without permission is a theft of the author's intellectual property. If you would like permission to use material from the book (other than for review purposes), please contact permissions@hbgusa.com. Thank you for your support of the author's rights.

Seal Press
Hachette Book Group
1290 Avenue of the Americas, New York, NY 10104
sealpress.com
@sealpress

Printed in the United States of America

Originally published in trade paperback and ebook in February 2010
Third Trade Paperback Edition: September 2019

Published by Seal Press, an imprint of Perseus Books, LLC, a subsidiary of Hachette Book Group, Inc. The Seal Press name and logo is a trademark of the Hachette Book Group.

The Hachette Speakers Bureau provides a wide range of authors for speaking events. To find out more, go to www.hachettespeakersbureau.com or call (866) 376-6591.

The publisher is not responsible for websites (or their content) that are not owned by the publisher.

Print book interior design by Linda Mark.

Library of Congress Cataloging-in-Publication Data has been applied for.

ISBNs: 978-1-58005-924-4 (paperback), 978-1-58005-925-1 (ebook)

LSC-C

10 9 8 7 6 5 4 3 2 1

Dedicated to Octavian Orion

CONTENTS

part three: In the Thick of It

part four: The Trifecta of Wedding Conflict: Loved Ones, Ceremony & Sanity

part five: The Wedding Itself

part six: As the Dust Settles

INTRODUCTION

How I Learned to Stop Worrying & Love the Bride

WHEN I SAT DOWN TO WRITE *OFFBEAT BRIDE* IN 2005, IT WAS A DIFFER-
ent era. It was the time of Friendster and Myspace. A time when
having a website for your wedding was still a new and nerdy idea—I
mean, you had to hand-code it! It was a time when marriage equality still felt like a distant, rainbow-striped dream in the hearts of
progressive Americans. A time before most of us knew the word
"cisgender." It was a time when many of you reading this may have
been teenagers!

Needless to say, a LOT has changed since *Offbeat Bride*'s first edition. For me, the little website I launched to promote my book tour
ended up becoming a global wedding planning resource that's been
used by 50 million people over the past twelve years. Offbeatbride
.com went on to spawn several other web publications, and in my
attempt to sell a few copies of a book, I accidentally founded a
media company that's kept me busy for almost fifteen years. Oops?

Technology has advanced in ways that, even as a nerd back in the
mid-2000s, I never could have imagined. Back then, you felt high
tech if your wedding favors were a CD-ROM of wedding songs
that you'd downloaded from a questionable online source. (Aww,
cute!) Now, we all deal with ubiquitous smartphone use, wedding
hashtags, app push notification overwhelm, and navigating social

media etiquette faux pas. (And here I thought I was fancy for asking my wedding guests to upload their wedding photos to Flickr . . .)

More joyfully, marriage equality is now legal across the United States—and in Canada, Australia, and the UK, too! Offbeat Brides of all orientations and identities can now marry their beloveds all over the world. . . . Yes, we still have a ways to go, but the political and legal progress of marriage equality in the past decade has been monumental.

One remarkable wedding industry shift is that, well, we kinda won the war against wedding homogeneity. Now it's not only accepted that your wedding will reflect your personality, it's almost assumed that of course you're going to have some references to your favorite bits of pop culture, or the place where you had your first date, or that song your dad used to sing to you.

For the most part, these days people understand that having an offbeat and authentic wedding is an option—even the more conservative folks who think *Offbeat Bride* is tasteless and "tacky." Alternative weddings have permeated American culture so deeply that even the most mainstream wedding media covers nontraditional wedding trends and nonwhite wedding dresses barely raise your mom's eyebrow.

So, does that mean *Offbeat Bride*'s work is done? Is that it? Time to just fold it all up, and call it quits? Mission completed, see y'all later?

That's cute, but there is still so much to be done. . . . Stuff like helping wedding vendors understand that gender essentialism isn't effective marketing. Stuff like ensuring that couples who feel underrepresented in wedding media can still feel supported in their planning process—this means representing couples with disabilities, couples who aren't slender or young or white. Hell, this means representing folks who are more than a couple—*Offbeat Bride* has a long history of celebrating polyamorous commitment ceremonies, too.

I love that in the time that *Offbeat Bride* has been around, marriage equality has become accepted to the degree that sometimes people are like, "Pshaw: What's offbeat about this lesbian wedding?!" Although I'm personally giddy that lesbian weddings can now be considered "boring" (equality means we *all* get to be as boring as we want!), I'm still wondering when gender-neutral contracts will become the standard for wedding vendors. I'm still grumpy about the sign-up pages on mainstream wedding websites having fields for [Bride's Name] and [Groom's Name], instead of just having [My Name] and [Partner's Name].

But there's no denying that, at least when it comes to aesthetics, being an Offbeat Bride may not be as much of a battle as it used to be. I wrote this book with a sense of reactionary urgency and rebelliousness—I wasn't just being myself, I was also pushing hard against mainstream weddings, trying to carve out something different! I was defying the expectations! I was standing up for my own vision!

Truth be told, I definitely used my uniqueness as a defense mechanism, coupled with a healthy dose of "offbeater-than-thou" posturing. I mean, when this book was first released, I made promotional shirts that said, "Offbeat Bride: Fuck Taffeta." I quickly learned that some offbeat people love taffeta . . . *and that's awesome!* I am sorry for my old taffeta-shaming ways.

In updating this book for its third edition, taffeta-shaming and dismissiveness toward more traditional-looking weddings wasn't the only old stuff that had to change. Back in the mid-2000s, most of us didn't have the language to talk about gender and identity in the same way we do now. Back then, I made jokes that make me cringe now. (You want some humble pie? Spend some time with your work from fourteen years ago. Ouch. What an education.)

Back in the mid-2000s, I interviewed fifty-plus "lab rats" to include their stories in the book, and, for this edition, I added the thoughts of dozens more Offbeat Bride readers. I wanted to share more perspectives on things like planning a wedding while working with disabilities, nonbinary identities, and the challenges of modern technology. You'll see these Offbeat readers quoted and referenced throughout the book—I'm choosing to identify readers only by their first names. I've learned better than to identify anyone by their full name when talking about the challenges of wedding planning. I've seen enough blog comments from angry family members who stumbled across something written about them on offbeatbride.com. Now I know better than to go offending family members.

These days, *Offbeat Bride* doesn't have to try so hard to offend anyone or be off-anything—it's about being inclusive, a place where "bride" is a state of mind, not a set of genitals (. . . because you better believe there are masculine-identified brides!).

Offbeat Bride is here to welcome you to the world of wedding planning and speak to you with respect for whatever your visions are. This book is about throwing the doors open, moving past reactionary rebelliousness, and helping you celebrate finding your way to a wedding that feels like you—whoever you are.

Offbeat Bride isn't about having the weirdest wedding, or being the first person to ever do that thing at the reception, or wanting guests to tell you "that was the best wedding ever!"

Offbeat Bride is about authenticity, whether that means your visions are super elaborate and wild or incredibly streamlined.

Offbeat Bride is here to cheerlead you in your wedding planning, support you through your challenges, provide inspiration and advice, and cultivate a sense of inclusivity.

Offbeat Bride is just about celebrating the ways each of us is offbeat and awesome—not about drawing lines around who's "offbeat enough."

Offbeat Bride is about not taking ourselves too seriously, and about respecting and celebrating folks who do things differently than we do.

Offbeat Bride is about inspiring you to do things in a way that feels right, regardless of whether that's over-the-top weird or quietly minimal. I understand now that offbeat isn't just a spectrum—it's a prism. I love all y'all's love, no matter what it looks like.

I guess what I'm trying to say is that *Offbeat Bride* is still here for you, all these years later, because although a lot has changed . . . a lot of the realities of wedding planning remain the same. The challenges of dealing with the dynamics of your family of origin and your families of choice, the complex project management of wedding details, trying to reconcile your identity in the face of intense community and cultural expectations? These are ubiquitous rocky waters to be navigated by everyone on their path to their own offbeat altar.

It's been my privilege all these years to be able to help . . . or at the very least, to entertain you during times of stress. Thank you for the honor of letting me be a part of your love!

—*Ariel Meadow Stallings*
Seattle 2019

part one

Otherwise Engaged

1. THE PRESSURE AND THE PROPOSAL

Knowing when (& whether) to say "I do"

ANDREAS AND I HAD BEEN TOGETHER FOR LESS THAN A YEAR WHEN THE questions started. I spent the afternoon of Christmas 1998 with my mother, two of my aunties, one auntie's lesbian partner, and Andreas's mother, Nancy. (Andreas was with his father for the holidays.) Auntie Cherie, perhaps wishing to make me squirm in front of the mother of my boyfriend, asked me whether Andreas and I planned to get married.

I stuttered through my evasive answer. "Well, we're really committed to each other and we might have a ceremony someday to acknowledge that, but I'm not sure if we need or want the legal institution of marriage to make it official."

There. Whew. I was committed, but we were nonconformists. The end.

No, not the end. The three lesbians in the room all commented on the irony that Andreas and I—a straight couple who could get married—would choose not to enjoy the legal rights for which so many committed gay and lesbian couples fight. At that point, Nancy and her partner, Susan, had been together for fifteen years, and Auntie Andrea had been with her partner for seven—and yet they couldn't enjoy spousal rights. The irony stung a little. But the idea stuck: a commitment ceremony might be okay, but marriage seemed weird to us, with our gay families and both of our sets of parents divorced.

By the time our third anniversary rolled around, my thoughts on getting married had shifted. We were basically already functioning as a married couple, so why not? I made a half-hearted attempt at a proposal. Andreas's response felt like both an acceptance and a rejection. "Oh, of course we'll get married," he said. Acceptance! "I thought we decided that a long time ago." Oh, I thought. So I didn't need to propose at all. We're already getting married!

Andreas wasn't done yet, though. "But we're not, like, getting married anytime soon, right?"

Oh. Ouch. So that was the snub: no duh we're getting married, but what's the hurry? It was delayed gratification with no timeline for a payoff, but I saw his point and agreed with the concept. Okay, so we'll do it someday, but what's the hurry? Why the rush?

Three years after that, however, it appeared that the pressure had grown to be too much. Our finances were screwed from filing taxes separately but functioning jointly. As terminal freelancers, it seemed like we never both had health insurance. And our friends and family, despite their nontraditional values, were itching for a party.

The *M* word and the *C* word—no, not that one

It all started one night at a steak house. Jerry and Sallie—Andreas's father and stepmother—had taken us out for dinner with their friends Alan and Char. (Please disregard the irony of us, a vegetarian and a vegan, being invited to a steak house for dinner. Sometimes these little issues must be overlooked in the interest of familial relations.)

Soon, we were also trying to overlook the attentions of Char, who asked us what we thought about "the *M* word." We glanced at each other with a little confusion at first. The *M* word? What *M* word? Char clucked at us. "Marriage, you guys! When are you getting married? Sallie and I are just itching to plan a wedding!"

We hemmed and hawed and tried to change the subject, reverting to our old commitment-ceremony lines and aware of the difference between the kind of wedding we would plan and the kind of wedding someone else would envision for us. I foresaw gold monogrammed napkins and a princess dress and knew it just wasn't in the cards. We would not be cornered into a steak house shotgun wedding.

The conversation got increasingly surreal from there, with Char going on to ask us whether we'd put any consideration into "the C word." This code-speak confounded me—the only C word I know is the one that ends with "-unt." I have put a lot of consideration into that particular C word, but of course that wasn't the one to which Char was referring. She meant children.

It wasn't just Andreas's side that started to apply the pressure. My mother had also reached a state of terminal frustration. She called me up one day to crow, "I don't care if you two never sign any papers—it's all bullshit anyway. I just want you to throw a party so we can give you presents and sing about how much we love you!"

Well, presents. Presents are hard to argue with, aren't they?

TIP: WEDDINGED YES, MARRIED NO

THERE'S NO REASON WHY YOU CAN'T HAVE A BEAUTIFUL WEDDING that doesn't include actually getting married. LGBTQ+ folks already know this, of course, because they were denied the right to marry in the United States until 2015. But many straight couples are opting to "get weddinged" and have the ceremony without the legal documentation as well. Offbeat reader Joriel and her partner, Ben, simply couldn't reconcile their frustrations with marriage-equality issues. They didn't want to get married, but they wanted to share their commitment with their families, so they opted to have a "union ceremony" and sign all the power-of-attorney paperwork, remaining domestic partners rather than husband and wife. They explained their decision to their families with this articulate essay:

>>>

We have chosen not to get married for a variety of reasons, none of which has anything to do with our feelings for each other or our commitment to a shared future. We do not require a legal contract or the blessing of a minister to make our commitment real and sacred.

We believe that God is Love, and that a union of love will necessarily be blessed. While we consider our relationship to be a bond between souls, neither of us follows a specific faith. Although we regret any distress this may cause for members of our families, it would be disingenuous for us to have a ceremony that followed the tenets of Christianity.

We are also acutely aware that marriage is not an option for everyone, and we are resistant to becoming part of an exclusionary institution. We both identify with and feel compassion for the thousands of gay couples in loving, committed relationships who would like to get married and cannot. Some of these couples are close friends. If the day comes when adults of any gender can marry, we will probably reconsider our choice regarding legal marriage.

This decision has not been made lightly and has not always been easy. It's a challenge to plan a ceremony that will be both meaningful for us and comprehensible to others. Most of all, it has been difficult for some of our loved ones to understand why we don't just "go ahead and get married."

Fortunately, our friends and families are pretty used to both of us being stubbornly idealistic.

Party planning to avoid party receiving

Our friends gave us very little grief, because, in keeping with typical overeducated urban coastal types, few of them were married either. Of my most immediate circle, only two close childhood friends got married when I was in my twenties, and only one of Andreas's childhood friends had tied the knot. Among our circle of aging ravers, intellectuals, music festival freaks, hippies, and geeks, we were one of the longer-standing relationships by years—our friends sure as hell weren't going to pressure us to get married when they were all busy dealing with their internet-dating snafus, hidden porn-collection crises, and catastrophic, caterwauling breakups.

But the pressure kept mounting. The most bothersome thing to me was that almost no one ever gave Andreas any shit about our unmarried state. It seemed that, as the owner of the ovaries, I was also the de facto prewedding planner. Because I didn't have facial hair, I was obviously the one who was picking out crystal for the registry and poring over bridal magazines, trying to decide which tiara I would wear once we were finally engaged and he gave me that big ol' rock. People sometimes harassed the both of us, but very rarely did someone corner Andreas to ask whether we were getting married.

The whole thing gave me the grits. Sure, I might be the girl, but that didn't mean I was the one who was dreaming of the ribbon-tied rose topiary that would be at the center of the white-cloth buffet tables.

Then again, maybe I was. I really wanted to get married, but not because I'm the one with the boobs—because I'm the one who thinks about health insurance. In our relationship, we had very well-defined roles: I was the vice president of logistics; he was the CEO of emotional support. He inherited a little bit of the absent-minded-professor syndrome, while my brain loves keeping track of the little details. I, meanwhile, can be moody and foul-tempered at times, while Andreas remains compassionate, supportive, and reassuring even in the worst of emotional storms. We balanced out well.

As vice president of logistics, it then fell under my jurisdiction to realize that we were both getting older and that having no health insurance was starting to be a bigger risk—a risk that separately we couldn't afford to surmount. If we were married, only one of us would have to have a real job at any given point, and we'd both have health care. Alternately, if we were paying for our own insurance, it would be cheaper as a married couple. These pragmatic, nonromantic reasons were what pushed our gushy sentimental affections over the edge to legal union.

That and my mother. Ever persistent with her "party and presents," she had called me in January 2004 suggesting that, because we seemed to be lagging in getting married, she wanted to throw us her own party. "In honor of your relationship," she explained.

"Sort of like an engagement party?" I asked her. "You know, we are getting married someday, so we're technically sort of, like, semi-engaged." My mother was satisfied with the semi-engagement-party concept, and so she asked me to talk to Andreas about it and see what he thought.

The CEO of emotional support wasn't sold on the idea. "I don't want to go to a party about us that's all planned by your mom," Andreas explained. "If there's going to be a party about us, I want that to be our party."

Andreas had thrown a party or two in his raver heyday—one called "Teddy Bears Always Say I Love You" and its sequel, "No Shoes & You Have to Smoke in the Kitchen." He knew a bit about the importance of theme and setting in the throwing of a good party. I was the consummate hostess myself—after all, had we not met at a party, one of my drunken tumblings around my apartment?

It should be known that my mother has thrown a lot of parties in her time, but her parties are called "rituals" or "gatherings," and they usually involve a sweat lodge, a campfire, and hand percussive instruments. They're great, profoundly touching events that have resulted in the formation of a cohesive community over the years.

But let's be clear: these are not our like-minded folk. Not all of them, anyway. Certainly there'd be some crossover between the people my mother would invite and the people we would invite. But if there was going to be a party, it was going to be our party, damnit. Not a steak-house wedding! And not one of my mom's "gatherings"!

So Andreas rejected his future mother-in-law's idea for a party. But don't feel sorry for her. I'm positive it was exactly what she wanted us to do. By pushing our rebellious, sassy asses, she totally forced our hand.

We would do it! We would throw our own party—so there!

2. OKAY, FINE: WE'RE GETTING MARRIED

Broadcasting the news via phone, e-mail,
social media, carrier pigeon, etc.

WE ANNOUNCED OUR ENGAGEMENT TO OUR IMMEDIATE FAMILIES OVER the phone. When I called my mother and told her, she didn't get especially excited. Personally, I think that's because she'd secretly been masterminding the whole thing and probably been visualizing the whole situation for months in an effort to manifest it.

My father got a little befuddled; he's a quick wit but a slow digester and couldn't get his head around it all right away. He called a day later to congratulate us fully.

Andreas's mother was a little incredulous—not about us getting married, but just of marriage as a concept. She'd been known to voice concerns that marriage can unexpectedly alter relationships, and so although she was excited about our engagement, she also seemed a little nervous in an if-it-ain't-broke-don't-fix-it kind of way. His father was pleased, and when Andreas told his twenty-one-year-old sister the news, she squealed so loudly that I could hear it through the phone line from across the room.

Announcements in the information age

We broke the news to our close friends over drinks, where the first rallying cries of "party of the year!" were heard. (Thanks, guys. No pressure, right?) And as for the rest of the world? I, of course, announced it on my blog.

There's no shame in admitting it: I am a huge geek and a devoted blogger. So of course I publicly announced my engagement on my blog. If you knew five hundred people of varying levels of acquaintance, wouldn't you make one simple announcement instead of calling people who may or may not care?

Thanks to my blog, guests I never would have thought would be interested came to the wedding. One of our guests was a former contestant from an online game show I helped with years prior. Other guests were blog-reading classmates from a summer course I did at Columbia University three years before. These were people whom I kept in casual touch with, but, after I posted on my blog, I found out that many of these folks wanted to come to the wedding—and what a treat! People flying across the country to come hang out! And all we had to do was feed them dinner one night! Then again, as you'll see in Chapter 21, managing the bloated guest list became a total nightmare.

The blog was a great way to announce the engagement. Andreas called his friends, but most of them read the blog anyway, so they already knew.

TIP: THE FIGHT AGAINST TRADITION BEGINS . . . NOW!

THE QUESTIONS AND ASSUMPTIONS ABOUT YOUR WEDDING MAY STRIKE within seconds of your engagement announcement. Offbeat reader Erin explained, "Both sets of parents immediately wanted to know our plans for the type of wedding—the how, when, where. We hadn't given it a bit of thought!"

Don't go into your announcement defensive or expecting a fight, but do be prepared to immediately establish boundaries when it comes to planning your wedding. It's perfectly acceptable to defer questioning with something like, "We're talking over ideas right now. I'll let you know when we're ready to dive into details." Granted, you may just be delaying the inevitable, but at least it focuses your engagement announcement on what's important: your exciting news!

Marriage boycotts and avoidance

We were lucky. Our situation would have been quite different if our friends and family had not supported our relationship. I suppose this is the big advantage of waiting six years to get engaged: by that point, everyone is mostly convinced of your compatibility, and the people who don't like your partner still have to admit that, well, you've clearly made it further than many marriages, so your partner is probably okay . . . and, well, fine, actually, he's probably very good for you . . . and, well, gimme a hug, that's just great news! The only "think twice" comments we got were about the institution of marriage—questions we'd asked ourselves as well.

One gay friend suggested that we hold off on our ceremony to protest the fact that not everyone could enjoy the social/civil privilege. This was hard to hear. We'd long debated about marriage equality, and we simply believed there were more effective ways to fight the battle. As Massachusetts representative Barney Frank told the *Village Voice*, "Too often people on the Left want what they call 'direct action' because it's more satisfying to them in some way. It's well-intentioned but not helpful. When two very good heterosexual people refuse to get married, I don't see how that puts pressure on politicians. Refuse to vote for people who won't let us get married. That's the way you address this."

I have the deepest respect and nothing but admiration for those who choose to protest by refusing to get married, but we elected to use our straight wedding as a political soapbox instead. More about that in Chapter 39, "Duck!"

We also heard from a friend who was grinding through a divorce and warned us what a pain in the ass it is to have the courts involved in your breakup. It's so much paperwork added to an already difficult emotional experience. With two pairs of divorced parents, we were aware of the risks. At that point, however, our finances and legal lives were already entwined. Separation would be a headache regardless—we might as well enjoy the benefits while we could. Big party! Fun dancing! Lots of prezzies! Streets paved with champagne! Sex in a conjugal bed!

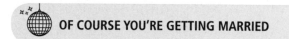

OF COURSE YOU'RE GETTING MARRIED

When you've been together for a long time, engagement announcing can be distinctly anticlimactic. Offbeat reader Leah recounted that when her fiancé called his mom to announce their engagement, her response was, "Of course you are." Her fiancé was a little hurt at his mother's lackluster response. Leah explained, "It felt as if it were somehow less special that we were getting married because we've been together for over five years."

If your engagement announcement meets with similar apathy, try upping the ante a little. Share a special aspect of the proposal or a romantic story about how you two finally decided it was time. If you can't get indifferent family to jump up and down in shock and awe, at least you can get them a little misty-eyed and sappy.

And if not, don't let it get to you.

3. LOCATION, LOCATION, LOCATION

Picking the where & when of the wedding

IN CHOOSING WHERE TO HOST OUR WEDDING, WE LOOKED AT WHAT WAS around us, the world we already inhabited. We crafted our wedding to be a reflection of that place. Why create some other world to live in for a day? Commitment is all about day-to-day partnership, the long years of companionship. It can be rough to get married in a fantasy land filled with horse-drawn carriages and then find yourself riding back to your apartment in a hatchback the next day.

For us, we wanted to reflect the two people we are and the space we inhabit, not some foreign dreamland that we could visit for a day before returning to our real life. We didn't look at wedding magazines; that's not our world. For inspiration, we looked at wedding photos from people who lived lives like ours, but, ultimately, we crafted our vision for the wedding based on the life we live and the people we live it with. And that vision started with the physical location.

Our venue was a study in taking the path of least resistance. I grew up in the shade, raised in a log cabin that my parents built in the rainforest of Bainbridge Island, which is a thirty-five-minute ferry ride due west of downtown Seattle. Thirty years ago, the community consisted mostly of old money and young hippies (guess which my parents were), but the population has since doubled, and the island has evolved into a more typical Pacific Northwest suburb, filled with polar fleece vests, overpriced SUVs, and latte-gripping mothers with frosted hair and the funds to pay a mortgage on waterfront property.

14

TIP: GET MARRIED WHERE YOU LIKE TO BE

ONE OFFBEAT BRIDE READER I SPOKE TO SUMMED IT UP BEST WHEN she said that in picking a wedding venue, you want "the kind of place you would actually go to if it wasn't a wedding." Is a church or synagogue the place you go to feel good and celebrate? If so, then maybe a religious locale is perfect for you. For many secular, untraditional types, however, there are numerous places where we feel infinitely more happy and at peace with ourselves—be that a forest or a pasture, a library or a museum, a restaurant or a theater. These places are just as holy to some couples as a temple is to others. And, in many cases, they're a better spot for dancing and squealing.

It's an insular community and as provincial as you would expect for an island. It's also unbelievably beautiful and the perfect place for a wedding—even if you weren't a cedar-sheltered Islander child, which I certainly was. The forests of Bainbridge Island drip with moss and lichen and the smell of living things becoming soil. And so we selected a venue where we had an abundance of space and the easiest access: my mother's ten acres of forested island property and her neighbor's small bed-and-breakfast. The vision, in other words, was limited to what we could already see.

Under the sea and other venues

There are varying degrees of extreme wedding venues. Many nontraditional folks I spoke with went the family-property route as well. I heard beautiful stories of grandmothers' farms and family backyards. Plus, offbeat weddings held on family property can be a great way of honoring your family without following its traditions.

But not everyone will have access to (or want to choose) such family-friendly venues. Offbeat reader Julie decided to marry her husband in their favorite place to be: underwater. As scuba divers, it was a natural choice.

According to Julie, however, her mother's first response was, "That's not fair!" She had a bit of a point: because Julie's mom didn't scuba dive, she felt that she was being pushed out of the ceremony. Julie and her fiancé made special efforts to include non-diving family members, renting a boat with a glass bottom and having parts of the ceremony performed above water so family members could take turns at readings. These efforts stand as an excellent lesson for all weddings held in untraditional locations. You can find ways to make your friends and family feel included, even if they're a little (or a lot) out of their element.

Julie's advice to others dealing with pressure from family about wedding venues was this: "It's helpful to be able to explain why you want to have the wedding where you do, but you don't have to justify it to your aunt, your coworker, and your mail carrier." It's important to set boundaries early on about your vision for the wedding. Explain what led you to choose your location and why it's important to you. Then stand your ground. Ask for suggestions on how you can make that location more comfortable for more traditional guests, but don't ever feel that you have to bow to others' expectations. It's okay to say, "This is where we're getting married. We want you there, and we'll do what we can to make you happy there, but this is where it's happening."

In thinking about locations, be sure to do your research and think of venues beyond those that advertise themselves as "perfect for weddings." You'll quickly learn that anything that has the word "wedding" attached to it costs twice as much—and that includes more traditional wedding venues like ballrooms, hotels, and private estates. Researching and brainstorming venues can be grueling work, but the payoff is worth it.

Offbeat reader Susan recounted, "Finding the venue was kind of a pain. I looked at gardens, parks, restaurants, ballrooms, and everything in between for months—most of which were way, way out of our price range. Then I thought of a museum I absolutely love in Portland, the Contemporary Crafts Museum, which is a gorgeous, wood-and-glass 1930s arts center. It's a very creative, open building with a very relaxed, modern vibe, and I could imagine how fun it would be to celebrate there. It was so much nicer than several of the places I saw charging four times as much, and so much more us."

You don't need to limit yourself to private property. Offbeat reader Matthew was married at the Seattle Aquarium. He explained that, "during the planning process, we discovered that a lot of places that seem 'exotic,' like the aquarium, are actually a bargain because they are considered city or state parks and therefore rent for cheaper than a corresponding hall. We loved getting married there—the best part was that whenever we had a 'transition' (such as from wedding to reception or whatever), there were otters to look at for the guests." When was the last time you saw otters at a church wedding?

The old proverb: "Wed where you pee"

In our case, we tempered my mother's homegrown forest eco-retreat with the relative comfort of her neighbor's bed-and-breakfast. Our ceremony and dinner were held on the safety of a manicured lawn, with the reassurance of flushing toilets, well-tended gardens, and brick patios to soothe the frayed nerves of more traditional family members. It wasn't until after dark that we led the troops down the hill to my mother's property, where things were a little wilder, both figuratively and literally.

Was it a little funky? Yes. Did our guests poop into sawdust-filled buckets? Why, yes, they did. But did they have a great time? Sure looked like it. And we didn't put ourselves in debt. Instead of paying to create a fantasy land, we picked the best things our everyday lives had to offer and crafted an extra-special everyday.

Our vision wasn't really very creative in the "working from the ground up" sense: we did the things that were easiest for us and made arrangements with the people we were closest to. Instead of trying to forge a connection with strangers, we called on the skills of many friends and family members. In this way, we tried to create a day that was a reflection and celebration of our community of ravers, hippies, academics, and urban hipsters—not an expensive day dedicated to our relationship narcissism.

Basically, I got married in the same forest that I used to pee in as a child. Maybe it was more special that way, because we were encouraging our guests to pee there as well.

Your location probably won't be as urine-centric, but just try to pick a venue that works well for you and your betrothed's needs—and then find ways to share it with your extended family. It might take a little extra work, but if Julie can share her underwater wedding with above-water family, then surely you can share your goth industrial-loft wedding with your non-children-of-the-night relatives.

TIP: BURNING WEDDINGS AND OTHER FESTIVAL NUPTIALS

OFFBEAT COUPLES LOVE TO GET MARRIED AT EVENTS LIKE BURNING Man, the Oregon Country Fair, and the UK's Glastonbury Festival. I spoke to lots of folks who'd fallen in love at these amazing events and saw it as only fitting that they would get married in the same surreal, fantastical environment where they'd first met. Festivals are wild venues for weddings—but be prepared for the fact that family and certain kinds of friends simply won't be able to make the trek. Also, these large-scale events can be expensive as hell. Do you really want to make your beloved Aunt Mert, who lives off of social security checks, pay hundreds of dollars for a ticket to Burning Man? Although I heartily encourage festival weddings, I also think festival couples should at least consider having a small, simple family reception in a more accessible location as well. See Chapter 27, "Something Borrowed," for more thoughts on having two weddings.

4. SAVE-THE-DATE CARDS

And other news-flash fun

SAVE-THE-DATE CARDS (SOMETIMES CALLED STDs, MUCH TO THE AMUSE-ment of some of us) are your introduction to wedding swag. For many folks, the save-the-date card marks the first chance to communicate to your guests just how offbeat your wedding might be. For those who are really into design and accessorizing, it marks the first opportunity to express the aesthetic of the wedding.

Save-the-date cards are a first step, but Lordy they can be a doozy. They mark the initial hurtle into the bride mind.

These pre-invitations force you to think about just who you're going to invite . . . and who your family may want to invite. Offbeat reader Jennie explained to me, "In order to make sure everyone got a save-the-date card, both our families were forced to provide their complete guest lists. This gave us 'hard numbers' to work with over the rest of the planning process. Yes, there was some eventual mother-in-law guest-list slippage, but the numbers were very helpful." Save the date cards herald the beginning of bridal database work: every engaged couple needs a nice spreadsheet of guest addresses. And doing these pre-invitations can help you get the work out of the way early.

Offbeat reader Susan said, "I was so glad we did save-the-date cards. It really took the pressure off, especially since all of our family and most of our old friends were coming from the other coast. It also meant that, for the most part, we weren't freaking out trying to round addresses up for our invitations at the last minute."

TIP: DOUBLE-DUTY CHEER BRINGING

OFFBEAT READER JANET BUNDLED HER SAVE-THE-DATE ANNOUNCE-ments with her holiday cards and got a great response. "I wrote a little cheesy verse after the holiday greetings: *'And after the snow has melted and the flowers have bloomed, please save-the-date to celebrate our wedding with us.'* It was great to make the holiday rounds and see the postcards hanging on people's refrigerators." Not only do you save on postage, but you also provide a little holiday cheer. That said, Janet noted, "I'm really glad we had them sent out at the beginning of December, to avoid the holiday hustle and bustle." You definitely don't want your save-the-date card to get ignored under a stack of other people's holiday letters and other season's greetings.

You don't need a physical card— the grapevine works, too

Then again, do you really need to do save-the-date cards? If you're worried about etiquette, don't. They're not even traditional. These pre-invitation cards are a relatively new practice, and, as such, it's outside the realm of heavily dictated wedding behavior. While some crafty types get really into doing magnets or clever thematic postcards, others opt for e-mail or phone calls. And for those wondering whether e-mails or phone calls are okay? Of course they are.

Offbeat reader Shannon opted to let her family do the dirty work for her, explaining, "Our families are grapevines, so we told our parents, and they passed along the message. We didn't bother with the save-the-date stuff."

The core of a save-the-date notification is to give guests an early heads-up. If your guests are traveling from out of state, or if you're aiming for a high-traffic wedding date (summer wedding–havers, this means you), it's good to give them a big heads-up—at least five or six months. If you want to do that via your family grapevine or a post on social media or phone calls, that's awesome. The goal here is to make sure guests know the date of the wedding far ahead enough to make travel plans. The goal needn't be to impress them with a curlicue font or witty wording—unless you want it to be.

Regardless of whether you do a standard printed card, a holiday card, an e-mail, or even just a phone call, you need to include only the most basic information: your names, the date, the general location (city and state), and the fact that a real invitation will follow. If you're a geek like me, you'll also include the URL of your wedding website. More about that in Chapter 7.

Set the tone

Because our families are relatively liberal and expected a freakfest wedding, we chose to give guests an initial peek at what was in store: our save-the-date cards looked like rave flyers. We thought they were sort of classy rave flyers, but one aging raver friend com-

---

TIP: SEALED WITH A KEEP IT SIMPLE, STUPID

IF YOU'RE PLANNING AN UNTRADITIONAL WEDDING AND HAVE TRADI-tional extended family, keep your save-the-date messages simple and to the point. Offbeat reader Jennie told me, "We deliberately didn't give a lot of information—just date, location, and our website address. I didn't really want people commenting on our plans." Or, as another reader, named Sabrina, more candidly admitted, "We really kept things under wraps to minimize the mama drama." You'll have plenty of time later to deal with concerned guests freaking out about untraditional plans. You want to give everyone an early heads-up about the date, but you may not want to give them a head start on their panicking.

mented, "They look really cheesy, but then I realized that was the point." Uh, thanks . . . I think.

One thing's for sure: have your location, location, location and date confirmed before asking folks to save-the-date. And if you're doing a short engagement (say, less than four months), it might not be worth doing save the date cards. Just send the damn invitation already!

5. ONE RING TO RULE THEM ALL

Who knew one piece of jewelry could be so loaded?

SHORTLY AFTER ANDREAS AND I DECIDED TO TAKE THE PLUNGE INTO engagement, I found myself in my underwear on my regular aesthetician's table, waiting to get my legs waxed.

The aesthetician and I were chatting amicably, and she asked how my boyfriend was, and I said, "Oh, hey! We got engaged!"

"Me too!" the aesthetician squealed, and held out her left hand so that I could see her ring. I, too, reflexively whipped up my left hand beside the aesthetician's, splaying my fingers out happily. (Is this the secret gang sign for engaged women?)

The difference was immediately evident: I was not wearing a ring. I don't really even like rings. Our proposal was a joint decision involving health insurance. There was no ring.

So why was I holding my hand up like a dumbass? I snatched it back down to my side. "Our engagement was more of a decision than a proposal," I said, and swallowed. "No ring."

As for the diamond ring tradition? It's not a tradition, it's marketing. De Beers kicked off a publicity campaign to establish diamonds as the standard engagement ring in 1938. Clearly the campaign worked, because here we are, eighty years later, still hearing nonstop from Tom Shane, our friend in the diamond business.

Offbeat reader Sabrina explained it to me this way: "I feel good about engagement rings as long as they are a token of commitment—and not of status. I worry about our traditional pattern of engagement: man shoves big rock under woman's nose and says, 'Will you marry me?' A lot of women seem to hear this as, 'Would you like to wear this really big ring and have a huge party?' Why, yes! Yes, I would, thank you!"

Simply stated, the diamond industry is creepy (I could write another whole book on that—but it's already been done), and the tradition of having a diamond engagement ring is just marketing. So then how in the hell did I end up with a diamond on my wedding ring?

Andreas and I thought about it a bit, and we decided that we liked the traditional symbolism of rings—I'm pretty dang agnostic, but what faith I have tends to revolve around cycles and circles. It's the shape of raindrops, of our pupils, of planetary orbits. It's also the shape of a hula hoop, and, even if I'm not sure about diamonds, I was big into hula hoops. And what's a ring but a little finger hoop?

In keeping with the rest of our wedding planning, we made the most of what was available to us. I had inherited my grandmother's engagement and wedding rings from her (cough) third marriage.

TIP: WHO NEEDS AN ENGAGEMENT RING?

EVEN AMONG NONTRADITIONAL BRIDES AND GROOMS, THERE'S A feeling that there needs to be *some* sort of material acknowledgment of the engagement. I spoke to Offbeat Bride readers who had everything from drugstore rings to simple silver moonstone-set bands to square-cut sapphires to enormous diamonds. One reader, named Amy, said, "My boy was quite concerned about the politics of diamond engagement rings. But I wanted *something* from him, something to prove this was a serious commitment, not just a passing whim."

Then again, it's not always a ring. Offbeat reader Sabrina bucked tradition completely by first proposing to her boyfriend and then skipping the whole ring thing. "I didn't get my fiancé an engagement ring, but . . . I did get him an engagement lighter. In fact, that's what we call it, saying things like, 'Where the hell is the engagement lighter?'"

The design made it eminently clear that Grandma had been married in Las Vegas in the late '60s while wearing a muumuu and a stylish wiglet, so we found a local goldsmith to help us redesign the rings.

Choosing something shiny, but with intent

I wholeheartedly recommend the experience of designing your own rings. Especially for those who like to dance to the beat of their own drum (or kazoo, or double-headed death-metal guitar), there's a deep satisfaction in having hands-on experience in the creation of a piece of jewelry you'll potentially wear every day for the rest of your life.

Gulp. Sorry to harsh your mellow, but seriously! If you want them to, these rings will symbolize one of the most important decisions of your life—so why not take the time to make them as unique as you and your partner? Our experience of sitting down and working with our goldsmith was reassuring and almost therapeutic.

I had to side with Offbeat Bride reader Jen when she said, "We couldn't have gone with boring, or picking something from a glass case. We really did have to do our own." She and her fiancé ended up designing rings that were "Alex Grey–inspired, with a DNA strand with a kundalini fire shooting through it." You're not going to find anything like that at the national jewelry chain store at the mall.

And what of diamonds? I hemmed and hawed over including one of the diamonds from my grandmother's original ring in my wedding band. Offbeat reader Joriel sums my feelings up best when she explains her reasons for not wanting a diamond: "De Beers sucks, and we didn't want to wonder whether anyone died for me to have a little bling."

I salved my political concerns with the fact that my grandmother's diamond was antique—my wedding ring wasn't putting any money in the De Beers coffers (or coffins), and the family sentiment was nice. Ultimately, however, the choice of stone (or whether there will even be a stone—or whether there will even be rings) is up to each couple. It's interesting to note the ways even the most offbeat of us buys into these material longings.

I guess the best advice I can offer is this: If you're going to buy into the concept, at least choose what you want carefully and with intent. If you want something shiny, consider all your options, from diamonds to opals to tinfoil and everything in between.

DIAMONDS ARE FORMED BY DEEP PRESSURE, BOTH GEOLOGICAL AND SOCIAL

A diamond engagement ring is a double-headed snake of two cultural pressures twisted together: it's about love . . . and money. Joriel told me a heartbreaking story about a friend who had a beautifully simple engagement ring "that featured a piece of rare bright-red sea glass—vaguely heart shaped—that she and her fiancé had found on a beach walk." Despite the beauty and richness of the ring's sentiment, the bride-to-be got incredible grief from friends and family members. Joriel recounted that "nobody could understand why she didn't want a diamond, and everybody seemed to judge her ring as somehow less than a true engagement ring. Some months later, shamefaced, she turned up with a diamond ring. The pressure is enormous."

6. LET'S GET THIS PARTY STARTED (OR NOT)

Bridesboys, groomsgirls & wedding parties

I'VE NEVER UNDERSTOOD WHY TRADITIONAL GROOMS CAN ONLY BE supported during the ceremony by guy friends, and brides can have only a gaggle of maids. It seems like this idea is born from the theory that, once you get engaged, you certainly can't have friends of the opposite sex, because, like, that obviously means you're having an affair and don't love your future spouse. Well, bullshit. One of my closest friends is a man who was my roommate for years.

Andreas and I were pretty sure that we didn't want to deal with the complexity of a wedding party, but we seriously considered it just so we could make a gender-political point about bridesboys and groomsgirls. I loved the idea of rows of our friends, all the ones on my side wearing ivory skirts and blue tops (including the men; they could wear ivory Utilikilts or something) and all the ones on Andreas's side wearing punk-rock tuxedos—including a tiny fitted one for Dre's friend Naomi, who's about five feet tall and a hundred pounds. Adorable!

I'm totally jealous of Offbeat Bride reader Maria, who actually went through with the gender-bender wedding party: "I had a bridesman, and my partner had a groomswoman. The bridesman wore the same tuxes as the other guys but carried a bouquet; the groomswoman wore a long black skirt and tuxedo jacket with a red shirt she made to match the guys' outfits. When they processed in, he was on her arm." I love it when people play with concepts of gender and identity, and weddings are no exception to this rule.

Ultimately, however, we decided that we didn't really need a ceremonial wedding party. It's just more people to coordinate and

28

clothe. As you'll see in Chapter 17, "It Takes a Village," our friends were all helping with the wedding and would be too busy to take the time to put on their matching outfits and stand there next to us while we said our vows anyway. So, hey, friends: Sit down, take a load off! We'll entertain you for our ten-minute ceremony. We won't make you pay a fortune for an outfit. We know that being in a wedding party can be expensive.

That said, functionally, we sort of had a wedding party—they just weren't part of the ceremony. My wedding party had titles like "senior camp counselor" and "upper location manager." They didn't have to buy matching dresses, but they all donated much of their love and time and attention to the wedding. I didn't want them standing next to us; I wanted them to just enjoy the ceremony from the lawn. They'd worked hard enough.

In this way, most weddings have a wedding party of sorts—a trusted inner circle of friends and family who are closest to the planning of the event. It's just that sometimes these people get more traditional titles and roles in the event. At Offbeat reader Jen's wedding, the attendants were known as "henchmen" and "supreme beings of chickness." People who support us in life come by many names.

This doesn't mean that wedding parties have to be traditional or that untraditional weddings can't have wedding parties. Offbeat reader Sabrina told me about how although her wedding party was a must for her, it was actually her untraditional mother who took offense at the idea!

Sabrina remembers, "My mother kept screeching, 'Bridesmaids?! Bridesmaids?!' like I'd suggested roasting babies over an open fire. But I wanted to get married with these women around me; they're part of who I am." Inviting loved ones into your ceremony and wedding with you can be a really affirming way of connecting with these people.

TIP: CHOOSE WISELY, GRASSHOPPER

WHETHER YOU GO TRADITIONAL OR UNTRADITIONAL WITH YOUR wedding-party concept, choose your attendants carefully. Consider not just the role in your life (best friend, sister, whatever) but also the time they have to give you, their propensity for weddings like yours, and so on. In other words, make sure they really want it. Weddings don't have to be agonizing or drama laden. Just choose wisely.

I spoke to one bridesmaid who got chewed out by the bride when the bridesmaid dared to get her hair cut during the engagement. Apparently, her new bob wasn't going to fit with the predetermined bridesmaid updo. If hair uniformity is really important to you, just make sure you have friends who are equally into this level of meticulous detail. A mismatch of personalities can be a pain in the ass when, honestly, honey, you don't need any more pains in that ass of yours.

Be clear in what you're asking

Offbeat reader Jennie offered this advice: "Examine your motivations closely. Do you want a bridal party because that matches your idea of what wedding photos look like? Do you want them to help you feel more special on your day? Do you want them there because you can't imagine getting married without them standing up for you? You need to be clear about whether wanting these people to fill a particular role is all about you or all about them . . . then I'd suggest being really transparent with them about that. Let them know what your needs and expectations are when you ask, in order to avoid bridal drama."

Jennie really wanted to have her friends and family close in her wedding but sadly admitted, "Almost the only stress I had [during the wedding] was from conflicts between bridesmaids." Now is not the time for it. A wedding is hard enough without people going the

TIP: IT'S OKAY TO PICK NONE

EXPECT YOUR WEDDING-PARTY CHOICES TO BE TAKEN TO HEART. I don't know why, but people seem to just love feeling hurt and excluded, so when it comes to having a wedding party, you *might* want to choose no one. As Heather remembers, "I just couldn't see us having brides-maids and groomsmen. We just aren't those kind of traditional people. We don't have one or two close friends; we have seventy-five close friends each."

stereotypically bitchy-ego route. The way I see it, part of the gift your wedding party should give you is their kindness, time, and patience. Infighting doesn't qualify. I don't mean to get all tsk-tsky on anyone here, but come on: let's make it common courtesy to treat everyone in the wedding with the respect they deserve. Deep breath. Let's move on.

The wedding bouncer

One important role for the wedding party is to act as your buffer, so pick folks who've got some chutzpah. At my wedding, I commissioned a former coworker (a workaholic who lives to move mountains and make things happen) to act as my bridal bodyguard. The day of my wedding, she hovered outside the cabin where I was getting prepared, telling people to back off, get out of the way, or help her find something I needed. At one point, just before pictures were being taken, I noticed that a number of people had arrived early and were milling about. I sent my bodyguard to go let them know that the reception wasn't starting until 4:00 P.M., and to ask whether they would mind helping us keep things clear until then. Unwittingly, I asked my bodyguard to shoo away everyone, which ended up including Auntie Andrea and her partner, who huffed that they were related to the bride and had every right to be milling about, thank you very much! Meanwhile, I was obliviously getting dressed and having my makeup done.

When I asked Jen about her wedding party, her experience echoed mine. "They kept a ton of drama from happening by saying, 'I'm sorry, you can't talk to the bride right now. Could you please go to another side of the building for a couple of hours?'"

See? I wasn't the only one who sicced my wedding party on family. That's part of what makes a good bridesmaid, groomsgirl, or supreme being of chickness.

7. OURWEDDINGFAQ.COM

Behold the "wedsite" & wedding hashtag—
evidence of a twenty-first-century wedding

I AM A GEEK. I MAY HAVE ALWAYS BEEN A GEEK. IN FACT, I MAY HAVE been predestined to be a geek: my father's primary sport in college was jump-roping. Need more proof of the geekiness in my veins? Dad started working with computers in the late '60s. I was doomed to have my first internet date in 1992.

A quick rundown of the geek history: created art on Apples in 1984, spent afternoons playing with Mom's word processor in 1987, obtained first family computer in 1991 and first e-mail address in 1994, found design for my first tattoo online in 1995, built first website in 1996, founded first blog in 2000, and then went on to found digital publishing company in 2007.

The blog started innocently enough: at that point, I was an urbanite living an hour south of Seattle in a house in the forest. To honor the city/country dichotomy of my own split personality, I called the blog *Urban Forest* and wrote about whatever I wanted, including dalliances and parties and things that no smart person should write about online in the Age of All-Seeing Google.

The blog began to gain momentum, getting linked on a few heavily trafficked sites. Suddenly, I realized that it was more than just my out-of-town friends reading my words. I toned things down (for god's sake, Stallings, tread carefully when writing about work, sex, and people! . . . which for me means always tread lightly, because those are the things I like to write about).

Still, I've continued to expose my least juicy bits online ever since. It's part of how I remember things. My short-term memory's not always so good. Write it down, write it down. Whatever goes unwritten goes forgotten. This translated into my wedding planning, too: suddenly I was making meticulous lists of every detail. Half these lists made it onto my blog, which was suddenly taken over by wedding planning.

Within a day of announcing our engagement on my blog, there were thirty comments to the announcement post and even more e-mails with congratulations—and questions. Oh, the questions. After a few hours I decided that I must do as busy, bothered geeks have always done: I crafted an FAQ.

And why not? Brides have some pretty common frequently asked questions, like, Are you keeping your name? What was the proposal like? I am not a woman of mystery. Information wants to be free and overabundant, and if you're going to make news public, you want to make sure everyone has every . . . last . . . nugget of information. My blog readers and our wedding guests were nothing if not overinformed.

Using our wedding website (adorably known as a "wedsite"), I filled guests in on every nuance, including what kind of apparel would be inappropriate (basically, you could show up naked if you wanted, but don't wear heels!), why it wasn't a great idea to bring dogs, and how to arrange carpooling.

Our website was an overkill explosion of information for guests, and you know what? I wish everyone's was. I want to know what other people are going to be wearing! Will we be at fancy tables outside under a tent or inside a warm dining hall? I tend to overthink things, and that goes for both attending and planning a wedding, apparently.

Rockwellian moderne

Regardless of how overzealous you may or may not be in the content development of your own bridally branded information portal, organizing wedding information into one helpful site makes the wedding organizer's life easier by cutting down (at least a little bit) on the never-ending nattering questions from guests. Plus, the sites can be a genuine treat.

Matt Haughey, founder of Metafilter.com, loves wedsites:

> I must admit I feel a second wave of excitement long after web-nerd friends announce their intent to marry: It's when the invitation arrives and there's a new URL to signify their love. you go to this intensely personal site meant only for a handful of family and friends, and you get to see photos you've never seen before, and often you see a new blog with comments from your friends' brothers and sisters—and you didn't even know they had brothers or sisters.

Wedsites are a great way to pre-introduce the members of your extended communities to each other. On ours, we listed all the people who were helping us, complete with a thumbnail photo and a little bio. I wanted to do family-member profiles too, but Andreas nixed the concept, probably dreading the idea of running our families through Ariel's Descriptorama Machine. Fair enough.

You may find that even the web-phobic are relatively okay with wedsites, as long as you keep your dot-com sensibility focused on simplicity. Offbeat reader Jennie told me, "More people than I'd expected looked at our website. Even the older, less technical people had been shown the site by their children or grandchildren."

See? Picture it as a cross-generational opportunity for shared family time around the ol' 'puter. Very Rockwellian moderne, darling.

For those of you who have your own websites, you know that the web is all about ME, ME, ME, and wedsites are about letting everyone know more about YOU, YOU, YOU and YOUR, YOUR, YOUR WEDDING.

That said, the web isn't just good for oversharing thoughts; it's also great for researching, planning your event from afar, investigating vendors, getting ideas, and kvetching.

Offbeat reader Maria said that she used the web to plan almost every component of her wedding. "I work in IT and spend a good ten hours a day in front of the computer. I even met my husband online, so as you can imagine, most of my wedding was organized over the internet. I found my photographer, florist, and limo on-line. . . . We sent our vows to the registrar for him to approve over an e-mail. The engagement and wedding were both announced over e-mails, and the ceremony at Glastonbury Festival was all or-ganized though the chapel's website. We also designed a wedsite, so that everyone who wasn't there (that's everybody, really) could see the pictures."

TIP: WHAT SHOULD YOU PUT ON YOUR WEDSITE?

I MIGHT BE EXTREME IN BOTH MY WEBGEEKERY AND MY NEED TO KEEP my guests informed, but it's safe to assume that if you're planning an offbeat wedding, your guests are going to have questions. Head them off at the pass by providing them with information to make them feel safe. It's easy to create a wedsite—there are numerous free services that make it as simple as picking a template, typing in some text, and press-ing Save. Just search the web for "free wedding websites." You'll find dozens of free services.

When figuring out what information to share with guests, consider this: a good wedsite makes it easier for your guests to enjoy themselves at your wedding. When crafting the mission statement for your own little dot-com, keep this line in mind: leverage information so guests can gain the most enjoyment from your upcoming nuptials. Wedsites can act as an impersonal tour guide. You may not have time to show out-of-town guests around, but you can give them the information they

>>>

need to have a great visit, aside from the wedding. Anything that keeps you from having to play tour guide when you're about to get married is a good thing.

Oh, and you definitely want to have lots of photos. Everyone loves photos. Fewer words. More photos. That said, your words may include things about lodging, registry information, transportation options, fun things to do in town, backstory of the happy couple, information about venues, and so on. Refer back to the motto: leverage information so guests can gain the most enjoyment from your upcoming nuptials. And take a look around the web at some of the hundreds of thousands of great wedsites out there.

#wedding #planning #hashtags

Your wedsite is also the perfect place to introduce your wedding hashtag if you want to use one. Hashtags are great for your guests on social media to tag photos and status updates they make about or at your wedding so you can find all the info in one place. People who can't make it to the wedding can follow along in real time as your guests update the hashtag. Plus, this is also a safe place to be as punny as you want without repercussions!

Be warned when choosing your hashtag, though: it has to be unique enough so that your photos don't get mixed up with the latest meme on Twitter, and easy enough to spell so that you don't have four slightly different variations to browse through.

Think about combining your names, referencing the name of the venue, your wedding theme, your hobbies, and so on. If you can't come up with your own hashtag, there are websites that can help you generate them. And don't forget about the websites that aggregate the hashtag use across social media sites, making it super easy to corral all those posts.

> **HERE ARE SOME HASHTAGS OFFBEAT BRIDE READERS HAVE SHARED:**

» My new last name is Handley, which sounds (a little bit) like "happily"—so we went classic romantic with our hashtag and chose #HandleyEverAfter

» I'm going to be a Howe, so ours is #HoweSweetItIs

» Last name Pham: #wearePhamily

» For last name Gidrey: #GidreyUp

» New last name Grey: #isupportgreymarriage

» Last name Wiener: #WienerTakesAll

» My name is Annelise and my last name is my fiancé's name is Alex: #bringyourAgame

» Last name Wilk: #WilkYouMarryMe

» Last name Pitts: #newPittsontheblock

» Last name Whiteley: #NiceDayForAWhiteleyWedding

» Brittany & Aaron: #Brittron

» I'm the Holsinger and he's the Webster: #theWebbingSinger

» Last name Blake: #takestheblake

What happens if you don't want your wedding on social media?

Hashtags are great and all, but what about those of us who don't want our guests to share our wedding with millions of strangers as it's happening? In Chapter 34 we'll talk about unplugged wedding ceremonies. If you have one of these, and explain to your guests via some combination of the wedsite, invitations, programs, ushers, and officiant that devices need to be kept out of sight, this will probably solve the social media problem, too. The most you can do is ask politely and explain to your guests why it's important to you. Ultimately, you can't control people's actions, but you can make your wishes clear and hope for the best.

TIP: SHARING YOUR WEDDING PLANNING ON SOCIAL MEDIA

REMEMBER WHEN WE TALKED ABOUT ANNOUNCING YOUR ENGAGE-ment in Chapter 2? Social media makes this even more complicated. Do you want to post a Facebook status update about your wedding? What happens if you start getting comments from people you have no intention of inviting? Did you post just after someone close to you went through something really rough? Or just after someone close to you announced their engagement?

These are all considerations when taking to social media for the announcement. And after the announcement, think twice before post-ing about planning. We live in the age of overshare and sometimes forget that not everything needs to be documented for everyone. It's better to keep those updates to a smaller group of friends and family you really know well so that nobody's feelings get accidentally hurt. However, you have every right to use social media the way you want to. Be conscientious and respectful (and throw in a GIF or two) and celebrate your news!

part two

Vanity, Fashion & Other Things We Supposedly Shouldn't Care About

8. THE PRINCESS INDUSTRY

Are you high maintenance?

I AM FULL OF CONTRADICTIONS WHEN IT COMES TO GIRLIE-GIRLNESS. I wax my legs but then go hairy months at time. I tweeze my brows yet rarely worry about my armpits. I get my hair colored but only wash it twice a month and barely brush it. I'm like a poodle with fancy sculpted leg puffs and a shit-stained, matted tail.

This incongruity was only magnified by wedding preparations. I planned to do my hair myself, winding it up in two buns to anchor my headpiece. And yet I got a facial and full-body wax (yes, even pits). The facial actually sort of sucked; the salon receptionist squealed at me, "You know what tomorrow is, don't you?"

I was stupefied.

"The Nordstrom semiannual sale!" She whined on, "I'm so superficial! It's my favorite day of the year! Shopping, shopping, shopping!"

I was clearly not among my people. I almost ran out of the salon, which was appropriately named High Maintenance. But I stayed and had my pores squeezed, feeling guilty and overly self-indulgent the whole time. It felt like I'd signed a contract when I walked in vowing to represent the salon's name, care deeply about Nordstrom's sales, and obsess over the color of the gunk in my pores.

I felt, in other words, like a sellout. Like I'd bought into the disgusting princess industry that exploits women by manufacturing vanity and anticipating every possible beauty need that blushing brides could possibly (not) need. Facials! Waxing! Manicures! Massages! Pedicures! Elaborate updos! Professional makeup jobs! Weight loss! Body buffing! Botox injections! Bridal breast augmentation! Where does it end?

It can be rough to reconcile. Offbeat reader Laura said, "I have a strong anti-consumerist streak, as well as a feminist distaste for societal expectations of women's appearance." But she admitted to worrying about how white her teeth were. She herself described her concern as "petty" and remembers how she felt guilty for indulging in a little vanity. She worried that she was buying into "just one aspect of the whole beauty-industrial complex that also pushes breast implants and anorexia." She's right, of course. She also still paid someone to do her hair for the wedding. Was Laura a victim, or was she a well-educated woman who chose her own path through the thorny forest filled with tested-upon animals?

I chose to believe the latter—but there's no denying that I could simply be justifying my own behavior to myself. The issue for most Offbeat Brides isn't wanting to feel like a celebrity or a princess or somebody else's image of beauty. It's wanting to feel your most lovely, whatever that entails.

Let's not kid ourselves: for most of us, a wedding is the most photographed day of our lives. And goddamnit, who doesn't want to look good for that? Hence, I have to pay someone a day's worth of my salary to squeeze my zits and pull hairs out of my follicles. As Offbeat Bride reader Leah said, "Somehow, many otherwise perfectly reasonable women become convinced that if you don't have a personal makeup artist, the perfect veil, the blue garter, etc., you won't really look like a bride."

Bullshit. All you need to look like a bride is to be standing next to someone you love deeply, someone to whom you're ready to commit. But even the humblest of us have thin streaks of vanity.

That postfeminist rebel–meets–snotty brat look

The biggest conflict Andreas and I had with our whole fucking wedding was over whether I should wear makeup. It's remarkable that, of all the arguments we could have had, the only one was over vanity.

I typically don't wear a lot of makeup. I have some amateurish drugstore goods that I smudge on (glittery eye shadow, candy-pink lipstick, other leftover raver sparkles) when I go out for a night on the town, but if I remember to use blush on my pasty Seattle skin before I head to work, it's a fancy day. I haven't ever owned powder or foundation.

However, we had a guest coming up from Los Angeles—and she happens to be a professional makeup artist. She does amazing work in Hollywood, and she once testified (supposedly from first-hand intelligence) that Justin Timberlake didn't shave his chest (he waxed). She wanted to do my makeup as her gift to me, and I was beyond excited. I used to do musical theater, and what's a wedding if not a mini-performance? And fuck it! I wanted to look good for my personal paparazzi. With this friend's brushes and magical powders on my face, it would be an honor as much as a celebration of my own pathological narcissism. Go vanity!

Upon hearing this plan, my *Free to Be You and Me* fiancé went stony and cold. He remembered how I'd looked after a friend's wedding when I had my makeup done at a salon. He was frightened by the plasticized foundation and the dark blush and could barely look at me all day. He told me it would look like I was wearing a mask to our wedding, so he requested a no-foundation-makeup rule.

Well, my skin's pretty clear, I thought. Maybe that's not a problem. But a makeup artist isn't like a sandwich artist. When I passed along Andreas's proposed rule, our friend made it clear that, as a professional, she required freedom to do what she needed to do for her best possible work. I respected that. I wanted to look good for my pictures, and I know that foundation can make that easier. My own internal froufrou glamour-puss and dirty-hippie-child sides were now externalized, with our makeup-artist friend playing my princessy side and my fiancé acting as the voice of down-home, progressive logic.

Andreas sets new standards when it comes to not being controlling (trust me on this one), so I knew the makeup issue was important, and the respectful, accommodating partner in me wanted to abide by his wishes. But my outfit was theatrical, I wanted to wear some dramatic makeup, and, for god's sake, just like I wouldn't ever let someone force me to wear makeup, I wasn't going to let someone forbid me from it! Keep your laws out of my body and off my face! Postfeminist rebel? Snotty brat? Who knows! I make no excuses for my behavior; I only offer possible armchair explanations. Really, it probably just came down to a toxic combination of stubbornness and vanity.

Andreas argued his case with well-crafted nuggets of romance, saying things like, "I want to be able to see the woman I'm marrying! I want to be able to see your face, the face I fell in love with. Not some sort of plasticky fake face!"

How could I argue with that?

But, of course, I did. Or rather, I let our friend the makeup artist argue for me. (See, the whole externalizing-internal-conflict thing works great!) She explained to Andreas that she was known in the industry for her work with skin tones, and, by god, she'd show him that in Los Angeles the standards are world-class high, and she's not some small-town Seattle salon aesthetician, and have a little faith! Mouthy makeup-artist friends are awesome.

I prevailed in the makeup argument, and the end result was to everyone's liking. Andreas was pleased with my subtle skin, and I was happy with the dramatic eyes. Our friend the makeup artist gave Andreas a hearty ribbing, scoffing, "See? I told you so!" And I had the gloaty knowledge that the gold eye shadow I was wearing had supposedly been Britney Spears's favorite on her last tour. I take my celebrity gossip in double shots, straight up with a rim of coarse salt. It's a vice.

Spa days and lake water updos

Although it's up to each Offbeat Bride to decide how much they want to rage against the princess-industry machine of hair, skin, massage, and nails, there is something to be said for the stress-reducing powers of pampering. Offbeat reader Leah went for a spa day with her bridal party and reported, "It wasn't something I would've done on my own (I'd never had a facial or a massage before)! But it was fun and relaxing, and it was a nice time with my friends. We got to hang out, relax, and enjoy each other's company for an afternoon." If the structure of paid pampering allows you to have some quality relaxation time before your wedding, do it. You need as much relaxation as you can get. More on that in Chapter 30, "Staying Sane."

The best is when brides find ways to feel pampered that work perfectly for them. Offbeat reader Brittany shared this serendipitous beauty regime: "I have naturally curly hair, which tends to take a lot of product to straighten or not look frizzy. Since I was having an outdoor lakeside wedding in humid August, I planned on using a lot of hairspray and gel to get it to cooperate, something I don't normally bother with. I spent the afternoon of my wedding day floating on a raft and hanging out in the water. When I left the raft to get ready for the wedding, my friend I had recruited to do my hair took one look at it and told me not to wash it, as the combination of lake water and sunshine had dried it in perfect small ringlets, and no frizz! She pinned it up as is, and

it was magically the best hair day of my life. No products needed!
The afternoon in the lake also made my skin look radiant and
glowing—no spa needed!"

To me, Brittany had the best updo possible, not just because it
was so low maintenance but because it was a natural extension of
her day and her life; she didn't borrow a vision (or a hairstyle) from
someone else.

9. CLOTHES FOR THE FEMMES

On pouf dresses and barefootedness

I LIKE TO PLAY WITH FASHION, AND, WHEN IT COMES TO SPECIAL OCCA-sions, my clothes border on costume. I like to use old clothes as new fabric, and I'm known for making weird things out of old sleeves and abandoned sweaters. I can't really sew, but I do have an old sewing machine that I use like a sports car: pedal to the metal and no road map! Faster, pussycat! Sew, sew!

I also wear my subcultural epaulettes on my sleeve. I haven't been to a big warehouse rave since Clinton was in office, but I still find myself wearing obscenely bright colors and platform shoes. I still like enormous fuzzy hats and sparkly makeup. I no longer wear the trademark phat pants that were the standard for ravers, but if you scratch right under the surface, you'll find I'm wearing rainbow socks and other bits of cartoon detritus.

Then again, I sometimes dress like the hippies who raised me. I dress up a lot, but I don't do semiformal very well or very often. I don't know how to walk in narrow heels, I always put runs in panty-hose, and I can rarely get my hair to look tidy. It was clear I would not be wearing the white strapless dress with a pouf skirt and heels that grace most bridal magazine covers.

I wanted to dress for my wedding the same way I would for my favorite kind of party, which is to say like a fairy-freakish electro forest queen. I have a passion for local independent de-signers—badass chicks with sergers and sewing machines doing things that I could definitely dream of but never accomplish.

One such designer had caught my eye. Her style was influenced a bit by Renaissance faires (not my scene, but who can deny the cleavage?) and a bit by postapocalyptic Burning Man madness. Exactly what I was going for! The designer's specialty was corsets.

I'd never worn a corset before, and I'm definitely not into the waist-training fetish thing. I reject restrictive clothing on principle, but, then again, I've always thought that corsets make women look hot. Somehow, an outerwear corset seemed like the perfect fashion centerpiece for this wedding.

I worked with another local designer (who happened to be an old rave friend) on the bottom half of the outfit, which consisted of a lime-green organza overlay ripped off a secondhand prom dress and a cream satin skirt. On my head and in my hair I wore a color-coordinated, butt-length ribbon pony fall/headpiece that substituted for a veil and made me look like a Renaissance alien.

The shoes were a pair of overpriced, asymmetrical low heels made by a trendy Spanish designer whom I should know better than to adore so profoundly. My only excuse is that I bought the shoes on eBay, so they were cheaper than they would have been new (but still too much). I'm a recovering shoe slut, and although I've effectively beaten most of the bad consumer habits out of myself, when it came to the wedding, I was a relapsed victim of my shoe impulses. I have deep admiration for the brides I spoke to who got married in kicks from Payless ShoeSource. I should have been one of these brides, but even smart girls fall prey to chick-lit shoe fetishism. My only excuse is that my day-to-day shoes are nursing clogs, so stereotypical shoe-lusting is only for special occasions!

Wedding gowns and wedding pants

Obviously, brides and other femme-types have deeply different needs when it comes to their wedding dresses. For me, it had to be relatively comfortable. It had to be able to work outside, feature reusable components (to justify the cost), and make me feel funky

TIP: DO NOT LACE UP AND DRIVE!

THE DESIGNER CINCHED ME UP DURING THE FITTING (A WELL-MADE corset should feel like a comfortable hug, and this one did), and I was so excited that I asked her if I could leave it on so that I could show Andreas.

Learn from my mistakes: driving in a corset is very difficult. I leaned my seat way back and sat up as straight as I possibly could, but I was constricted to the point of getting flushed and slightly light-headed. I had to roll down the window for the last few miles of the drive.

Don't go getting all Victorian while driving. It is not ladylike to swoon while operating heavy machinery.

and sassy as hell. One bride I spoke to didn't know what she wanted until she found herself inspired by her sister's hand-me-down sundress from high school. Offbeat reader Jen needed something she could move in, because her wedding involved a lot of dancing, running around, and trapeze swings. She also required a skirt that could be ripped off as part of her reception's first dance, revealing a pair of red hot-pants.

Others opted for less opulence and more of a classical look, wanting something that they wouldn't look back on and regret in twenty years. As for me, I'm not afraid of being the butt of a good joke. Our wedding was a representation of exactly where we were when we got married, and, as such, it will stand as a relic of the era. I love my parents' wedding pictures from 1974, with my bearded father wearing a shirt embroidered with a lion and my mother five months pregnant and crowned by a wreath of daisies. The question to ask yourself is whether you want a zeitgeist wedding.

Even those with varying needs seem to agree on one thing: having your clothes custom made is truly a luxury. How often do you get to wear an outfit made to your specific measurements? Why spend your money on a designer gown when you can put it in a local seamstress's pocket and have the best-fitting outfit ever? Many brides told me that their custom clothing cost them more than they would have ever spent for something off the rack but that they felt good about working with the artisans who actually created the garments—an increasingly rare experience in this era of Old Navy. You get emotionally resonant bonus points if your dressmaker is a friend or relative!

Custom-made gear can potentially also let you skip the whole bridal-shop experience, which may or may not be your thing. You know your tastes best, but, as one Offbeat bride recounted, "The first shop I went to put me in a meringue, stuck a veil on my head, gave me a fake bunch of flowers, and put me in front of a mirror. I think they expected me to cry." She didn't.

If, however, you think you will find a dress that will make you cry (in a good way), then a trip to a bridal salon might be a worth-while, even sentimental, moment. I heard beautiful stories of brides smiling into mirrors at themselves in dresses they'd never imagined liking, their mothers in tears at the sight. If that doesn't rock your boat, don't bother with boutiques. Offbeat reader Amy told me that she hit what she called "white blindness" pretty quickly while looking at traditional gowns, eventually giving up "in disgust, con-vinced that every single dress looked exactly the same: hideous!"

And what's with the white? I spoke to brides who wore red, cream, green, gray, and blue dresses—and just about every color in between. There are no rules.

What about when there's more than one bride? For some lesbian couples, it means going the two brides / two dresses route. Offbeat reader Kym wore a bright green dress, and her partner Ema wore a pale pink gown at their Pacific Northwest fairytale-inspired wedding, and they had an officiant who cheered their queerness. "Ema and I wrote our own vows," Kym explained, "and at the end, Ema's sister pronounced us 'gay married'—which brought down the house!"

Of course there are plenty of queer brides who forego the gown and go dapper instead. Offbeat reader Sarah explained that, though her partner Holly would be wearing the pants at their wedding, that's not a comment on her role in their future marriage: "Regardless of the fact that my future wife will be wearing the pants at our wedding, that doesn't mean anything except . . . she likes wearing pants. I mean, who doesn't?" Obviously, loads of people like wearing pants— brides, grooms, gender nonconforming and trans people, too!

Offbeat readers Kim and Jamie set out to make their vows to one another "legally official" at their intimate wedding, with Kim in a white gown and Jamie in a three-piece suit with contrasting waistcoat, no tie, and Converse. Then there were Käri and Roz, who both wore pants, ties, and button-ups, and had a great idea for avoiding gendered terms in their ceremony: "Because we didn't want any of the 'I now pronounce you . . . kiss the bride . . . ' stuff, our officiant gave us a wink and we kissed and were married!"

Regardless of whether you're wearing a skirt, pants, or something else altogether, wear something that makes you feel like you could take over the world. Because, in the right outfit, maybe you could.

🪩 A BIG-BRIDE SURVIVAL GUIDE

For plus-size brides, the sartorial landscape looks different. Offbeat reader Natalie wrote this time-honored survival guide:

> When I got married I was a fat bride. In fact, I was fat when I got en-gaged—I was even *gasp* fat when Nick and I met! Despite having a well-established, recognized, and loved body shape before getting mar-ried, I copped a huge amount of pressure to lose weight in the lead-up to the wedding. For some reason, I had it in my head that my wedding

day would be a celebration of love and happiness between Nick and me; however, it seemed that foolish me had little idea of the true wedding agenda—basically some kind of reality TV show where the ugly duckling turns gorgeous siren.

There would be no end of helpful clicks and tuts on hand to whip me into shape (I maintain that rectangular with bumps is a shape, dammit) for my reveal . . . wait . . . wedding day. My hairdresser at the time barely let her congratulations fly past her lips before she'd cornered me and asked how much weight I was losing. She lost the job. Bridal stores have ALL KINDS of euphemisms for asking about your weight loss plans. My favorite was the ever so polite "Now, are we planning on losing or gaining any weight for the big day?" Not to mention the hushed murmurings of "big girl," "solid build," "flattering," and "voluptuous." You know what? I walked out of all of those places. I wanted a bunch of supportive people helping me look even more fancy on my wedding day, not a wake of frowny-faced vultures picking over the fat girl.

I wanted to share a few things that helped me survive as a fat bride, because if you're not used to speaking up, it really can be intimidating and upsetting. I had a crystalline vision of how I wanted to look on my wedding day and I wasn't ashamed of my body, nor did I have plans to change it consciously before the date. Being somewhat blunt and quite confident, I had few real issues with the barrage of concerned but unhelpful people who just wanted me to look fabulous when I got married. I understood that they were coming from a mind-set held by most brides, a world where a slimmer bride must be the more beautiful bride, but I was not convinced of that!

1. COME OUT AS FAT TO ALL OF THE PEOPLE INVOLVED IN YOUR WEDDING PARTY.

Lay down some ground rules when it comes to your body—that is, it's none of your business. I also told my bridesmaids that I would not entertain negative body talk during the fittings. If they waited until I was out of the room, that was fine, but I didn't want dress fittings to be railroaded by unproductive and negative discussion!

2. LOOK AT SOME REAL-LIFE WEDDINGS.

Offbeatbride.com is one of my favorite wedding websites because there are so many different bodies all happy, celebrating, and looking great! Glossy magazines are fine, but if you don't want to have a traditional Western wedding, you'll be left feeling empty! There are heaps of wedding blogs out there to help you with ideas for garments, decorations, themes, and locations.

>>>

3. TALK ABOUT YOUR IDEAS WITH YOUR WEDDING PARTY.

This is especially important when it comes to garments. Different bodies like to wear different things!

4. BRIDAL STORES GENERALLY CARRY TWO SIZES IN "TRY ON" DRESSES—10 AND 18.

I think I only went to one store, where I definitely did not fit in the 18. I figured that if they were going to assume that they could just grade a smaller sized pattern up to "fit" me, then they could go jump.

5. INVESTIGATE A DRESSMAKER.

This is what I did—my mother and I asked an assistant at a local fabric shop for her recommendations and she gave us the phone number of the amazing Gloria, a couture seamstress and pattern designer. Gloria only took petite and plus-sized clients, and had incredible pattern drafting skills, which she used to outfit women who didn't fit within mainstream sizing. Instant brownie points! Working with Gloria was a great experience—I had designed my dress, but with her guidance we made it epic! We also designed the bridesmaid dresses in such a way that the design would be adapted for each of the girls' personalized slopers (a sloper is like a basic pattern created to fit your measurements). I wanted my sisters and my friend to feel special on the day, with a gorgeous dress that they felt great in.

6. IF A VENDOR BOTHERS YOU ABOUT LOSING WEIGHT, DROP THEM.

If you feel up to it, you can always say something like, "I'm not planning on losing weight for my wedding." You don't need to sass them back or come back with a quip that will make them regret ever saying anything to you. You don't have time for that, and you'll feel rotten afterward. Focus on your main goal—getting this theatrical monster of a wedding on the road.

7. LISTEN TO PEOPLE, BUT DON'T FORGET THAT YOU ARE THE AUTHORITY ON YOUR BODY.

Plenty of bridal (and plain old everyday fashion) assistants have plenty of things to say on what's "flattering" or "suitable." There seems to be a metric buttload of rules and regulations, and if you bother following all of them, you'll basically wave goodbye to any sense of individuality. If you really want to wear a dress that's cut a certain way, ask the assistant or the dressmaker whether there's something close if they absolutely veto your first choice (or dump them). Tell them why you want your neckline just like so. Be assertive and use "I statements"—"I feel confident when I have cap sleeves" or "I feel really gorgeous in a strapless dress." Push for what you want, or else you're having someone else's wedding.

>>>

8. WEAR COMFORTABLE SHOES THAT FIT YOU CORRECTLY.

Most wedding days go on for twelve hours—you don't want to be wearing unsupportive shoes that make you snarl. Alternatively, take your damn shoes off. I did that, because my gorgeous Italian slingbacks kept slipping off! Unfortunately I also stood in dog poo, but, uh . . . what can you do when you can't see your feet, let alone half a meter in front of you?

9. YOU DON'T HAVE TO WEAR THE GARTER BELT.

I really did not want Nick to dig through my skirts and pull a rotten scrunchy off my thigh, only to throw it to his mates. The whole idea grossed me out. What I did was arrange to slip it to him with my magical sleight of hand during the whole garter toss show. I was going to pin it inside my skirt, but I didn't get a chance! Of course, if you hate this part of the reception—nix it. You're not really beholden to anyone to include anything on your wedding day besides the bits required by law during your ceremony!

10. HAVE FUN!

After months of planning, your wedding day should be when you take the pressure down. If you've been true to yourself and your relationship, you should be feeling completely at ease—surrounded by all the people who love you and wish you well.

10. CLOTHES FOR THE NON-FEMMES

Thinking outside the tux box

MY GROOM AND I HAD VERY DIFFERENT SENSIBILITIES WHEN IT COMES to fashion. I can't get over my penchant for raver colors and sparkles, and Andreas dresses like the Midwest academic feminist he was raised by. He leans toward comfortable, functional, and usually natural fabrics. He had a brief period of making his own parachute pants in the late '80s, and he has a weakness for certain European shoes, but he's a pragmatist when it comes to clothing. This is one of the few ways we fall along stereotypical gender lines.

Our contrast in style meant that, while I dreamed of getting married in gold-brocaded corsets and headpieces made from strips of fabric and organza ribbon, Andreas mentioned a simple pair of linen pants. We each were thinking the same thing: we wanted to be dressed like we were going to a really big party. Only for me that meant "sparkle-pony cosplay outfit," and for him it meant "comfort shoes and dancing pants."

Andreas was certainly more practical. We were, after all, getting married outside. Our wedding was going to be distinctly low key, with mismatched chairs and blankets as seating. I realized we were having a nice, casual wedding in the forest, and although Andreas's clothes might reflect that, I was going to show up looking like I'd gotten lost on the way to a Mad Max cyber-brothel. My groom and I would clash.

But Andreas had a trick up his sleeve! He found inspiration in the form of a faintly remembered Sprite commercial from the late '80s. If you were of a certain age watching TV at a very certain time, there's a tiny chance you might remember the ad as well. It featured a punk kid with a mohawk and a slashed tuxedo, playing the violin in a park. The chorus reassured the kid that we liked the Sprite in him. He was that perfectly precious soft-drink rebel.

Apparently this advertisement had a profound effect on the adolescent Andreas. He had Sprite in him too! He was the punk-rock classicist, the ass-kicking spacy savant who wasn't afraid to say who he was or play his metaphorical violin in the alley or marry his weird-ass girlfriend!

And so it was that Andreas would be married in tuxedo tails with sleeves artfully ripped off and given a distressed finish by our seamstress friend Chaya. The spin on the traditional was the perfect complement to my outfit, and we coordinated by using the same material for my underskirt and his pants and by making his cummerbund out of the same lime-green organza as my overskirt. We were freaks united in love and green accessories!

Andreas struggled a bit with the shirt. He had envisioned something slightly piratey as a nod to my corset. As the wedding approached, however, the only shirt he had found was a flouncing costume pirate shirt that laced up the front. It was from International Male, a fabulously tasteless catalog that seemingly caters to gay escorts living in Miami who need things like bejeweled banana-bag thongs and lace-up pleather hip-huggers.

TIP: MATCH YOUR SKIRTS!

ONE POPULAR WAY FOR GROOMS TO PUT A TWIST ON THE OL' TUX IS to wear kilts . . . especially Utilikilts. I'm biased, because they're made in my hometown of Seattle, but these amazingly badass kilts are like the bastard offspring of a pair of Carhartts and a traditional kilt. They can be dressed up exquisitely, and isn't it nice for both of you to show off your legs?

When the shirt arrived, Andreas blanched; after trying it on, he broke out laughing. It was too much even for my costumey tastes. The pirate idea was scrapped, and Andreas instead ended up in an imported Afghani shirt made from thin cotton. We still receive mailings from International Male, though. I wrap gifts with the pages of the catalog, the best pages being the ones with hot pants that feature butt-enhancing ass-cheek pads.

Men often get short shrift in fashion—padded hot pants being the exception. Luckily, Offbeat Brides often end up with offbeat grooms—men who know that a little black eyeliner would look great with their tux or want their long hair braided back in an Elvish style that would make Legolas green with envy. One off-beat groom simply said he wanted to look like James Bond.

Although there are some grooms who are willing to play Ken doll, the goal here is that everyone feels good about themselves, and a guy with even half an inkling of vanity in him will find his own way to look good (a way, in fact, to make the whole wedding look good). One Offbeat Bride commented that she was hit with a sense of pride when her fiancé said, "When I picture myself as a groom, I see myself wearing this . . . " Why don't more little boys dream of the outfit they'll get married in?

Offbeat reader Amy remembers, "When it came to our color scheme, he decided my tastes couldn't be trusted—I would have made the whole wedding shocking pink and flaming orange! He chose a mellow lavender and green color theme. He also picked out a white linen suit (after briefly toying with seersucker), a purple shirt, and a blue tie: the very picture of a Southern aesthete."

There may, however, be limits for some people. I heard legends of a bride who'd talked her husband out of his dream outfit—a nod to his alma mater, with an orange-and-maroon tailed tux, a ruffled shirt, and a tie covered with small turkeys. Another wore a yar-mulke decorated with Grateful Dead dancing bears. Again, the goal is for everyone to feel comfortable, and if standing next to someone with a turkey tie makes you a little uncomfortable, then it's time to speak up and look for a compromise.

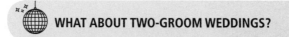

WHAT ABOUT TWO-GROOM WEDDINGS?

What about two-groom weddings? Turns out they're as varied as off-beat wedding attire.

Offbeat readers Jeffrey and Kevin's huge masquerade wedding on Halloween featured the couple's eleven groomsmaids and two groomsmen, all in complementary outfits complete with masks. The couple recited a love spell during the ceremony, and a psychic gave readings at the Haunted Mansion–inspired reception.

Offbeat Bride readers Kalisto and Ohanesian's Egyptian gothic meets *Frog and Toad Are Friends*–themed wedding included pagan elements, ornate black sherwanis as groomswear, and a trip to a history museum in a Rolls Royce.

After fourteen years together, offbeat couple Jeff and Don made their marriage official in an intimate Christmastime ceremony with just ten friends in a candlelit living room. They said their vows by the fireplace in elegant suits with festive ties.

Wayne and Jeffery did a wardrobe change at their Bollywood-inspired wedding on a yacht in Florida. After their ceremony (which featured their dogs as ring bearers), they changed out of their tuxedos into Swarovski-bedazzled traditional groomswear from India.

11. HERE, WEAR THIS

Dictating fashion to guests, friends & family

REMEMBER THE BRIDESMAID I MENTIONED A WHILE BACK, THE ONE WHO got chewed out because she got a haircut that didn't fit the bride's updo-able standards? When I got engaged, I swore to all things holy that I would not be that bride. But there comes a time in every bride's life when she must tell others what to wear.

Because they knew our wedding was going to be so weird, I wanted to give the guests some guidance on how to prepare, including at least a general sense of what to wear. I wrestled with this: what if, because we didn't have a wedding party, I was taking out strange, control-freakish updo-ability issues on the guests? What if I was that bride clutching her bouquet and sobbing through her Tammy Faye mascara about how she just couldn't believe that her aunt had come wearing last year's Prada? Such an embarrassment, and now it's going to be immortalized on film! Someone! Call the Bentley! I want to go back to the bridal suite and sob!

That's usually about the point when I emerged, drenched in sweat, from my fever dream and restrengthened my resolve to be the woman I wanted to be while planning this wedding. I reminded myself that I could be helpful without being a controlling, superficial rageaholic.

But I really did want to give guests an idea of what to wear. Especially when you're holding a nontraditional event that may be confusing for certain guests, you want to hand out as many life preservers as possible. For our hippie/raver freakfest wedding, we ripped off the invitation wording written by Mightygirl.com's Maggie Mason, who encouraged her guests to dress "creative casual." We took it a step further and went into a little bit more detail in our wedsite's FAQ:

> We're encouraging guests to go for what we call "wildly creative casual." Two things we discourage you from wearing:
>
> 1. High heels (They'll sink into the grass, and you'll have trouble walking.)
> 2. Super-fancy clothes (Our dinner will be served pic-nic-style on the lawn, and we don't want anyone wor-rying too much about their silk finery.)
>
> Ariel and Andreas will be getting freaky in clothes created by local designers Red Ant and DaintyCore. Take a look at their websites to get an idea of what we'll look like, and then plan ac-cordingly. Come in Birks, come in a tuxedo, come in Burning Man gear, come in drag . . . we just can't wait to see you!

See? Helpful without dictating in a way that felt control-freakish, like, *Dear Guest, Please Only Wear Blue. We Mean It.* It was a weird balance to try to strike. We wanted people to be com-fortable and have fun, but it felt a little awkward to instruct them on their footwear. I'm still not completely sure I nailed the FAQ writing, but dear lord, leave it to the writer to obsess over the copywriting for the wedsite FAQ. Just wait until you hear about the typo on the invitation.

I'm not the only one to have worried about guest attire. Offbeat reader Jennie told me, "I did have a moment, when I heard that just about all our close female relatives had decided to wear pink. I was worried people would think I'd asked them all to wear pink." See? No one wants to feel like a little dictator.

For traditional family members going to costume or themed weddings, knowing a little about what to wear can actually be a fun way to come together. Offbeat reader Echota told me about how she and her husband encouraged guests to dress in Renaissance costumes (if they wanted to): "We knew darn well that there was no way our families (other than my brothers, who had to because they were in the wedding) were going to dress in Renaissance costumes," Echota said. "And on the very day of our wedding, my mother, my husband's mother, brother, and sister were all donning Renaissance costumes in support of us. It was a huge and very happy surprise for us to see them all dressed up like that." Don't assume your family will rise to the challenge—but you might be pleasantly surprised.

For those who have a wedding party, the joy of dictating fashion to others gets even more complex. Issues of updo-ability may become very real, depending on the kind of bride you are. (Untraditional doesn't mean unmeticulous!) If you're the sort of style-conscious rockabilly girl who needs to maintain that perfect retro-kitsch fashion aesthetic, you had better be ready to tell your girls exactly what shade of fire-engine-red lipstick they need to wear.

Money, of course, factors into the issue. I keep hoping that the American tradition of making bridesmaids pay for their dresses is on its way out, because there's nothing worse than being forced to wear something you can't stand—and having to pay for it. When attendants are paying for their own clothes, I think it's only considerate to take their styles and body shapes into consideration—or, hell, let them pick out what they want to wear. Nobody wants to be immortalized in photos wearing an outfit that makes them feel awkward.

TIP: GUESTS ABSOLUTELY NEED TO KNOW
WHAT TO EXPECT.

COUPLES GETTING MARRIED OUTSIDE, ON BOATS, OR IN OTHER VENUES
prone to shifting temperatures, uneven walking surfaces, or other en-
vironmental surprises really should give guests a solid idea of what to
expect so they can pick their attire and footwear accordingly. A small,
tasteful insert in paper invitations can do wonders for your guests' comfort. Offbeat reader Jen noted that she's a guest at "too many weddings
when poor Grandma showed up and then kept sinking into the soft
ground or froze to death because there was nowhere to go inside."

Physical comfort is the priority, but making guests feel fashionably
comfortable is important too. Jen noted that even weird indoor events
can benefit from a dress-code insert: "When you do something nontraditional, it's fun for you . . . but you also want your guests to have fun.
Some of them won't have a clue what to expect—so you need to give
info and provide for them. They'll have a much better time if you do."

Boho coordination makes everyone happy

Years before I got married, I'd been asked to be a bridesmaid at a
childhood friend's traditional wedding. I accepted but immediately
warned her that I had really outlandish hair (at the time, it was
braided with a blinding array of Froot Loops–colored extensions).
I also reminded her about my tattoos on both shoulders. My friend
has always tended toward coordinating her socks with her cardi-
gans, and I totally respected the fact that I might clash with her
vision for the wedding and simply look too weird for the in-laws.

She insisted, however, that she wanted me in her wedding—and
the wacky hair was perfect. She then went out and found matching
floral dresses for me and the maid of honor. In keeping with my
friend's tastes, the matched dresses perfectly coordinated with my

candy-colored hair—and I couldn't help but notice that they had short cap sleeves that exactly covered my tattoos.

Thanks to the bride's dress choices, my weird hair looked like it had been specifically coordinated to the wedding (instead of the other way around), and the bride's dictating of the fashion was so perfectly suited to me that it was almost a gift, a sign that she really understood my style and could find a way to integrate me into her more traditional vision. My friend got everything she wanted: her bohemian friend in her wedding *and* precision color coordination.

Be prepared for some surprises, regardless of whether you take a totally laid-back approach or a detail-oriented, meticulous one. Jen recalled, "I didn't know what the groomsmen would be wearing, and that ended up being . . . interesting. One wore a yellow old-fashioned jacket, and the other wore a red Hawaiian-print shirt and a sparkly silver skirt. I just about fell over." And this was coming from a bride in a red, sparkly flamenco dress!

TIP: SOME PEOPLE WANT TO BE TOLD

OFFBEAT READER LEAH STUMBLED ACROSS THE OPPOSITE PROBLEM. She asked each of her three attendants to wear whatever they wanted, which worked just fine for two of them. "But the third had an unexpected problem!" Leah went on, "After trying to convince me to choose matching dresses for them, she tried to talk the other two into buying matching dresses, but they stood firm. After saying she was just going to wear jeans, I think she finally went shopping and found her dress about a week before the wedding." Some people apparently don't trust their own fashion choices. You may want to help these folks out.

part three

In the Thick of It

12. I AM WOMAN, HEAR ME ORDER MONOGRAMMED NAPKINS

Is "feminist wedding planner" an oxymoron?
Or, how to deal with your impending bridentity crisis

I HAD SOME TROUBLES GETTING INTO THE WHOLE BRIDAL IDENTITY thing. Despite my vanity, I wasn't into many of the stereotypical trappings of a bride—no ringlets in my hair, no big, poufy white dress, no special monogrammed ring pillows. I was the same woman I was before we decided to throw a party.

. . . Er, wasn't I? I had been writing FAQ copy telling my guests what to wear to my special daaaaay. Oh, god. Bridentity crisis!

Offbeat reader Phyllis was so uninterested in her own bridentity that she initially described her wedding as "a family event," explaining, "It was hard for me to say 'wedding' for the first few months of our engagement. As much as I loved my groom and was excited to marry him, I didn't feel like a bride, and the idea of a wedding embarrassed me."

I shared many of those feelings and thought of myself as sort of an embarrassed bride. Despite that, I was deliriously stereotypical in at least one way: I am an obsessive planner. I love lists and calendars and exact time frames in which to get my work done. Lucky for my sanity, I figured out years ago that the feeling of procrastination was much more painful to me than the feeling of just doing whatever needed to be done. Procrastination guilt is like my version of original sin. This meant no waiting until the last minute to plan our wedding; I was immediately full steam ahead. We had six months, and I was going to make that shit happen! On schedule!

See? No bridentity issues there.

This is one of the ways in which Andreas and I fell right on target with all the gender stereotypes: I am the bridal taskmaster, he the groom goer-with-the-flow-er. Once things got going, I was the one making most of the phone calls and doing the calendar keeping. I delegated, delegated, delegated, assigning projects to Andreas and tracking the progress of my own allotted wedding tasks.

But, whereas this bossy, ambitious, go-get-'em attitude normally makes me feel like a strong, independent ass-kicker, somehow, when I was applying those same aggressive, ass-kicking skills to wedding planning, I felt guilty of falling into a predetermined bridal role.

Oh, there I was, discussing what kind of cake to serve. Oh, there I was, wrestling up mugs for people to drink champagne from. Oh, there I was, compulsively gazing for hours over gold-filigreed napkins with our initials . . .

. . . *Kidding!*

There were no monogrammed anythings at our wedding. This was crucial to me, because somehow my line in the identity sand was that I was obsessively planning an *offbeat* wedding. Instead of monogrammed napkins, I was figuring out where our friend would set up his geodesic dome in the meadow where we would dance all night. So, sure, I was still the stereotypical bride, dictating and delegating and obsessing . . . but I was offbeat!

Project management by any other name . . .

My theory about demented bridal-control issues is that they come into stark relief when women typically denied power in their lives get a taste of it. Suddenly they're the commanding princesses, and everyone has to obey—and women unused to giving orders and being in control risk getting intoxicated by the power. Things can get warped awfully quickly.

In my dream world, these women realize that they secretly want to be organizing board meetings or starting their own small businesses. After the wedding day is over, they pour that energy into founding their own LLC. Sadly, however, it seems like many of them just fall into a funk (see Chapter 45, "Postweddin' Depression," for more).

My hope is that those of us who are headstrong bossy-faces in our daily lives have more experience in how to get things done without breaking down in manipulative sobs at a floral boutique or screeching over mismatched manicures. As someone who spends a lot of my daily life project managing, this was just another project to be managed. Tasks! Time lines! Resources! The only sobbing necessary was a private stress-release valve, not a controlling, explosive outburst to get something I wanted.

For brides who find themselves willingly stepping into project-management roles for their weddings (it's not a default role; if you're not interested, for god's sake, don't do it!), it can actually be useful to think of your wedding planning like any other chance for skill

TIP: UM, *HELLO?* I'M MORE THAN A BRIDE

ONE OF THE WEIRDER ASPECTS OF BEING A FIANCÉE IS THE BRIDE WORship. Offbeat reader Mary Ellen grumbled, "It drives me up a wall when everyone thinks that to become a bride is the be-all and end-all of my life, when no one seems at all excited about my professional achievements." For brides who are ambitious outside of their wedding-planning lives (which, if you'll excuse my bias, really should be every bride!), be prepared to feel belittled. Thank bridal worshipers for their excitement and then steer the conversation toward all the other things in your life that you're excited about, such as your academic, professional, or creative accomplishments and successes. It can work wonders to say something like, "I know, it's so crazy to be getting married the same year that I'm also founding my own engineering firm!" Graciously remind well-wishers that your bridentity is far from your only identity.

development: Make it an autodidactic process. When you're at the bookstore looking for wedding books, grab a couple books about time management and productivity, too.

If you're inclined to, think of your wedding as a chance to teach yourself some business skills. Project management, event coordination, conflict mediation—these are aptitudes MBAs pay big bucks for! Chances are that even if you've got a small budget, your wedding involves a bigger chunk of change than you're normally tossing around. When was the last time you spent $5,000 (or even $1,000!) on an afternoon party? If you're business or management minded, your wedding doesn't have to be a bridentity crisis—it can be a great opportunity to flex management skills you never knew you had.

FOUR MYTHS ABOUT BEING AN OLDER BRIDE: A.K.A. WHERE'S MY LIFE ALERT REGISTRY GIFT?!

The senior editor of Offbeatbride.com, Catherine, has this to say about planning her own wedding as an older bride:

> I've been a wedding blog editor for seven years now and have never actually been married myself. I'm now engaged and planning my own offbeat wedding for next May. This is the first marriage for both of us, and, pearls clutched, we're older. By the time I get married, forty will be staring me in the face. This isn't very old when it comes to first marriages, but it is older than the average in the US, which is about twenty-seven for women and twenty-nine for men. I'm also a city dweller, so that also means my chances of being married by that age are way lower. I don't feel weird about it at all, and I'm far more confident in my ability to choose a partner at this age than I ever was in my twenties.
>
> I anticipated that it would be a little different getting married later in life (what with the Ensure cocktails and shuffleboard reception), but it is taking some surprising turns. Here are some myths about being an older bride that I have discovered:
>
> **MYTH: YOU'LL HAVE TOTAL FREEDOM**
> My biggest misconception about having a wedding as an older bride was that I would have the freedom to do pretty much anything I wanted.

>>>

I figured that since I wasn't beholden to many people for financial help and that we were taking a slightly different route by having our first marriage later in life that folks would just let us run the show any way we liked. We're youth-impaired now, and a lot of it just seemed a bit . . . youthful to me.

I figured I wouldn't have to open gifts at a shower (we have too much shared stuff anyway), go partying at a hen night (are we in by 9?), or have to invite everyone we've ever known to the wedding itself. A lot of it just felt irrelevant since we're both in our later thirties and are already well established in life.

The truth is that I'm lucky enough to have many people who have been anxiously awaiting my wedding day for years or even decades (centuries?!) and they want to celebrate it RIGHT, silly hen nights and all. I'm not giving in to every tradition and pre-party (no shower, teeny tiny hen night, non-traditional wedding, small guest list), but I am definitely seeking to find a compromise with those traditions that I assumed would be optional for me as a more aged lady.

MYTH: MY PARTNER WOULD ALSO BE SEEN AS OLDER

Nope. He's just a normal dude getting married. Obviously this is a hetero-specific issue that plays on societal expectations and gender roles in relationships (and I'd LOVE to hear how you're seeing it play out in LGBTQ+ relationships, too!). We are about the same age, so I assumed that he'd be having the "finally" talks just as much as I was. Despite the fact that most of our friends are married, most with children, some even divorced, he's still viewed as a typical groom, age-wise. His more traditional friends and family are happy that he's "finally settling down," but, on the whole, his wedding planning experience hasn't been affected much by age factors.

MYTH: I'D HAVE TO HAVE AN "OLDER BRIDE" WEDDING

There's a stigma to second marriages where couples feel like they can't whoop it up the way they did at their first wedding. They have to tone down their look, opt out of a big ball gown, or keep the guest list smaller than they'd like. This is all bullshit, of course, and you can do what you like at your second, third, whatever wedding.

But there is an element in the back of my mind that almost thinks of a later-in-life wedding in the same way. Keep it small, keep it demure, don't be a blushing first-time bride of twenty-three. This one was pretty easy to squelch, though, as literally no one has implied that I need to keep anything smaller or less intense. As seen in the first myth, it's been quite the opposite.

>>>

MYTH: I'D KNOW WHAT I WAS DOING BY NOW

A wedding blogger who has been to many weddings and waited a thousand years to partner up? She's got to know how to plan a wedding.
Nah. I have zero clues. I like to say I've seen enough to know I've seen
too much and all of the weddings I've edited (literally thousands by
now) are a blur of loveliness and quirkiness that I haven't been able to
filter into something usable for my own wedding planning. And that's
totally okay. I've been using this blog as if I'm new to it when it comes
to wedding planning tips, and I'm loving it.

At times I feel very much like a young bride just getting started in life and
love, but, really, I'm a wizened old crone who scoffs at some traditions
and still swoons over others. Having a foundation of a bit of extra life
under my belt and a solid education on being authentic to myself from
this blog and others, I feel pretty ready to creak down the aisle with my
Life Alert at the ready in case I fall and can't get up.

13. OFFBEAT GROOMS

Wedding gender egalitarianism is hard,
even when he's a bigger feminist than you

IF YOU THINK THAT YOU, AS A FREETHINKING WOMAN, HAVE STRUGGLED with your bridentity crisis, think about how many grooms might feel. Many well-intentioned grooms get turned off of wedding planning because they get constant, chronic messages from friends, family, and the wedding-industrial complex that they don't have the right to an opinion on anything wedding related—that this is a woman's world.

In an article called "Being a Feminist Groom," *Mountain View Voice* writer Bill D'Agostino expressed frustration that the message he kept getting was, "This is not your gig, you hapless groom." He fought the assumptions about who would do the wedding planning, explaining, "One photographer we interviewed spoke only to my fiancée, Carrie, and talked about his goal being to make his 'girl' happy on 'her big day'—emphasis on her. The truth is, I want to be involved, and not just because I think it's fun."

Bill's interest was also a political statement: "Every step Carrie and I take toward gender equality is . . . two steps closer to sharing our lives equally." Wedding planning can be a fantastic opportunity to turn the cultural boat around and have one man at a time get more involved in planning his wedding.

Hopefully our children will find themselves in a world where their boyfriends are grunting over *Groom Gear* magazine. In the meantime, we can each allow and encourage our fiancés to be as active as possible in the planning. Offbeat reader Derek told me, "I think that members of our generation have an expectation of equality in all things, so brides should assume their grooms will be involved. If he's not, maybe he's getting bad advice from his family or society in general. Tell him you want your wedding to be as equal as you want your lives together to be."

Play to your strengths

If you're a woman marrying a man, hopefully your groom will be responsive. The sad reality, however, is that for a variety of socio-cultural reasons, you may end up planning a lot of your wedding. And maybe you like it that way. Offbeat Brides have numerous explanations for why they ended up in the planning role. "My husband and I divided the planning between us," Offbeat reader Jennie remembers. "I probably did more, but that's because I enjoy organizing things—not because he refused to do it."

In the spirit of egalitarian relationships, it seems like the easiest way to keep everyone happy is to divide the tasks. "Since both of us work full-time jobs, getting involved was almost a necessity," explained Offbeat reader Rich. "My wife was a mother, bride-to-be, and full-time employee. Unless I wanted to see her head explode, we needed to divvy up the tasks."

Rich went on to say, "As a DJ and a writer with some design skills, I thought I could bring a lot to the table in certain aspects, namely the music and the invitations. Even though we paired up on most things and made joint decisions, I definitely 'owned' those two aspects of the wedding planning, since they were my passion." The ideal is for each half of the couple to do what they're interested in and good at—and then evenly divide the shit work that no one wants to do.

Offbeat reader Deana argued, "I refuse to see the wedding plan-ning as primarily my responsibility, even though I'm focused on it way more than he is. I tend to throw myself into research when I get excited about anything, and so the same obsessive need to find

books and resources, write outlines, etc., that helps me in my work
is coming into play here."

Just because you plan the wedding, however, doesn't mean that
your groom won't be interested or appreciative. Offbeat reader Susan recounted, "I felt like planning the wedding fell to me both as
a traditionally female thing and as something I happen to be good
at, and that my husband wasn't as invested or as minute-to-minute
interested in it. On the other hand, the weekend of the wedding,
Andrew really stepped up and ran errands and took care of logistics stuff while I went to my crafty shower and got my nails
done. Also, I know he had a great time and really appreciated that
I pulled the whole thing off . . . and under budget, as a bonus. If
he had been totally oblivious, it would have been no fun at all, I
would have abandoned everything midplan, and we would have
done something really low key."

Not all brides get wrapped up in wedding planning. If I were less
of a control freak, maybe I would have let someone else organize
our wedding. As Rich said, "I think most modern-day men offer
their services at the beginning of the process—and some may be
fortunate enough to get certain tasks assigned to them that they
can call their own. But if you get enough criticism about stuff 'not
being right' or 'taking the wrong approach,' it's only a matter of
time before they bow out completely." Don't commit the sin of
asking your fiancé to get involved and then dismissing their ideas.
No one likes to work with a micromanager.

One bride described how her fiancé "realized that he had a
dream wedding in his head that he had never recognized before."
In my perfect gender-egalitarian world, partners would be matched
in terms of their interest levels. I guess it's up to each of us to pick
our gender battles, and if wedding planning is the place where you
want to wage that war, I say go for it. The world needs more men
with dream weddings.

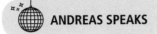 **ANDREAS SPEAKS**

Wait a minute, why *did* I do most of the wedding planning? Was it some sort of latent sexism lurking in my relationship with Andreas? How is that even possible? He's a bigger feminist than I am! Here was his explanation:

> While I'm aware that some of the logistical stuff that Ariel took care of fell along typical gender roles, I wasn't going to upend the ways in which we support each other in this relationship just for the sake of fighting the gender paradigm. Relationships are about sharing talents and utilizing and balancing each other's skills to come up with a better whole than you would on your own—isn't that the goal of marriage too? That the sum of the whole is bigger and better than its individual parts? So if you have certain talents, you utilize them.
>
> So in some ways, the wedding planning fell out in terms of our stereotypical roles—Ariel was in charge of cards and communication, sort of like she always is. Then again, I made sure the wedding went the way I wanted it. Serving a vegan dinner was a big deal to me, and having total control over my own clothes was very important.

The moral of the story seems to be, "Don't necessarily avoid doing what you're good at just because it's gender stereotypical." But examine your motives, avoid assumptions, and make it a choice instead of a default.

14. LGBTQ+ETC.

Wedding planning with a non-het identity

BACK IN 2004, SOME OF OUR FRIENDS SUGGESTED THAT ANDREAS AND I consider boycotting marriage completely, until all our queer friends and family could also legally get married. In Chapter 1, I mentioned Offbeat readers Joriel and Ben, who had a union ceremony and acknowledged that they might reconsider getting legally married when "adults of any gender can get married."

Thankfully, marriage equality finally happened in 2015, when the Supreme Court legalized gay marriage in every US state. (Canada was way ahead of us on legalization, but at least we beat the UK and Australia!) And yes: Joriel and Ben did indeed go on to get legally married, just like they said they would.

The Supreme Court ruling was not just momentous—quotes from it also make great readings at weddings. Take this one that Offbeat Bride readers Healey and Allie used in their Virginia wedding:

No union is more profound than marriage, for it embodies the highest ideals of love, fidelity, devotion, sacrifice, and family. In forming a marital union, two people become something greater than once they were. As some of the petitioners in these cases demonstrate, marriage embodies a love that may endure even past death. It would misunderstand these men and women to say they disrespect the idea of marriage. Their plea is that they do respect it, respect it so deeply that they seek to find its fulfillment for themselves. Their hope is not to be condemned to live in loneliness, excluded from one of civilization's oldest institutions.

They ask for equal dignity in the eyes of the law. The Constitution grants them that right.

After marriage equality swept across the United States, some folks started saying things like, "Now that it's legal, why even differentiate gay weddings at all—aren't they just weddings?" And although, yes, some queer couples reveled in the right to have "just a wedding," others wanted to make it clear that their weddings were both very legal and very, very gay.

As queer couples have attained the right to legally marry (and even found an increased visibility in wedding media), many still want to acknowledge and even highlight their non-heteronormative identities at their weddings. When Offbeat readers Betsy and Tiffany were planning their Atlanta wedding, they wanted to make sure that they acknowledged what made it different from other weddings: "In the fight for marriage equality, there's a risk that the thing that makes queer lives different will get lost in the shuffle. We wanted to celebrate the gayness of gay weddings and the importance of our broad family-of-choice to our lives."

Alternately, there are queer couples who want their weddings to more closely resemble a more traditional aesthetic. Some folks may expect queer weddings to be radically different or untraditional just because of the couple's identity—and that just doesn't jibe for some couples. When Offbeat readers Kristy and Flora were planning their North Vancouver lesbian beach wedding, they were surprised to find that their family and friends balked at their more traditional decisions, like having a bridal party and a father-daughter dance.

Flora wondered, "Some people expect [queer weddings] to be different, for a variety of personal reasons and pop culture assumptions. We hear more about the challenges couples face with their nontraditional wedding plans, but how about the challenges/

criticisms/judgments we face when we choose to include tradition?" She worried that she wasn't living up to some unwritten rule that seems to apply only to queer weddings:

> I was hurt—do they think my wedding is less cool now that they know there will be flower girls and a father-daughter dance? And I was confused—WHY should a same-sex wedding be so different from a straight wedding?
>
> Maybe because heteros have had a few thousand years of the right to marry, they feel freer to mess with tradition, whereas same-sex couples may feel the need to take it more seriously . . . to prove to their parents, friends, themselves, and society at large that this is a "real" wedding.

The pressure to conform to expectations of "what makes a wedding a wedding?" can seem like a double dose of shitty no-wins for queer couples. Is this gay enough to be a gay wedding? Is it wedding enough to be a gay wedding? If you want your queer wedding to include more traditional aspects because they reflect you and your partner more authentically, remember that your union, relationship, and lives are valid regardless of public perception. Your wedding is not a contest to prove you fit anyone else's expectations. There's no one way to be an Offbeat Bride!

Okay, but what about the BTQ of LGBTQ+??

Of course, it hasn't just been gay and lesbian couples "getting weddinged" since marriage equality became legal. The rest of the alphabet soup in LGBTQ-etc.-etc. have found their own ways of making their celebrations uniquely theirs, too.

Couples where one or both people identify as pansexual or bisexual (helloooo there, my fellow bisexuals!) have made it clear how important it is for them to make their identity visible at their wedding. Offbeat readers Fran and Siobhán wanted to acknowledge all types of queer love at their UK wedding: "Living a nontraditional life meant our guests weren't expecting a traditional day from the start, so we had complete freedom. We're bisexual, so it was important our day was a celebration of not just our love . . . but of love generally. The top table included a sibling's wife and girlfriend from their poly life, with a toast to the fact we could even have a legal ceremony."

Sometimes acknowledging the legality of the union can be a motivator. Offbeat reader Karalyn and her genderqueer partner, Ali, decided to move the date of their Brooklyn wedding up to celebrate their community and lift everyone's spirits after the 2016 presidential election. Their officiant spoke about the importance of support from a community when she said, "We have survived against all odds and this . . . this is what we have left. Queer love, defined most broadly, is what we have left. And not just romantic queer love, but queer friendship, and queer community. It is all we have left. And it is everything. This is what we celebrate today."

Queer weddings can also be a chance for the couple's friends to feel safe to express themselves in ways they typically can't. At Offbeat Bride readers Molly and Caleb's femme/transfeminine "celeGAYtion," both partners wore gowns and encouraged their guests to dress however they pleased:

We have a big, supportive community of friends, chosen family, and relatives who came out to celebrate our day. My favorite aspect was how queer it was! We explicitly told our guests to wear whatever clothing was most gender affirming for them, and it was wonderful to see so many of our loved ones (who often don't get to be themselves at big family events like weddings) get to rock their genders on our wedding day.

Couples where one or more members is transgender have shared stories about choosing to make part of their ceremony honor other trans people who may not yet feel safe enough to be out. Offbeat couple Liz and Elly held a moment of silence during their ceremony, which took place on Transgender Day of Remembrance. The ceremony included this prompt: "In recognition of the hard paths the brides have walked, of the paths their transgender sisters past and present have walked, and the paths their children may someday not find a little easier, please be silent for a moment of prayer."

Liz added, "At our local Transgender Day of Remembrance event, a friend of ours read an announcement of our wedding at the open microphone . . . in order to provide a beacon of hope and love and help lift up the spirits of our transgender community."

DEALING WITH QUEERPHOBIC GUESTS BEFORE THEY ARRIVE

If you've chosen to invite family members or friends who you know struggle with queer weddings as a concept, you may want to address the issue before your wedding. As a lesbian couple getting married in Spokane (a somewhat conservative city on the eastern side of Washington State) Offbeat Bride readers Sarah and Holly used their wedsite to broach the topic with their guests, ultimately explaining that they're not welcome if they're going to be assholes:

> As you can imagine, being part of a two-chick couple is not always simple on a cultural level. Holly and I are incredibly fortunate to live in a time when it's fairly accepted and generally safe for us to be together openly. We also live in a state where's it's been legal for two ladies or two dudes to get married for over a year. Yay, Washington!

> While we have a great group of friends and family that love us and are extremely excited for us, there are plenty of people who still struggle with accepting that us being together can be both normal and good. Perhaps you're one of them. You might also be unsure if you're going to be comfortable coming to the wedding . . .

>>>

Is the quality of the relationship more or less important than the quantity of men or women in it? If you believe it's less, I'll be the last person to ask you to compromise your beliefs or to share in our special day. Peace and love be with you. But, honestly, after seeing my share of abuse, infidelity, and broken marriages, I think we shouldn't just assume God is onboard at every boy-girl wedding we attend.

But, even if you cannot fully celebrate the quantity of ladies in our marriage, maybe you can be part of a celebration of love and commitment between two fellow humans.

Because, against all odds, by design, tradition, or accident, people still like to couple up. And, when the coupling is characterized by love, willingness, mutual respect, honesty, faithfulness, and joy, I think that's a win for humanity all around.

Asexual and polyamorous people get weddinged, too

Asexual people can find it challenging to navigate the sexualized aspects of wedding planning that don't interest them (like all that "wedding night" talk in Chapter 41!). Offbeat reader Gwendolyn told me she hadn't thought there was much reason to get married, because she'd always thought marriage = sex. Then she realized that it's up to her and her partner to define what marriage could be for them.

Her inspiration came from her own future family: "My future mother-in-law didn't need to get married again, but as she got older she realized she desired someone to 'build mutual memories with,' a companion rather than a live-in f@$%-buddy. I've always found her and her partner's relationship interesting since they're rarely in the same room together, they don't often eat at the same time, they're not all over each other; they're individuals who share their individuality with each other. I liked that! So my partner and I decided to really buckle down and figure out what marriage would mean for *us*, rather than what it meant to the rest of the world."

Again: *Offbeat Bride* is about finding what works for you, your relationship, and your wedding . . . even if the relationship doesn't look like what many people expect!

On the other end of the spectrum, there are polyamorous couples and throuples . . . and even quadruples! Sometimes polyamorous folks choose to involve their outside partners in their weddings or have commitment ceremonies for the whole group. Obviously, not all couples practicing polyamory choose to be "out" to their wider communities or extended families, but some polyamorous folks feel safe enough to make their multi-way commitment central to their weddings—even if the commitments are not legal in the certificate sense.

Massachusetts triad Brynn, Kitten, and Doll's ceremony made tongue-in-cheek reference to the pearl-clutching a polyamorous lesbian wedding could evoke, but it was their historical and religious references to multiple marriage that grounded their ceremony:

Today we have gathered to witness the union of Brynn, Kitten, and Doll. We are here today to offer them our love and our blessings as they embark on the next phase of their lives together. To some, they represent the "slippery slope" we were warned about. In truth, what they are about to do today is as old as mankind. While modern humans may have invented the word "polyamory," or "many loves," we certainly didn't invent the idea. Multiple adult relationships are as old as we are as a species.

Every major culture on the planet has had some form of multiple marriage. Every major religion has allowed it at some point, and some still do. Numerous holy men from the Old Testament had multiple wives. Arjuna, a Hindu hero in the Mahabharata, shares his wife with his brothers, one of whom later marries as well. To modern Pagans, all acts of love are holy to the Goddess. Ecclesiastes 4:12 says that though one person may be overpowered, two can support each other, and a cord of three strands is not quickly broken.

Three strands.

Today, Brynn, Kitten, and Doll will forge their own three-strand cord. This ceremony is very much their creation, a modern blend of the old and the new, to mark the new beginning of their lives together as a family.

If you're not comfortable being out to your wider community, Offbeat Bride readers Briana and Joshua's wedding offers some ideas. When they got married, the third member of their triad, Tony, acted as Joshua's best man. (Tony also made Briana's bouquet!) The trio then had a secret ceremony immediately afterward, so that they could quietly honor their three-way union without alarming guests who weren't in the know:

> After our legal ceremony (which all our guests attended) Joshua, Tony, and I snuck off with a few close friends to have a second ceremony officiated by my maid of honor. It was a handfasting, binding all three of us to each other.

A multistranded cord is clearly a great metaphor for multi-partner weddings!

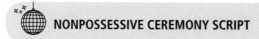 **NONPOSSESSIVE CEREMONY SCRIPT**

Offbeat reader Chelsey shared this script she used at her Vancouver wedding to her long-term partner. She wrote it drawing inspiration from Buddhism, which her partner practices.

Officiant: Welcome, everyone. We have gathered here today to rejoice and celebrate the love and commitment two people exhibit. [Name] and [Name]

>>>

have decided to choose a path together, to share in some of life's incredible moments, and to assist in making each other's dreams into realities.

Before going further, I wish to acknowledge the ancestral, traditional, and unceded Aboriginal territories of the [insert first nations band specifications for your region].

This marriage is being created through equality, mutual respect, and love. [Name] and [Name] bring with them the experiences which drew them together and their dedication to their personal growth. They bring the intentions of their hearts as a treasure to be shared, and they bring with them the ability to view the world, themselves, and each other with patience, liberty, and a loving sense of humor.

Legally required wording to be married [in Canada, fill in your own here], repeated by both parties:

Both Parties: I solemnly swear that I know of no lawful reason why I, [Name], should not be joined in marriage to [Name], and I ask those present to witness as I take them to be my lawfully wedded [wife/husband/spouse/partner/person].

Officiant: Will you please turn to face each other as you share your vows.

[Insert personal vows here.]

Officiant: Your wedding rings are a symbol of your intentions toward one another. There are three of them to remind you that yourselves, each other, and your connection are all of importance to both of you.

Let these rings always remind you both that you are choosing every day to be part of something you both care deeply about, understanding that just as we are a mystery to ourselves, each other person is also a mystery to us. These rings symbolize a pledge to be curious, to seek to understand yourselves, each other, and all living beings, to examine your own minds continually and to regard all the mysteries of life with curiosity and joy.

You can each repeat after me, and place the rings on each other's hands as you do:

"I am giving you this ring as a reminder of the ethics we are associating with our relationship—that we are committed to supporting and engineering what each of us wants, together and as individuals. We are architects."

You may now kiss, if you want to. Congratulations.

Being an ally and acknowledging marriage equality at your hetero(. . . ish) wedding

At my wedding, I knew I wasn't interested in tossing my bouquet into the crowd, but I wanted to find a way to take the bouquet tradition and twist it for my own devious purposes.

. . . Well, some people might see the twist as devious. Is it devious to transform a tradition into a way to further your own political or personal agenda? Perhaps. But what better way to make a point?

I'd read about some brides handing off their bouquet to another couple at their wedding, often to the pair that has been married the longest. This is a nice way to honor a commitment that's stood the test of time, and I considered that option before eventually deciding that, no, the couple in our family that most deserved the honor was Auntie Andrea and her partner of fifteen years, Stacy.

See, shortly before we announced our engagement, Andrea and Stacy were married in San Francisco during the few months in 2004 when Mayor Gavin Newsom managed to convince the city clerk to issue marriage licenses to gay and lesbian couples. This was what the road to marriage equality looked like: furtive little exceptions to rules. That spring was an exciting time for the gay and lesbian community in San Francisco—my favorite photography websites were filled with beautiful portraits of smiling couples standing on the steps of the courthouse, showered in rose petals thrown by activists and onlookers.

My aging aunties' wedding had been a pragmatic affair: They'd shown up early in the morning with lawn chairs and thermoses full of coffee. Bundled up in wool jackets and hats, they sat in line for hours and were heckled by a few protestors as they waited their turn to commit to each other and be legally wedded. They had no reception, no wedding dresses. Nor was there any bouquet, so

I decided that I might as well get some good use out of mine and pass it on to them.

It was also an excellent opportunity to make Andreas's and my perspective on marriage equality very clear to our families and friends. So, after everyone had finished their toasts, Andreas and I stood up, and I explained that I didn't want to throw my bouquet, but that I wanted to pass it off to the newest brides in our family.

As everyone applauded and cheered, I crowed about how much we hoped that soon everyone would be able to enjoy the privileges of marriage—privileges like wedding-planning stress and expenses.

Then I handed off my bouquet and gave each of my aunties a kiss. It was one of my favorite moments of the wedding.

There are those who might criticize us for using our wedding as a pedestal for our political agenda. For better or for worse, we live in a time when fundamentals like love and commitment have become political issues for, well, fundamentalists. Our wedding was the most politically charged events I'd ever planned. I was buying into an institution that my partner and I both have a lot of misgivings about, and therefore we opted to use our wedding as a soapbox.

We certainly weren't the only ones to do this. Offbeat reader Maria did exactly the same thing at her wedding. She explained, "My lesbian aunts were waiting for marriage to be legal. Our ceremony invocation was from the Massachusetts Supreme Court ruling legalizing gay marriage in that state, but I knew I didn't want to do the bouquet toss. I haven't been excited about participating in it as a catcher since I was eight, and I didn't want to single out my single female friends for potential embarrassment, nor did I want the bouquet to land on the floor after every woman sidestepped it. Though it wouldn't have been in keeping with the general attitude of our friends and family, I have also seen the bouquet toss look surprisingly like a rugby match. So it was natural for me to stand up, explain that I didn't like the traditional bouquet toss for the above reasons, and ask my aunts to take it instead."

See? Even when you're offbeat, you're like everyone else. Maybe Maria and I are starting our own tradition of handing bouquets off to lesbian aunts.

Obviously, the wedding-planning climate for LGBTQ+ people shifted dramatically in the fifteen years since my wedding. Hell, you can get Martha Stewart–branded "same-sex wedding" advice now! In most ways, the differences seem to be for the better . . . but there are still shitloads of brides of all genders and sexualities dealing with bigoted and ignorant family members, institutions, and even vendors. It may be easier to find examples of gender-neutral vows or brides in pantsuits these days—but the discrimination that kept gay marriage illegal for so long is still very much alive.

Because of this, you might want to think about including obvious support for marriage equality and support for LGBTQ+ rights in your wedding, whether or not you or your partner are members of the community. Here are some lovely options we've seen at ally weddings:

- Accept donations to activist causes and charities in lieu of gifts.
- Make donations on guests' behalf instead of favors (as a bonus, this solves the problem discussed in Chapter 19 about having to deal with useless wedding trinkets!).
- Add a special reading or acknowledgment in the invitation, programs, ceremony, and so on.
- You could always adopt my tradition of dedicating the bouquets or boutonnieres or first toast to all those for whom marriage is and has been a hard-fought right.

If you're not a member of the LGBTQ+ community and you want to honor marriage equality at your wedding, consider talking to your LGBTQ+ friends about it—without asking for ally cookies! (Google it.) Let them know your intention behind your desire, and invite them to be involved if they'd like. Remember that they're allowed to say no—they're busy people, too! Be thoughtful and do your homework about ways to acknowledge the community that feel like a good fit for you, your wedding, and the community.

Whether you're LGBTQ+ or some other identity, take to heart what Sarah from Spokane said: "When the coupling is characterized by love, willingness, mutual respect, honesty, faithfulness and joy, I think that's a win for humanity all around."

And isn't that what we're all aiming for, regardless of what kind of wedding we're planning? Being an Offbeat Bride is a state of mind that transcends gender, sexuality, class, race, weight, chosen subculture—everything. Anyone can be an Offbeat Bride, as long as they believe in everyone's right to make their wedding just as weird as they want it to be.

 MR., MRS., MX.: GENDERQUEER AND GENDER-NEUTRAL WEDDING WORDING

Offbeat reader Aeron has some insight about making the very gendered world of wedding wording more neutral:

> Weddings aren't a strictly gendered thing, as all of us reading *Offbeat Bride* are likely aware of . . . but many of the words around weddings and marriage are very gendered. Even if you're having a completely gender-neutral wedding, it's really hard to talk about it without using gendered verbiage. But I've tried to find some ways around that!

> Sometimes gender-neutral wedding wording already exists, and sometimes there are gender-neutral or other-gender words that somebody else has coined.

> Here are a few of the ideas I'm playing with to try to de-gender some typically gendered wedding words . . .

>>>

BRIDE/GROOM:

The most obvious words are the hardest to find gender-neutral replacements for. I've thought about mixing the words "bride" and "groom" to make "gride."

HUSBAND/WIFE:

"Spouse" is the generic word for husband and wife. But words like "partner" are more common, if you don't need to specify that you're married.

FIANCÉ/FIANCÉE:

Luckily, the pronunciations of these words are exactly the same, so when you're speaking, they're gender neutral anyway. Words like "betrothed" have a very old-fashioned, romantic feel, and you can always just call them your "spouse-to-be" or similar.

MRS./MR.:

Titles come up as an issue for genderqueer people way before weddings, but there are some wedding-specific issues. Some people don't like the sound of Mr. and Mr. or Mrs. and Mrs., or the fact that the order is always Mr. and Mrs. Other title options include Mx., which uses the *X* for "none" or "other" and sounds like "mix" and "misc.," which is short for "miscellaneous."

BRIDESMAID/GROOMSMAN:

The generic name is "attendant," and you can have a bit of fun with words like "crew" or "team" for the whole group. If you do have a bride and groom but have other-gender attendants, words like "groomsmaid" or "bridesman" can just swap them around. Likewise, you can follow "bride" and "groom" with a neutral word like "mate" or "peep." If you have a gender-neutral couple and a word instead of "bride" or "groom," you can follow that with any of those words or make up a new word that matches your bride or groom word replacement.

BEST MAN / MAID OF HONOR:

Like "bridesmaid" and "groomsman," there's the option to swap or replace "maid" and "man," but there's also a lot of fun to have. You might have chosen your "best friend," "best cousin," or even your "best Alex"! "Maid of honor" can become "made of honor," or another quality like "awesome." "Chief" (as in "chief bridesperson") is gender neutral, so everyone can be given titles to match their roles; you can have a "chief ringbearer."

>>>

HEN/STAG NIGHT:

Hens are female chickens, and stags are male deer—any gender-neutral animal name would be a gender-neutral replacement, and animals like fox work well. There's also the option to use "chicken," "rooster," or "cockerel" instead of "hen," and "deer" or "doe" instead of "stag."

BACHELOR/BACHELORETTE PARTY:

Moving away from animal names, and away from the UK, "bachelor/ette" or "bachelor(ette)" are one way of making "bachelor" and "bachelorette" gender neutral. "Bachelor" is technically neutral like in "bachelor of arts," but it is used for men in this context. The "-ette" ending is used to feminize "bachelor," like "-ess" is commonly in English (princess, hostess, waitress), so a similar ending would make an other-gendered third word. Easy options could be "bacheloren," "bachelorelle," "bachelorine," or even just "bachelorre."

If all else fails, I like making up my own words; someone had to coin every other word, after all!

15. PRIORITIES & PERCENTAGES

The buzzkill of wedding budgeting

BUDGETING YOUR WEDDING IS SORT OF LIKE SAFE SEX: A BIT OF A BUZZ-kill when you're in the height of excitement (. . . gawking at wedding porn, perhaps?) but critically, crucially important. And like safe sex, if you don't think about it and talk about it right up front, you might find yourself sick or screwed over and dealing with the ramifications for a long, long time.

When Dre and I got engaged, I was working a contract job and he was freelancing. Although neither of us was carrying around extensive debt, neither of us had any savings, and our incomes were definitely not in the high-roller category.

Our first budgeting decision was simply that we would not go into debt for our wedding or our honeymoon. For us, it just didn't feel worth it to trade the strength of our shared financial future to throw a big party for ourselves. We would use only the funds we had.

Of course, this made it immediately evident that our wedding would be low budget, firmly rooted in scraping things together and making the most of what we had.

After conversations with our families, our parents agreed to match the funds we'd collected, bringing our budget to a grand total of $6,000 (for more about accepting money from family, check out Chapter 28, "Whose Wedding Is This?") felt like SO MUCH MONEY! I mean, seriously, when was the last time I spent more than a day's pay on a party, and suddenly I've got thousands of dollars for food and booze and good times?! Call in the clowns and the balloon artists! We're going to throw one hell of a party!

Of course, I quickly realized that our wedding budget was roughly one-fifth the national average.

And, as I spoke to other people planning their weddings, I also learned that wedding budgets are regionally influenced and deeply relative to the cost of living. If you're planning a wedding in New York, your idea of a "budget wedding" is going to be drastically different than if you're planning a wedding in Omaha. Weddings in both locations can be done fabulously on a limited budget, but what "budget" means to you is going to vary—a lot.

Because "budget" for us meant $6,000, we decided that the best way to determine how to divide the money was to think about priorities and percentages.

Before agonizing over specifics, we looked at the aspects of our wedding that mattered the most to us. And when I say "matter," I'm talking about REALLY important issues. It's easy to get caught up in all the details—but what really matters?

As Offbeat Bride reader Jessica told me, "Too many people get caught up in the 'stuff' of a wedding and forget that it's about the relationship and commitment. Having spent under $1,000, we're just as married as a couple who spent $30,000."

In thinking about prioritizing the "stuff" of our wedding, it broke down like this:

- 25 percent: Dinner, booze, and catering
- 15 percent: Honeymoon airfare
- 10 percent: Venue
- 10 percent: Photography
- 10 percent: Fashion
- 10 percent: Rings
- 5 percent: Invitations
- 3 percent: Decorations and flowers

- 2 percent: Officiant fee
- 10 percent: Random stuff

You'll notice some things completely missing here—what about cake and music and makeup? They were priorities for us, but we had friends who donated their time and skills to make them happen. As you may have guessed, the biggest way we kept our budget down was by asking our amazing community of friends and family to skip the candlesticks and serving dishes and give us the gift of their time instead. I'll get into this in more detail in the next chapter.

Some of our other percentages might seem insanely low. For instance, spending only 3 percent for decor and flowers was made possible by picking a venue that was already filled with flowers (yay for getting married in a garden!), and we figured nature was pretty enough. We simply didn't care that much about fancy decorations.

That's what I mean by priorities—if it's not important to you, don't spend money on it, no matter what the wedding-industrial complex tells you. If you don't care about, say, a ring pillow, you don't need it! Don't let anyone tell you what you MUST have at your wedding.

Wants and needs and must-have-or-will-dies

But what about when you do care strongly about something, and it's not in your budget? What about when a long-standing wedding dream feels completely out of reach?

Well, just as you should feel free to cut out whatever wedding details you don't care about, you also have to think outside the box about how to attain your high-priority bits.

Our primary way of dealing was to make the most of the materials and community skills we already had available to us, but other

Offbeat Brides have been imminently craftier in their efforts to keep their costs down.

"I knew I wanted really awesome pictures but couldn't afford the price of a swanky venue," Offbeat reader Lucy told me. "We were getting married in an old community center run by square dancers."

Her solution? "We booked a room at the fanciest hotel in town (on discount, of course) and took a ton of glamorous pre-ceremony shots!"

Squeeze the most from your budget

Offbeat reader Raina, a graphic designer, kept costs down by keeping the wedding tiny and scrapping the idea of a reception.

"We live in Brooklyn (high rent!) and our parents didn't have money to give us . . . so we just had to get creative," she told me.

"The first step was to cut out guests and the whole idea of a reception. I wore my mother's wedding dress from 1979. The only expense there was to have it taken in slightly and cleaned up a bit. Mike wore his grandfather's wedding band, my mom and I did the flowers ourselves, and we had one of our good friends take all of the photos. Add in the cost of dinner for nine people, and we spent under $600 on EVERYTHING!"

If you're thinking to yourself, Oh, that poor girl. She only had $600 and had to make so many sacrifices, spare Raina your pity. As she says, "Yes, our wedding was small and intimate, but the day was so memorable because of it. Everyone involved had a part: my brother was my man of honor! I couldn't have hoped for anything better."

If you've got time, you can also save a fortune by slowly accumulating your supplies. Offbeat reader Jami explained, "I kept it cheap by collecting things I needed over the span of a year. We used recycled jars for vases and filled them with flowers we planted in the spring at my fiancé's mother's garden."

When it came to Jami's reception, she skipped the expensive entertainment and opted instead for low-budget good times: "We hosted a game-night reception so it could be more interactive for everyone. We bought most of the prizes on sale, nearing $200, but still saved a lot by not hiring a DJ or band, which comes with an added cost of a dance floor and lights."

Offbeat reader Sara, who had a wedding for $2,000, made it clear that working within a tight budget can be about much more than saving money—it can actually become a statement about your relationship.

"We wanted our wedding to be about sincerity, authenticity, connection, and a celebration and proclamation of love and commitment. We didn't want it to be about monogrammed napkins and excessive amounts of fondant. In all honesty, we didn't want to let our wedding overshadow our relationship."

You can also use your budget limitations as a way to celebrate your community. Sara asked her friends and family to donate their old gold to an environmentally friendly jeweler "so that we could incorporate a piece of their history into ours. The company melted the donated gold, credited our account, and created new rings. Our invoice came to $157."

Getting creative with your wedding doesn't necessarily mean DIYing everything and spending months in the craft aisle of your local hobby shop. It can also mean getting truly inventive about where you look for what you need.

Offbeat reader Helen, of Bristol, England, decorated her wedding with leftover holiday displays: "I filled the loft where we got married with these really lovely white paper Christmas decorations that had been used by a massive UK department store chain. I asked the local store what they were going to do with all the decorations after Christmas—they were going to go in the trash!

"I arranged with the manager to get the decorations from several different stores. They looked so fantastic! They didn't seem Christmassy at our summer wedding in an art gallery—they were in such a completely different context. It's so crazy to think that they all just would have been thrown away."

Clearly, there are a lot of ways to get creative about how to squeeze the most from your wedding budget. Still, the key is to understand your priorities. Helen may have saved a fortune on her decor, but she still put in the time to track it down. If decorations aren't something you or your fiancé care about, slide them to the bottom of the priority list, or eliminate them altogether.

Battling against the consumer pressures of the wedding-industrial complex can make some brides feel like they're somehow planning less of a wedding because they're spending less money. Don't fall for this bullshit! When you find, after your carefully budgeted wedding, that you're not $20,000 in debt for an afternoon party, and that you can move forward with plans to go back to school, buy a house, or travel the world . . . all the budgeting buzzkill will be worth it.

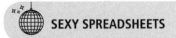 **SEXY SPREADSHEETS**

Google Sheets lets you create and update spreadsheets that save automatically in the cloud and can be shared with any number of collaborators. They're perfect for keeping track of not only your budget but also your guest list, seating chart, RSVPs, thank-you cards, gift registry, packing lists, vendor comparisons, and even a day-of timeline. These spreadsheets can be your fully customizable cloud wedding binder.

16. GATHER AROUND THE GLOWING SCREEN

Strategically using tech for your wedding planning

WE LIVE IN THE FUTURE. EVEN BACK IN 2004, I USED THE WEB TO PLAN almost every aspect of my wedding, and things have only gotten nerdier.

There's really no need for a three-hundred-page bridal magazine when you've got the internet. It's a bride's best friend, and although your bridalhenchfolk may rock, chances are good that they're going to be pretty pissed if you, say, call them at 3 A.M. with a question about Wiccan handfasting ceremonies or how to make a DIY chuppah from copper pipe. The internet, meanwhile, will be happy to tell you everything you could ever want to know about both these things—and it's got some tools and apps to help, too.

Techy Offbeat reader Marian and her husband, Elliot, had a techno-joy wedding in (where else?) San Francisco. They met on OkCupid (of course) and used just about every app imaginable when planning their backyard wedding—from a ride-share app for their day-of transportation to task contracting apps for jobs large and small. They even rented their backyard wedding venue through Airbnb.

Modern wedding planning makes heavy use of the web and your smartphone, which means the days of the gigantic wedding binder are behind us—I mean, unless you're into that kind of thing, of course. (If you're into scrapbook play, chances are solid you may be a wedding binder size-queen.)

For those of us who aren't into paper, this twenty-first-century shift away from wedding binders is good news for trees and can make the process way more streamlined . . . but it can also lead to wedding overload. Your planning tools are always right there in your pocket, vibrating and push notifying and oh-so-helpfully reminding you of all the things. More on that later, but there's no denying that apps have made calculating, hyper-organized wedding project managers out of even the most casual of brides. And, hey, developing new project management strategies and organization habits while wedding planning is great! These are skills that can help you way after the wedding's over. Win-win!

Wedding techno-joy: big-picture strategies for using apps and websites to plan your wedding

Okay, so that's great . . . but which apps to use? There are approximately 15 trillion apps and wedding resources available online, and it can be difficult to sift through to find the ones that suit you best. One nerdy Offbeat reader named Sunny shared her list of must-have functions for any app she would use to plan her wedding, and it serves as a good reminder that these apps are meant to simplify—not further complexify!—your wedding planning process.

Sunny's wedding app deal-breakers were as follows:

- Free!
- Usable on the go: "I have to travel a lot," Sunny explained. "So I want aids that are accessible on all of my devices (and on my sweetie's devices, too). This means things accessible on Windows, macOS, Android, and iOS." Be aware that some web-based resources are not always easily usable on mobile devices.
- Back up everywhere: "I want everything to automatically back up and sync across all our devices," Sunny said.

- Easy learning curve: "I don't want to spend a lot of time figuring out something that is only relevant to the wedding!"

Sunny's priorities may help you narrow your search for apps a bit—but spend some time thinking through what your priorities are.

Thanks to the ephemeral and ever-changing nature of tech and the internet, specific apps and websites may have come and gone by the time you read this; here are the kinds of apps and tools we suggest exploring:

- The almost-all-in-one, Google Drive: Use Sheets for lists and budgets; use Docs to collaborate on scripts; use Forms to collect RSVPs; use Slides to make a wedding slideshow . . . this suite can do almost anything.
- Inspiration boards: Pinterest, Instagram, and other image-focused apps allow you to bring everything in your vision to one place. These help especially when describing your wants and needs to vendors.
- Project management: Apps like that focus on to-do lists, scheduling, collaboration, and assigning tasks. Choose ones that allow saving in the cloud and multiple collaborators.
- Budgeting apps: Beyond Google Sheets, there are tons of apps for wedding budgeting.
- RSVP management and registry management apps: These single-use apps offer specific services to keep everything separate and organized, but you could integrate these tasks into Google Drive, too.
- Review apps: For researching vendors and venues, these apps can help narrow down choices of donut shops for your donut-tower wedding "cake" even while you're on the go.

- Music apps: If your budget doesn't allow for a DJ, make a playlist in your music app and have your device be the DJ. Just make sure to have a backup plan in case something goes wrong.
- Live-streaming apps: Set up a tripod and live-stream your wedding using an app so those who can't make it can still tune in and watch your ceremony.
- Apps for hiring people for single jobs: From last-minute tailors to chair-wranglers the day of your wedding, there are apps that can help connect you with people you can hire as vendors or just as an extra set of hands.

Even small weddings can benefit from the organizational tools apps offer. As Marian in San Francisco explained:

> While I've never been the type to dream about my wedding since I was old enough to form a coherent thought, I did turn into a slightly crazed version of myself in the days and months leading up to the event. Even with a casual, thirty-person backyard party, there are still a million balls in the air, and I don't wish the stress on anyone. The people we hired and the websites we used and the apps we downloaded saved our asses more than once.

Saving your ass: there're several apps for that!

Wedding overload and knowing when to de-screen

Websites like Pinterest make it all too easy to voraciously collect wedding inspiration like a dragon who hoards cake-topper and guest-book ideas. Eventually, the sheer number of ideas and amount of inspiration can blur into overload and make you feel inadequate.

What's going on when a bride buys a dress, and then finds another dress, and then picks a third dress because they keep seeing dresses they love? What's going on when people come up with five different wedding themes over the course of two months and still can't *quiiite* decide? What about when Instagram commenters' enthusiasm for someone else's wedding starts to slip over the edge from inspiration ("ooh, I might want to integrate something like that in my wedding") to duplication ("I MUST HAVE THOSE EXACT GREEN BOOTS WHERE DID YOU GET THEM TELL ME NOW NOW NOW!"). It worries me a little . . .

When wedding planning, you should never feel bad about the decisions you've already made about your wedding. That last thing you want when you plan your simple outdoor gathering is to start feeling like, "OMG, that girl painted her shoes and they look amazing. Why don't I paint my shoes? What's wrong with me that I'm just wearing a pair of pumps that I bought on eBay? What about those green boots? Where can I get them? OH MY GOD!"

What I'm talking about here is wedding fetishization—when things slip over from inspiration to fixation. Wedding inspiration shouldn't be the unattainable weird fantasies that keep you up at night with frustrated longing. I don't want people to scrap their perfectly lovely plans because they saw something else, something better, something MORE while poring over wedding inspiration online. After all, Offbeat Bride is about real folks doing their real best to cobble together weddings that reflect who they really are.

Ideally, wedding inspiration is here to inspire and delight—not ever to make you feel dissatisfied, unworthy, or disappointed in yourself. If it's doing that, you've reached wedding overload and need a break.

HACK YOUR WEDDING PLANNING WITH TECH-ADJACENT METHODS

Software engineers and developers have tricks up their sleeves that, when applied to wedding planning, can make the process smoother for even the most Luddite-like among us.

Offbeat reader Stacey is a software engineer and approached shopping for her wedding dress like one would approach problem-solving using the Agile method:

CUSTOMER PROBLEMS:

» I don't have a wedding dress.

» I'm a 4 on top and a 10 on the bottom (small boobs, great booty).

» It may be as hot as 90 degrees with 100 percent humidity.

USER STORY:

I am an Offbeat Bride and need a wedding dress that will make me feel beautiful without killing me in the Florida heat.

Requirements:

» allows legs to breathe

» suits my back tattoo

» is lightweight

» takes advantage of breeze with flowing fabric

» will not fall off me (small boobs)

» is not super traditional

» feels nice to the touch (lace looks nicer than it feels)

» $3,000 or less

STRETCH GOALS:

» no bra needed

» shows off my legs

She put herself in the position of "customer" and set about solving the "problem" of finding a wedding dress with her specific "requirements" and "stretch goals"—needs and wants, basically. This method helped her prioritize when shopping for her dress and let her keep her goals front and center.

>>>

Offbeat reader Hannah and her partner, Chris, used a specific type of Agile approach called Scrumming to plan their Seattle wedding, and she says that, because of it, the planning process was joyful in and of itself:

Our wedding planning process was smooth and enjoyable in large part due to my husband's and my day jobs. He's a software developer and I've been a "Scrum master." It sounds like a made-up title, but it's actually a real thing. "Scrum" is a popular methodology used in software development and manufacturing, and my husband and I found it was perfect for wedding planning as well.

Scrum makes use of something called "iterative planning," which simply means doing the most important things first. Think of it like this: What would you need to get married tomorrow? Maybe it's a marriage license, rings, an officiant, and a pretty spot under a tree at your favorite park. Sure, it may not be your dream wedding, but, technically, you could get married tomorrow with just those things. Let's borrow from software again and call that "version one," or "v1."

I'm guessing that you'll want to expand from there (I know my husband and I did). For us, v2 included guests! And, of course, with guests we had to have a few more requirements: invitations to send to them, a venue big enough to hold them, and a plan for feeding and watering them.

V3 included more fun things like wedding clothes, a killer playlist, and fresh flowers.

Of course, we kept adding new versions for as long as we could. Everyone will have different priorities. The point is, each iteration gets you closer to your dream wedding, but each iteration is also entirely independent of the next. It made me feel better to know that, once we'd nailed down those basics, at pretty much any point we could stop and have a wedding, and it would be great.

⁂

Wedding planning is all about balancing the shit that needs to get done with the fact that, honestly? That "shit" is mostly optional, and it's all just a way to celebrate and share your partnership.

If looking at endless Pinterest boards, Instagram hashtags, or even our own beloved offbeatbride.com posts ever makes you feel disappointed in yourself, or like your wedding doesn't quite stack up, or like you're not offbeat enough—please, please, PLEASE remind yourself that your wedding is not a contest.

If getting push notifications from your wedding planning apps on your phone makes you break into panic sweat, then it's time to practice some solid digital hygiene: go into your app settings and disable some notifications. Better yet, turn off your device completely and go hug your partner and tell them how much you love them and how excited you are to celebrate that love with your family and friends.

Remember: the wedding tech is here to serve you. You are not here to serve it.

17. IT TAKES A VILLAGE

With friends like these, who needs vendors?

I KNEW THAT I WANTED TO ENJOY MY OWN WEDDING, AND THAT I DIDN'T want to set myself up for a situation where I spent the whole day doing what I tend to do at parties—which is to circulate, madly trying to make sure that every single person at my party is having a really good time, and, Oh, that person seems to be feeling awkward, let's introduce her to this person over here, and, Oh, are you cold? Let me grab you a sweater, and, Who needs another drink over here? Another round, folks? Alrighty, then!

I have an über-hostess streak in me, and I refused to let it take over my wedding. Not that I don't get a sick pleasure out of throwing (dare I say "engineering"?) a truly killer party, but I knew that on my wedding day that particular pleasure wasn't the kind of happy I wanted. I wanted clear-minded, joyful happiness, not that "strategic win" feeling that I get from overplanning and controlling. I'd spoken to so many newlyweds who said they barely even remembered their wedding days, thanks to the fact that they were crazily running all over the place. I wanted to have the wherewithal to just enjoy the day.

And so, despite my obsessive project-management lists, I decided to relinquish some control in exchange for the increased sanity of letting magically skilled friends and family take over. I loosened the reins of my own neurosis and indulged in the intoxicating bliss of not worrying. In other words, I delegated my worries to others, and most of those people were not worried at all. I kept a bit of my control freakishness—exacting firm control over who would help me with a given facet of the wed-

108

ding. But, once that was decided, I resigned myself completely to their visions.

I picked exactly the minds and hearts I wanted working on the wedding, and then I tried to just sit back and bask in their magic-making ways. I am spoiled by being surrounded by some amazing, resourceful, skillful folks—but I really think we all are surrounded by amazing people with magical skills. It's just a question of figuring out who wants to help you in which way and then figuring out whether you want their help.

We made it clear that we didn't need a lot of wedding gifts. Six years of cohabitating is a long time to have lived without, say, plates. After living together for six years, what basic need could we possibly not have filled? If they're happy about a wedding, people get excited and want to pitch in. When we announced our engagement, everyone offered their help, and we took them all up on it— letting them know that their help was the best gift they could give.

We're certainly not the first to have thrown a wedding this way. Offbeat reader Melissa took many friends up on their offers of help and called the core group the "wedding steering committee." It was composed of friends who'd offered their help as their wedding gifts, and they did everything for her, from wedding photography to cutting up tissue paper for traditional Mexican flags.

Super-surprising help

If you let them, people will amaze you in the ways they honor your commitment. People love to shower you with affection during a wedding, for all sorts of different reasons. It's an amazing blessing to let them do so. As Offbeat Bride reader Phyllis reminisces, the portions of her wedding that friends contributed "ended up being the most impressive, beautiful, personal, and touchingly tangible elements of our day." She remembers one family member whose

TIP: DON'T BE SHY ABOUT TURNING DOWN HELP

IT'S OKAY NOT TO WANT PEOPLE'S HELP. OFFBEAT READER JENNIE, A self-described "research fellow, type A" told me, "My husband and I did all our wedding stuff ourselves and were happy about this. I have my own tastes and actually enjoy little crafty projects. Everybody loves a wedding, and if I'd let them, people would've been shoving their fingers in my pie." So ask yourself: Do you like fingers in your pie? If not, Jennie suggests her technique: "Ask someone for ideas on something you don't really care about, consider them carefully, then do whatever you wanted in the first place." You may get some great ideas and help on lower-priority parts of the wedding, and at the very least you've given interested parties the chance to have their say.

simple offer to take care of the wine was "a gift we never would have asked for, but a better gift from her we couldn't have received."

You also save a buttload of money when you let people help you with your wedding. Seriously. I would guess we cut the cost of our wedding in half by letting our friends help us with things.

Offbeat reader Greta summed it up best when she advised, "Get a group of family and friends who are unbelievably talented and happy and even eager to share their talent at your wedding. Have friends and family who will sing, dance, play music, help organize, design invitations and programs, arrange flowers and decorations, read their writing, and shamelessly bedeck themselves in imaginatively festive outfits—and who are extraordinarily good at all these things. Do not do this because it will save you money (although it probably will). Do it because it will make your wedding yours. Do it because it will make your wedding a unique reflection of your own life together, at its very best."

The best part of relinquishing control to your friends and family? You'll get help in surprising ways. Phyllis recounted a baker friend who offered to make her cake. "After she asked if she could make the cake, she called to ask if she could make us a cupcake tree instead. Um, duh? No plates, no forks, no awkward cutting ritual. Be ready to be pleasantly surprised when your friends come up with way better ideas than yours ever would have been. And remember that they can't do that unless you let them.

Ask (nicely!) and receive

There's taking the first step of accepting offered help, but then there's the next step: bridal begging. I hunted down several friends and specifically asked for their assistance on certain tasks. Um, that was difficult and took all the social graces I had—and probably could have used some graces I didn't have. It's a fine line between asking someone for help and announcing to your friends, "Y'all are throwing my wedding for me, okay? Ready, set, go!"

I always started by telling each person why I wanted their help. I came at people with my arms outstretched, singing their praises. Everyone likes to be acknowledged for a skill, and calling your friends out on what they do best and asking them to show it off in front of a whole community of people has the potential to be a win-win situation.

Of course, some of the people I asked for help respectfully declined. A family friend declined to help shuttle people from the ferry. There were a couple of people who backed out for various reasons—my adorable teenage cousins were out of town and had to relinquish their parking-attendant duties to some other close friends of ours, who made up for the swap by acting like adorable teenagers. Responsibilities evolved and shifted. But everyone who wanted to help did.

The geeks worked away on invitations, programs, and logos. The expert partiers started brainstorming where the dinner tables and late-night beanbags would be. The DJs started grooming their music collections for the perfect tunes. The artisans worked on sewing and jewelry-making, the foodies clucked away in their kitchens over cakes and buffets, the poet wrote verse, and the old hippie with the goofy name made a bamboo altar.

Many members of our communities had something to contribute, and those gifts were the sort that could never have been given by anyone other than the giver. It's amazing to see people create an event out of love for you, and it's a privilege to witness it firsthand—especially when mostly all you have to do is ask and brainstorm and say, "Yes! I love it!" to everything. Everyone rose to the challenge, and it was a great time to share.

Offbeat reader Jen recounted, "I think our community actually grew tighter from our wedding, and a lot of people thanked us for letting them be part of it."

Bridal beggars can't always be choosers. In order for the "It takes a village" technique to work, your intent needs to be "I want this person to be the one doing it." Whatever "it" is, you have to release attachment to how it might turn out. Then there's no room for disappointment. As long as that particular loved one is the person playing the trumpet for your processional, who cares if it was a little flat? You must completely relinquish your control issues and completely trust and appreciate your helpers. If you don't think you can do that, this technique may not be a good one for you.

Our wedding wasn't just about voicing our commitment to each other but also about voicing our commitment as a couple to our community. By making our wedding a collaborative project (instead of imposing our vision on everyone), I think we created an event that truly reflected our ideals and our community's values.

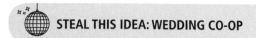

STEAL THIS IDEA: WEDDING CO-OP

Offbeat reader Susan teamed up with a few friends to develop a great idea: the wedding co-op:

> My friends and I banded together the summer we all got married to share the cost—and the hassle—of renting and dealing with all the glasses, silverware, tablecloths, and napkins we each needed for our weddings. It worked out beautifully once we divided everything up. Erin bought glasses and silverware for two hundred people at IKEA, and I found seventy yards of white cotton fabric for a dollar a yard and sewed twenty tablecloths and two hundred napkins. Nicole joined our co-op a month later and chipped in too, sharing plenty of her decorations and extras—plus, she stored everything in her basement all summer long.
>
> Our rule was that no one had to wash dishes after her own wedding, so we helped each other set up and take down and then got the favor repaid when it was our turn. It was so great to know my friends would be taking care of all the details for our reception. Everything looked fabulous at each of our receptions, and it was fun to see all the things we'd helped with too.
>
> At the end of the summer, another friend, Jess, heard about our arrangement and borrowed some of everything for her wedding, pitching in some cash toward the total. Once all of our shared gear had made its fourth appearance, we chose what we wanted to keep and then sold the rest off on Craigslist. When we did the final math, we ended up paying so much less than what the rentals for just one of our weddings would have cost, and got so much help and support in the bargain.

18. THE SWAG, PART 1: INVITATIONS & RSVPS

How to run your own decorative-paper
assembly line . . . or say "fuck it" & use e-mail

FOR ANDREAS AND ME—TWO PEOPLE WHO FELL IN LOVE WHILE MAKING out at a warehouse party—it was understandable that our wedding invitations would blur the line between rave flyer and invitation.

We did not stand outside clubs passing them out, but one jaded midthirties raver friend scoffed, "Wow, those multicolored spheres floating on a cloud of stars totally look like old-school flyers."

Despite their bright colors, our invitations were a far cry from the flyers that entice ravers to warehouses weekend after weekend. One of my dearest college friends happens to be a graphic designer, and she agreed to design them for us. She worked with our ideas and followed our suggestions, so, yes, they were full of color. Yes, they were glossy. And, yes, there were multicolored spheres. But there were also silhouettes of young lovers and a darkened forest under the stars, all hand-rendered by a prodigiously skilled someone who loves us, and how many rave flyers got made that way? There's no denying that, because we were throwing our favorite kind of party, our invitations looked sort of like flyers for, well, a forested hippie rave. In the spirit of my favorite raves, it was an epic, memory-making, high vibe gathering, to be sure.

Because I'm a writer, it was instinctive for me to carefully word my invitation. I read other people's invitations online and knew what I didn't want—things like our parents' names presenting ours, or curlicue fonts. Parents are traditionally listed on invitations when they pay for the event, hence the whole "Mr. and Mrs. Bride's Parents invite you . . . " thing. If your parents are paying for the majority of your wedding, you may want to acknowledge them somehow, although putting parents' names first on an invitation for people in their thirties has always struck me as a strange thing. I like it best when people say things like, "Bride and Groom, together with their families, invite you . . . "

Offbeat reader Ryan echoed my experience, agreeing that "traditional wording often sounds stuffy and old fashioned."

Amen! But what to replace it with? I loved the way some brides instilled a sense of humor into their invites, saying that the ceremony was scheduled for "as close to 8 P.M. as we can manage, what with our penchant for catastrophe and all . . . " or teasing guests with promises like "festive intoxication!"

We did not list our parents, even though they were splitting the cost with us. There was no drama over the wording, because I used the "don't ask, don't tell" philosophy and just did it. It worked, though I don't think I'd recommend it. I may have come off as rude and unappreciative, and your mileage with that technique may vary.

I toyed with what language felt genuine and what felt hokey; what was sincerely touching and what seemed contrived. I also wanted to emphasize the circular theme (which you'll hear more about in Chapter 23, "Decor Fetishist"). I ended up with this:

Ariel Meadow Stallings & *Andreas Tillman Fetz*
would love you to join them at their wedding.

August 7, 2004
Bainbridge Island, Washington

After almost seven years, we've decided it's time to voice our commitment to each other and our community. You're an important part of our circle of friends and family, and we hope you can be here to celebrate with us. Come camp in the Island forest for the entire weekend, or simply join us Saturday evening.

Garden cocktail reception at 5 P.M.

Ceremony at 6 P.M.
Dinner and all-night dancing to follow

Then I went on to include exact location and contact information, instructing people to "Get more lots info and RSVP" on our wedsite. Yes, "more lots." I almost fucking died when the invites came back from the printer.

Just accept it: typos happen. In my endless revising and rewriting of my invitations, I missed cutting a word when I rewrote for the five-hundredth time, hence, "more lots." I just didn't see it. Neither did the designer. Neither did my outlaw mother (as she prefers to be called), who framed a print of the invitations! My eye skipped over the error, and, guess what? So did everyone else's.

Typos are so prevalent that our eyes read right around them half the time. Just expect that some error will be a part of your invitations. Only errors concerning the date or the location really matter. If, as a writer and perfectionist, I can live down the humiliation of a typo, then anyone can. The reality of the situation is that no one cares as much as you do. If you can live with it, then the chances are pretty good that everyone else can, too.

RSVP and save the trees

You'll also notice that, yes, I instructed people to RSVP online. I included our phone number as well, but I figured 90 percent of our invitees were savvy enough to get to a website, type their name, and click a button that said "RSVP."

There's a lot of hullabaloo about the etiquette of wedding communications. Offbeat reader Elle mailed her paper invitations out and included stamped response cards for the non-geeks, but she made it clear that e-mail RSVPs were perfectly fine and encouraged guests to use them if they were comfortable with it. It's all about

TIP: MOVING BEYOND THE WHO,
WHAT, WHEN, WHERE

SURE, THERE'S THE OBVIOUS STUFF THAT GOES ON YOUR INVITATIONS:
date, time, location, RSVP information. But are there other things guests
might need to know?

   A website address can direct invitees to get more information online, but you may want to consider enclosing things such as information
about accommodations, detailed directions with a map, and information
about activities in the area. These enclosures can be personal and fun (I
spoke to one bride who took the opportunity to hand-draw a map to the
location). It's a great way to inject a little life into a piece of folded paper.

knowing your audience. Elle pointed out that, because she and her
fiancé met online, "there are plenty of e-friends who saw a delicious
irony in responding via e-mail to our wedding invitations."

   It's nice to give folks the option of replying by paper. . . . Otherwise, you might have to deal with the hassle that Offbeat Bride
reader Heather went through. Guests kept RSVPing by tele-
phone, even though Heather had set up an online RSVP service,
and she said that she kept thinking, "People, get a clue! Just hit
the Yes button!" Some folks have crossed over into the twenty-first
century; others have not. Make allowances for both. Paper is the
security blanket that keeps guests from freezing their confused,
computer-illiterate asses off.

To fold (and fold and fold and fold) or not to fold

Many Offbeat Bride readers I've spoken to named invitations as
one of their favorite aspects of wedding planning. Even the most
uncrafty start dreaming of home assembly-line paper artistry, and if

you have any sort of inclination toward design, the arts, or writing, oh, ho, ho: a feast of obsessive adventures awaits you.

Your invitations are how your guests know what to expect, so they should reflect your event. Is it a laid-back, efficient affair, and are you an unfancy type, your fiancé a fan of simplicity? Then don't break the bank going for some frilly-ass, vellum-covered, bow-adorned overkill. Get some simple white invitations on quality paper stock with black print. They do the trick wonderfully.

If, however, you're into having a theme wedding and having the perfectly matched novelty invitation (say, a message in a bottle for a nautical wedding), then that's exactly right for you. I heard about message-in-a-bottle invitations that were so nicely made that the mother of the groom refused to open it, displaying it as an objet d'art instead.

Couples who are inclined toward designy projects have great fun with invitations. Much of the rote labor of assembling and addressing invitations can be enjoyed as a bonding exercise with the fiancé or a social activity with friends. But if sitting around with friends and folding paper didn't appeal to you before you got engaged, chances are it won't appeal to you afterward, either, so just order your invitations online or from a catalog and save yourself the trouble. One person's fun is another person's paper-cut agony.

 ACKNOWLEDGING THOSE WHO CANNOT BE PRESENT

Some offbeat couples choose to acknowledge those who cannot be present at the wedding by designating a seat at the ceremony, or even the reception. Offbeat readers Alison and Jeremy saved a seat at their ceremony in honor of loved ones who had passed away by leaving a sign and a flower arrangement on the chair. Others set out an altar with candles and photos, and others carry possessions of their loved ones with them. Incarcerated family members can be honored this way and feel as though they were there in spirit.

19. THE SWAG, PART 2: MARITAL MARKETING

Programs, favors & other bridal branding

THERE'S A WHOLE INDUSTRY BUILT AROUND CUSTOMIZED, PERSONAL-ized, specialized wedding swag. Your names monogrammed on napkins. Embossed chocolates. Engraved champagne flutes. Little metal hearts with the wedding date painted on them. Your wedding hashtag on the place cards. Every year, there's some new trinket for couples to distribute on their wedding day, but if you swap out the curlicue fonts for sans serif and the champagne flutes for commuter mugs, it becomes immediately apparent that this stuff is bridal branding. If your wedding were a company, this stuff would be called marketing swag.

Or, in the case of my former coworker's wedding, marital propaganda. The groom created a photo-personalized button for each guest and set them at the dinner tables to show us where to sit. We all wore our buttons the way you would wear a candidate's pin. *Vote Doug and Susan!* Because the groom is extremely politically active, it made perfect sense.

Perhaps, given the bloated cost of the average American wedding, it's appropriate that brides often seem to treat them as a fully incorporated LLC, complete with their own little marketing department and promotions team. Despite our lefty leanings, we fell into this just as much as anyone else. Sure, we skipped many of the marital merchandise items (no fancy party favors; no seating-assignment cards), but our wedding did in fact have a logo. An honest-to-god logo! Call the board members: we're taking this thing public.

I also obsessed over our program to an unnatural degree. Because our wedding was so nontraditional, I felt the need to arm guests with as much "day of" information as possible. We went for small (5" × 6") and low-cost (black text on standard white office paper), but the programs were eight pages long (Eight pages! Talk about overkill . . .) and included a ceremony outline, the menu, a map, a ferry schedule, the DJ lineup with bios, and a page of thank-yous.

Perhaps, given the logo and the overabundance of information, we should have provided our guests / board members with a budget for the fiscal engagement year and our goals for the first year of marriage: "65 percent increase in happiness, 20 percent postmarital weight gain, 70 percent increase in church-and-state approved visits to the conjugal bed." Perhaps we could have closed with a nice slogan like, "Securing tomorrow's marital bliss . . . today!" All joking aside, corporate America did help us out a great deal with our bridal swag. My employer at the time unwittingly donated not only paper and printing for the program but also the skills of several talented graphic designers who teamed up to help me lay out the document. Unwitting employers are so generous when you don't ask them first.

I'm not actually encouraging you to take advantage of your employer this way (or, wait, maybe I am). I'm just saying that, at times, corporate America has its own wedding gifts to provide. There are those who go so far as to get certain aspects of their wedding sponsored ("Delicious catering by Yummy Bites, Inc.!"), so can it really be long before brides start looking like NASCAR drivers? Hey, if that's your thing, rock it.

Brand cohesion and muglies

My biggest offering at the altar of bridal marketing was the branded stickers. The same beloved friend who designed our invitations isolated one component of the design (our logo: profiled silhouettes of the two of us sitting on a circular background), and I had a company that specializes in flyers and brochures slap the design on five hundred full-color vinyl stickers. These stickers were then used to seal invitation envelopes and were applied to an appalling collection of horribly mismatched mugs that we forced upon our guests.

You see, although there are those who spend copious amounts of money on fancy filigreed guest favors, in our case, a couple of friends trawled secondhand stores for heinously ugly old mugs. We then stuck our wedding logo stickers on them and called them "muglies." There was no trademark on the word, but I should probably be in touch with a copyright lawyer about the idea. Someone get the legal department on the phone!

One of my designer friends whipped up a gorgeous little sign that sat next to the confusing table full of random stickered mugs:

MUGLIES
For beer, wine, cocktails
  How this whole thing works . . .

1. Pick the mugly of your choice. (Remember, they're not actually ugly mugs: just eclectic!)
2. Write your name on the sticker affixed to the mugly.
3. Refill your mugly with beverages throughout the evening!
4. At the end of the night, the mugly is yours to take home (our special gift as a celebration of the many unique characters in our community of beloved friends and family).

See what I did there? I tried to make the fact that we didn't have much money to spend on favors into a commentary on our eclectic, unique community! It's not an ugly floral mug from the late '70s, it's a beautiful keepsake commemorating a patchwork of bohemians! It's crafty! And each one cost us only about a quarter.

As you might imagine, we had a lot of muglies left over at the end of the wedding. I guess a few of our guests saw our favors for

what they actually were: ceramic monstrosities. But here's where the
true craftiness comes in: because we'd encouraged people to write
their names on their muglies, we could harass them for "forgetting"
their favor at the wedding, and we could threaten to return it.

There's also a great satisfaction to helping myself to a cup at a
friend's house and opening a cabinet to find a mug with teddy bears
on it. The wedding logo stickers didn't stand up to the test of time
very well, unfortunately. I'll be reporting back to the marketing department about that.

Wedding favors are going the way of the matchbook

With Offbeat Bride readers, there seems to be a trend away from
doing favors at all. As one bride cynically crowed, "I challenge anyone to describe a wedding favor that gave them any joy beyond the
first five seconds of use." Many wedding guests I spoke to struggled
to remember even one favor from a wedding.

Wedding favors come in and out of vogue. One elder offbeat
statesman, Tracy, recounted that in the '80s, when you ordered the
invitations, you always ordered coordinated matchbooks with the
couple's names on them. She laughed, "I remember having stacks of
those around, from my wedding and any other wedding I attended
in the '80s. But that's fallen out of fashion, which I don't think is
necessarily a bad thing."

The most common favor at early 2000s weddings was wedding CDs with music from the ceremony and reception, but
these have gone the way of the matchbook. Offbeat reader Melissa elected to skip favors completely, remembering that she and
her fiancé "had gone to too many weddings where we ended up
with tchotchkes and CDs of the couple's favorite music that we
listened to on the way home only briefly while waiting for radio
stations to kick back in." Many of us now have stacks of wedding

photobooth pictures (so many fake mustaches!), and they may well be the CDs of the future.

This is all to say, trends come and go. There's no guarantee that your favors are going to impress anyone, so do what you can to have fun with them. Offbeat reader Crissy gave her guests kazoos and reported that, six months after the wedding, "friends are still pulling out their kazoos and serenading us at random moments." Unexpected and fun favors like this go a long way toward lessening bridal budget overloads and maximizing guest involvement.

Handcrafted or homemade favors also tend to get a little extra love. One friend made her guests peanut brittle using a special family recipe and reported that guests were fighting over the bundled sweets. Guests fighting for your favors is pretty much the best-case scenario.

That said, watch out for favors that create inordinate amounts of work for you or someone else. I spoke to a bride who elected to knit a scarf for each one of her thirty-seven guests. The idea is incredibly thoughtful, but I couldn't help but marvel at her stamina to become her own little knitting factory.

TIP: PUT YOUR FAVOR MONEY WHERE YOUR MOUTH IS

SOME COUPLES OPT NOT TO DO FAVORS, INSTEAD MAKING A DONATION to a charitable organization of their choice and letting guests know in the program. This can be an especially great way to honor family members if you use language like, "In lieu of favors, we have decided to donate to [Whatever Foundation] in honor of [Whomever, including their relation to you], who is a survivor of [a disease or other hardship]." You get the idea. This is a great way to make your little Wedding, Inc., a bit more like a nonprofit.

20. FORK IT OVER

Wrangling a registry, online or off

TRADITIONAL REGISTRIES MAKE THE MOST SENSE FOR COUPLES BUILDING a house together—probably harking back to the days of dowries, because, god knows, if you're gonna stick the neighboring family with another mouth to feed (i.e., the bride), at the very least you could give 'em a goat and an acre or two, right?

After six years together, we did not need a goat. Nor did we need any sheets or things like plates or candlesticks. We had collected our own mishmash of secondhand flatware and had purchased several sets of our own sheets. We didn't need any crystal or china. I loved presents, but wedding presents felt like a different beast.

Registries are a hot topic for Offbeat Brides, many of whom have values that contradict mainstream materialism. Offbeat reader Erika recounted, "A large number of the wedding websites I browsed seemed to focus very heavily on the registry and showers, and less on the actual significance of the event. For me, that's a turnoff—the idea of having my seventy-year-old grandmother there is far more important than whether or not she sent me a gift, especially when we live in a world where so many people don't have anything and many others, even in this country, have very little."

Or, as one anonymous bride told me, "I feel really uncomfortable dictating to other people what they do with their money. Money is always tight for me and my husband, so I am pretty conscious of it for other people. I was worried when I heard that my grandmother felt she couldn't afford a good enough gift for us, worried that my no-frills in-laws would think our registry too chichi, and selfishly frustrated at figuring out what to do with all the hideous crocheted wall hangings and pink-cheeked figurines that the farm-family relatives gave us." She summarized, "Most of the problem was me and my confusion about money and my discomfort with material culture."

It's strange: despite the ways many of us rebel against the standard American wedding (sexist! capitalist! bleah!), so many of us still fall prey to the consumerism of wedding gifts. Offbeat reader Leah admitted, "One thing that really surprised me was how conscious I was (and am!) of who gave us gifts, what they gave, and especially who didn't give us a gift. I really didn't expect this, and it's not something I like about myself. I recently talked about this with a friend who got married around the same time as I did, and she was feeling the same way. We both were like, 'Who doesn't bring a gift to a wedding?' followed by, 'Wait, we shouldn't care about this. . . . ' and then, ' . . . but we do!' I don't know, I guess my friend and I both bought into the materialism of the wedding-industrial complex or whatever."

I bought into it too. We registered with Amazon (they'd just launched their wedding registry option and it seemed very fancy) and agonized over what to put on the list, stabbing out at whatever we could find. (More sheets? Sure, they're nonperishable!)

To add to the confusion, I got a call from a couple of guests saying, "I don't want to get you something boring off your registry—what do you *really* want?" What I really wanted was a night of sleep where I didn't wake up before dawn and start mentally running through my to-do list. What I really wanted was all our friends and family in one place at the same time, celebrating with me.

We browsed for ages to find a seven-dollar vegan cookbook, and . . . I guess we could include a knife set—sure, add that. We lackadaisically clicked around Amazon, adding unneeded martini glasses from Finland and a subscription for "fruits of the month" gift baskets because, *Hey! We like fruit!* We added some kitchen counter-top thingamajigger called the Wandering Chicken of Pistoulet and a cheese grater and a robotic vacuum cleaner. Each of these things felt silly, because they were all, to varying degrees, silly. I had lots of things that I wanted for myself, but I didn't feel quite right having a My Little Pony sleeping bag on the wedding registry.

Finally, friends started giving us suggestions. An enormous, gorgeous world atlas. A modular RPM blender. A new comforter. (We learned that guests love pimping out the conjugal bed. There's something about weddings that makes it okay for shy family members to winkingly give you a mattress pad with little comments about what might happen on it. Sympathy for the asexual brides!) Before we knew it, the tide had turned, and we couldn't stop adding things to the registry. We wanted everything! Our itchy trigger fingers couldn't stop clicking!

Of course, then I started feeling a bit uncomfortable in the opposite direction: maybe we were being greedy for even having a registry. There are those couples who defer wedding gifts, asking instead for charitable donations through any number of websites. Oh, how I admire these people. Oh, how I long for their truly altruistic, nonmaterial joys. But I love presents. I am a glutton for gifts. As rough as the registry was, I would soldier on! I would feel sort of guilty about it, but I would sally forth with my disgusting consumer gimme-gimme bridal greed.

Give your guests guidance and avoid thirty-four crystal vases

Just know this: guests accustomed to buying gifts will get confused and crabby if you stay mute on the subject. There's a legend of the

TIP: WHAT *CAN'T* GO ON YOUR REGISTRY

THE TYPICAL REGISTRY, MADE UP OF DOMESTIC ITEMS, IS YET ANOTHER tradition that's ready to be ignored. I spoke to couples who had his-and-hers Xboxes on their registries, and wedding guests who had shopped through Target registries filled with things like cases of Coke, panty liners, and laundry detergent.

I talked to one couple that included Hostess Ho Hos on their registry as a joke. On their wedding day, they received hundreds of Ho Hos; most guests bought a couple to toss in with their "real" gifts just for the fun of it. Moral of the story: although technically there's nothing that *can't* go on your registry, be careful what you wish for. You just might get it, and you might get a lot of it (ho ho ho!).

bride who refused to register and ended up receiving thirty-four crystal vases. Offbeat reader Erika commented about her registry, "I comforted myself with the knowledge that the things guests got me were things I needed (and, you know, not covered in pastel flowers) and things that were, for the most part, under twenty-five dollars (especially for my older, fixed-income relatives). It was still a little bit squicky for me, but at least I felt like by offering suggestions I could help steer things in a practical, inexpensive direction. . . . I certainly didn't complain about expensive gifts or ones that weren't my taste, but by giving people some inexpensive options, I felt a little bit less guilty about it."

For those who decide not to register, there are some great alternatives out there. In addition to the charitable-donation concept, some couples use honeymoon registries to to register for experiences. Other folks ask guests to give themed items (one I spoke with told guests that the only gifts that were needed were Christmas tree ornaments, turning every Christmas into a chance to remember their wedding and their guests). That idea has the advantage of being both sweetly sentimental enough to appease grandparents but affordable enough to pass muster with those of lower income.

For better or for worse, guests expect some sort of guidance about gifts. If you choose not to have a traditional wedding registry, have a nice little explanation prepared for confused guests. Something like, "Please resist the urge to give us gifts of any sort. If we receive even one pair of crystal candlesticks, we vow to use them as lewd 'marital aids.' So unless you want your gifts used this way, please, for the love of all that is holy, do not get us any wedding presents. Thank you and goodnight."

21. THE GUEST LIST

Feeling like the bouncer of your own elitist nightclub

WHEN WE FIRST STARTED ENVISIONING OUR WEDDING, WE KNEW WE wanted the ceremony to be relatively intimate. We have a large community of friends and family whom we wanted at our open-invite reception, but it was important to exchange our vows in an environment made up of the people closest to us. Our solution was to break the wedding into two halves: the ceremony/dinner (the sacred/expensive part, which we kept relatively intimate) and then the all-night dance reception, extended as an open invitation to our community of friends and colleagues and coworkers and blog readers and all the other amazing people we know and love.

When I first talked to my parents and the in-laws about invite lists, I made it clear to them that we were keeping this wedding small, casual, and weird—and that, therefore, "now probably isn't the time to pull long-lost second cousins out of the woodwork." I invited everyone our parents requested, and, after tallying up our friends, our guest list was about right: one hundred people. To us, that felt intimate—when you pull the thread of wedding invitations, your concept of intimacy unravels quite quickly. One guest quickly becomes eight, eight become thirty, and the next thing you know, you're feeding the state of Arkansas a catered meal.

Just when I thought we had our list locked down, family members started popping up—including some very sweet in-laws whom, in almost seven years of being with Andreas, I'd never met. These guests then extended invitations to other family members I hadn't yet met. I learned that many couples hit up against this "unknown family member" issue.

Some folks theorize that this is a generational difference in the concept of family. Contemporary brides obviously appreciate blood ties, but what often matters most is shared time. A long-lost aunt might not garner an invite, while a close family friend who's been around since you were four years old is a shoo-in. For couples who have found themselves part of the emerging "urban tribe" concept of creating a family out of friends from your peer group, it can feel odd to invite blood relatives whose names you may not know instead of the people who make up your self-selected family unit. The concept will not seem odd to extended family members, however. I guarantee it.

There's also the money factor. It costs a fortune to feed people—even when you go the budget route like we did (with a friend catering and shopping at bargain grocery outlets like Cash & Carry). If you do favors, count on a few more bucks per guest. When including extended family turns a $2,000 wedding with fifty guests into a $10,000 wedding with two hundred guests, frugal brides can't help but be aware of the costs. If your family is paying for your wedding, then maybe they're happy to spend the extra money to feed networks of cousins you've never met. But if you're paying for it yourself, you may find yourself making a different decision.

As I clucked over qualifications ("An uncle, sure! But if they're so related, why didn't I know their name until this week?"), I realized that I was starting to turn into one of the people I used to loathe most: a club bouncer.

During my days as the editor of a rave magazine, I spent a lot of time talking to bouncers. They determined whether I could get into a given event to do my job as a music journalist. I hated the assholes who turned me away because—despite the fact that I'd been invited to the event, despite the fact that I was there as a favor to the organizer—they didn't like how I was dressed. Or they were just too lazy to check with a higher-up if it turned out that my name wasn't on the regular guest list. And all of a sudden, here I was, checking VIP access and plus-ones. Suddenly a blood relation wasn't good enough. Had you called on at least one birthday? Do you know my husband's middle name? Can you tell us how we met? Nope? Then you don't know us well enough to come. Please stand behind the red velvet rope with the rest of the plebeians.

If you're aiming for a truly tiny wedding—say, fewer than a dozen people—ugh, I wish you strength. I spoke to brides who recounted horror stories of trying to say no to requests—only to ultimately buckle under the pressure.

I buckled too. If I was a bouncer, I wasn't an especially good one: I backed down on every extra family member. I was gracious and welcoming, if a little dismayed. As the last few RSVPs trickled in, I was stunned to see our acceptance rate from guests at 90 percent—even higher, when you consider the folks who invited themselves. It was wonderful and exciting, and in the end I concluded that it reflected the fact that our community was supportive of (or just plain curious about) our freakfest wedding. That said, we were so to capacity that I got a little nervous. Would there be enough food? Would there be enough booze? Who were all these people? Eep!

"Just one extra guest" and other famous last words

If the family side of the guest list was getting long, the friend side was even worse. Unless we knew their significant other quite well, guests invited to the ceremony didn't get plus-one invitations. This, of course, caused no end of problems. Friends wanted to bring roommates we didn't know! Friends wanted to bring boyfriends we'd barely met! And when we said no, other friends stepped up to tell us we were being unfair.

That's when I almost lost it. I freaked out on one infinitely well-intentioned friend, snapping at him via e-mail: "Can I request that this be the last time we talk about the guest list and your thoughts about who we should and shouldn't be inviting?"

. . . Meow! But in the last few weeks before the wedding, the guest-list issue started feeling seriously fucked up, and the pressure was intense from both friends and family. Both my fiancé and I got a little freaked out that what we had envisioned as a relatively intimate, focused ceremony and dinner had bloated to about a third larger than we wanted—with people still wanting to make it bigger.

And, of course, all this happened months after the invites went out, months after folks could have talked to us. Just one extra guest here, just one extra guest there. For some people, that's just how weddings are. For me, it was not. I was undoubtedly rude to a few people, but I'm certainly not the only one. Offbeat reader Jennie remembers that she had "one person e-mail the day before to say he couldn't come (with a crappy excuse), and that, I'm ashamed to admit, flipped my evil-bride switch, and I sent quite a nasty reply, asking how he was going to pay for the meal he was wasting." In Chapter 30, "Staying Sane," I contend that you will freak out at least once. For many people, it's the guest list that gets them to that point.

Offbeat reader Leah recounts inviting one of her mother's cousins and the cousin's daughter. When she received their RSVP, she was dismayed to see that the cousin had written "probably 5" in the blank next to "Number of Guests." Offbeat reader Amy remembers a casual acquaintance who expressed a lot of interest in the wedding and went so far as to offer to be best man. She and her husband hadn't been planning to even invite the guy but made room on the guest list because his interest was so touching.

Amy remembers, "And then? Never showed up, never sent a card, never called, never made any effort at all to excuse his behavior or even talk to us ever again. I ran into him on the street a few months later and told him he owed us seventy-five dollars."

Expect a few flaky types and a few party crashers. Almost every wedding has both, and a good club bouncer knows how to deal with grace and muscle.

TIP: PICK A CHAIR, ANY CHAIR

OUR WEDDING ACCOMMODATED BOTH RSVP FLAKES AND WEDDING crashers, because we opted not to do assigned seating. Couples go back and forth about seating charts, and the decision includes factors like the size of your wedding, the amount of seating available, whether food is served or buffet style, etc. In my experience, guests do just fine without seating charts, and it saves you a *lot* of trouble.

"I wanted to do assigned seating, but when I didn't have it done at 3 A.M. on the day of the wedding, I said forget it and went to bed," recounted Offbeat reader Andrea. Instead, she opted to do things her own way: "I had an area at the sign-in table set up with the guest book and some place cards. I made a sign that said something along the lines of, welcome to our wedding/celebration. We're all friends here, so please decorate a name tag and seat yourself."

She offers this tip: "Make sure whatever you choose looks intentional, even if it happened by chance. There are so many different ways to do weddings now that most can be explained away as a new trend."

22. DISABILITY-FRIENDLY WEDDINGS

Owning your aisle, whether you're walking or wheeling

SPEAKING OF WEDDING GUESTS AND FEELING LIKE A NIGHTCLUB BOUNCER, let me tell you about one of our guests. I first met Echo in 1997, where I usually met people when I was in my early twenties: in front of a speaker stack at a very loud electronic music event. At first glance, she looked like your average '90s raver girl (bobbed haircut, very small shirt, very large pants), with one exception: she was holding a balloon between her two palms.

"I'm Ariel," I shouted over the bass. Echo looked at me and shook her head, still holding her balloon in her hands like a ball.

"I'm Echo," she said. "And I'm deaf. I can read your lips, but you have to talk slowly and face me."

Over the course of the evening, Echo explained that she was holding the balloon because, while all of us feel the bass of the music, the balloon allowed her to feel the vibrations of the higher treble notes that she couldn't hear. I was vaguely jealous: my new deaf friend was having a more nuanced experience of the music through her hands than I was having through my ears!

Flash forward to our wedding . . . Echo had become a dear friend over the years, and we wanted to make sure we accommodated her as much as we could at our wedding. We couldn't afford a sign language interpreter for the ceremony, but I wanted to provide her with a copy of our vows so she could follow along. Here's what Echo had to say:

> Ariel gave me a Word document with her and Dre's vows. She made me swear not to read it until the very moment of the ceremony. But

I knew I wouldn't be able to watch and read at the same time—it would have made me miss the very important visuals and nonverbal communication between bride and groom. So I cheated and found a quiet space on the ferry ride over and read it by myself on my way to the wedding. I'm so glad I did because it was so beautiful watching the ceremony.

Accommodating Echo's needs at our ceremony helped me understand the whole day in a different way, through a different perspective. Most of us planning weddings will have at least a few guests who will need special accommodations like this—at the very least, grandparents who may not want to sit on the grass at your picnic wedding or a nephew on the spectrum who needs a quiet place to retreat to during your reception. Furthermore, many of us may have our *own* disabilities to work with during wedding planning.

 FIRST-PERSON TIPS FOR PLANNING A DISABILITY-FRIENDLY WEDDING

Offbeat reader Rachel shared her first-person tips for disability-friendly wedding planning, for those with and without disabilities:

As you've probably discovered, images of brides and grooms with disabilities will not be easily found within the pages of popular magazines. So there are probably very few examples to generate ideas and reminders for all of the details you'll need to incorporate into your event.

That's why you should check out these tips for planning an accessible ceremony, disability-friendly considerations for your reception, and accommodating guests with different needs . . .

ACCOMMODATING YOUR GUESTS

First, determine whether anyone on your guest list has special needs or accommodations. Does anyone use a wheelchair, walker, crutches, or mobility equipment? Or do you have anyone elderly attending? Making sure

>>>

your guests are comfortable is just as important as making sure your own accessibility needs are met.

CHOOSING A VENUE

Make sure that your venue is accessible for both you and your guests:

> » Visit a handful of venue options ahead of time.
>
> » Walk the entrances and exits that both you and your spouse will be using and that guests will be using in case you have anyone coming with special needs.
>
> » Visit the dressing rooms and bathrooms, practice walking down the "aisle," and so on.
>
> » Bring a notebook with you to record the little things that you will want to discuss with the venue coordinator to ensure they can accommodate your needs.
>
> » Keep in mind that historic churches or buildings can present potential difficulties in accommodating wheelchair users.

WORK WITH YOUR VENUE TO MAKE THE SPACE WORK FOR YOU

Think about what you want to request of the people managing your ceremony and reception space. Perhaps bring a trusted friend with you who knows your needs, as well as the needs of your guests, to help you remember to ask all the right questions.

Do not rely on the opinion of those who are managing the space. What they may say is "accessible" could, in practice, be inaccessible, depending on your needs. Although you may be able to enter and exit the facility without a problem, getting to the altar, maneuvering into a receiving line, or navigating narrow hallways and pews could pose problems for your guests.

Remember, it never hurts to ask! What may seem inaccessible at first could have an easy fix that the venue coordinator is willing to work out with you. Setting clear expectations will help ensure there are no unexpected surprises and will help you find out how your venue can best accommodate your needs.

PLANNING YOUR CEREMONY

Think about whether you will be staying in your wheelchair to say your vows or whether you will be "walking" yourself down the aisle or having someone else walk you down. Also consider what you want the aisle arrangement to look like. Your officiant can offer suggestions to help make the venue work for you as well.

>>>

Plan a practice run-through with the person who will be escorting you down the aisle and with your officiant the night before the wedding.

Carefully consider whether you'd like to carry a bouquet. Get creative when it comes to carrying your bouquet—lay it in your lap, attach a strap to connect it to your wheelchair, or make an extended handle so it's easier to grip.

If you are doing a sand- or unity candle–type ceremony, think about having the items placed on a table that you can steady yourself at, if needed, and at a level comfortable for you.

YOUR RECEIVING LINE

After you say "I do," some couples choose to have a receiving line for their guests to greet and congratulate the happy couple. Consider arranging your receiving line with plenty of wide-open space for guests who may use mobility equipment as well to ensure they can get through the line to congratulate you with no problem.

THE RECEPTION

Keep the same considerations in mind for your venue space as you did for your ceremony in terms of accessibility, ease of access, your and your guests' needs, and the flexibility and willingness of the reception venue of your dreams to work with you.

IF YOU ARE PLANNING A SEATING CHART

Think about those with special accommodations, and try to place them in more convenient seats—not in the far back corner—with plenty of room between seats, and so on.

THE FIRST DANCE

If you're just not into dancing, or any other traditional reception activity, don't feel pressured into going through the motions. If you DO want a first dance, or other firsts, then go for it and have fun! Practice together at home with your spouse to prepare for your first dance to figure out the best way to dance together.

CAKE CUTTING

Place your cake on a firm table or other surface. If you need to steady yourself while performing the cake cutting, you will want to ensure there's something strong and reliable to support you. Make sure the table is at a height that is comfortable for both you and your spouse and placed in the room with plenty of space to get around the table and provide an optimal photo-taking angle.

"Invisible" disabilities

Although my friend Echo was very clear about her deafness, you may not realize how many people at your wedding are hard of hearing: Inviting your grandparents and a handful of other octogenarians who pinched your cheeks when you were a baby? Expect some of the over-sixty-five crowd—30 to 40 percent, specifically—to struggle to some extent with hearing the toasts, ceremony, and reception chatter.

The digital hearing aid industry aggressively courts the senior citizen crowd, but not all seniors are receptive to their message. Be subtle in your accommodations offers: Print out a few copies of the entire ceremony, and make them available near the wedding venue entrance. Add a statement like "Printed copies of the ceremony are available—simply request one when you RSVP" to your invitations. After all, it's just like planning your catered menu with options for gluten-free, kosher, diabetic, or low-fat diets.

If you can afford it, having a sign-language interpreter at your wedding can help your deaf guests—but remember that not all hard-of-hearing folks know sign language. Writer Aimee Chou of deafREVIEW reminds us that planning for your or your guests' hearing needs can extend to the bachelorette parties and other prewedding celebrations, too:

"A good ol' raucous marital send-off ain't just for the hearing. But most strip clubs are dark, noisy places. Not an ideal spot for speech reading, especially if a dancer sidles up to someone, whispering into their confused ear. If you're lucky enough to live in a city with deaf-friendly strip clubs or adult entertainment venues, bachelor/bachelorette party planning is a whole lot easier. You also just might find a dancer who, coincidentally, has taken a few years of sign language. Another approach: e-mail a local pole-dancing instructor. They are well connected to many dancers and can make friendly referrals. Can't find one? Consider utilizing an interpreter for the party." (More about prewedding parties in Chapter 24, "Pre Funk.")

Accommodating your own abilities and limitations

Invisible disabilities can require extra planning that might not immediately come to mind—even to the people dealing with the disability. Offbeat reader Vyktoria learned a lot from her experiences of wedding planning with several disabilities (impaired hearing, nerve damage, chronic fatigue, social anxiety, plus various joint and muscle injuries), and offered these tips for couples dealing with their own ability limitations that may not be immediately obvious to others:

1. Insist on checking all the hotel facilities. The bridal suite might be lovely, but if you can't physically climb onto the bed or use the bathroom you're going to have a lot less fun.
2. Schedule plenty of breaks. Try to fit in twice as many as you think you'll need, and start early in the day. Resting once you've already crashed isn't as effective as not crashing in the first place.
3. Make sure you know what your medication can be mixed with, and try to find alternatives just in case you accidentally end up drinking alcohol.
4. Make a day-of kit with spare meds and anything else you might need (plasters, painkiller gel, etc.), and give it to someone trustworthy.

5. Charge someone else with keeping an eye on the time. In the heat of the moment, you might forget to eat for eight hours. It's easier if someone else reminds you of those things.

6. Expect to explain yourself. People expect the bride and groom to float through the day serenely, and if your guests are people you haven't seen for a while (or have never met), you're likely to get the "why are you limping / using a cane / wearing dark glasses / not making eye contact?" This is especially true if you have a chronic or invisible illness.

7. Make sure your officiant really understands your condition. In the UK you often don't get to meet the officiant until just before the ceremony. I didn't properly explain my need to lip-read and ended up swinging my head around like I was at a tennis match.

8. Double your worst-case estimates. We thought a room without lift access would be okay as long as we wouldn't have to climb the stairs very often. However, because of finicky keys, we spent a lot more time traipsing back and forth.

9. Try to make sure people know before they start drinking that you have physical limitations. I do love to dance, but I bruise very easily. The reception was mostly rock, metal, and '80s, which resulted in a lot of exuberant dancing, and I got thrown around a lot without the opportunity to decline. Over a week later, I was still covered in bruises.

Those with chronic illness have specific needs when it comes to wedding planning, too. Planning short photography sessions, having comfortable attire, and choosing a mobility-compatible venue (with easily accessible restrooms) are key. Offbeat reader Lexie reminds us that you can get a lot accomplished with tech these days: Camera phones can take pictures of venues, dresses, or cakes when you can't make it out and about. Sites like Etsy and eBay allow you to be as weird and wonderful as you wish, all from the comfort of your bed.

Speaking of Etsy: Remember when we talked about getting your outfit custom made? That can be an ideal solution for those with mobility issues or those in wheelchairs. Offbeat reader Andy's advice for being comfortable and looking amazing in a wheelchair on your wedding day? "Do your homework and get a dress designer, rather than just a seamstress. A designer can come up with ideas you wouldn't have thought of. Pay the price you have to pay to feel beautiful—it is worth it! A custom dress will be fitted to YOU and can be designed around your wheelchair."

TIP: CELEBRATE YOUR DISABILITY AT YOUR WEDDING

YOUR DISABILITY IS A PART OF YOU. IT HAS HELPED SHAPE YOU INTO who you are and maybe even led you to your future spouse. Celebrate it! Honor your disability by working into your wedding—below are some ideas:

» Personalize your wheelchair by hanging tin cans behind your wheels for a photo op or special "Just Married" signs on the backs of your wheelchairs.

» Decorate your equipment—consider adding a fabric train to the back of your wheelchair or wrapping your walking devices in flowers or ribbons.

» Personalize your M&Ms with a stamp of a handicapped symbol to scatter around your table for favors.

>>>

A little creativity and a lot of patience planning a wedding as a non-traditional couple can guarantee a great day, no matter your ability. However you get down that aisle (and on the Offbeat Bride website, we've featured wheelchairs, custom modified canes, crutches, and more!), the goal is to feel like you're as YOU as you can be in that moment.

23. DECOR FETISHIST

Getting from here to pretty without
tripping over your taste

YOU MIGHT REMEMBER THAT ENGAGEMENT RINGS AREN'T REALLY MY forte, but circles certainly are. Almost immediately after Andreas and I got engaged, I started sketching ideas for themes and general decorative concepts. All the sketches were of circles . . . not rings but hoops.

And so our theme was born—it would be circles! Someone informed me months later that the word for our theme was "armillary," which means "pertaining to, or resembling, a bracelet or ring; consisting of rings or circles."

This theme made things easy. The plates people would eat from? Circular! The rings we would say our vows with? Circular! The focus of the poem I asked my father to write for the ceremony? Circles! The bamboo hoop altar a hippie friend of the family made for us? Circular! The hula hoops guests would dance with? Circular! Circles everywhere.

But wait: What's up with the hula hoops, anyway? Well, erm, I was obsessed with them. Not the little flimsy kind you get at Toys "R" Us. No, I was inspired by hula hoop dancers who use larger, heavier hoops handmade from irrigation tubing. When I first picked up a hoop, I was immediately, irrevocably hooked. Hooping is a blast—like rolling down a grassy hill in preschool. I like the metaphor of the hoop (return, revolution, the cyclical nature of life), and it was meditative and calming, exhilarating and reassuring. And fun as fuck. In other words, all the things I envisioned for our wedding.

Thus I stumbled across a decor theme that was visual, meaningful, and really easy. Sure, weddings with more complex themes are great! But you can't go wrong with a simple theme. Stars for an evening wedding. Clouds for a spring wedding. Stones. Paths. Simplicity. The more kindergarten your theme, the easier (and cheaper!) it is to execute. Revel in the minimalist theme!

The easy-as-a-circular-pie theme wasn't the only way we cheated on decor. We also cheated by picking wedding venues filled with so much natural beauty that we could have skipped decorating completely and still had a lovely location. The bed-and-breakfast where we were exchanging our vows and eating dinner was surrounded by meandering gardens; we didn't really need any flowers, because we were surrounded by them. There's definitely something to be said about picking a beautiful location—when you start with lovely, you keep your efforts streamlined.

Streamlined remained a focus for our decorations. Other than some boxes of used Christmas tree lights, our decorations were limited to what our dedicated friends could pool. Lucky for us, our friends include a lot of festival scene chill-space / dome / environment creators. Thanks to these amazing people, we had access to weird inflatable furniture, fabric lanterns from a friend's trip to India, and even a geodesic dome–ish structure that was draped in a parachute and Indian bedspreads—straight from Burning Man's Black Rock City to our wedding. We pulled together everything we had access to, and our friends shined it all up with lots of love and enthusiasm.

We had two friends named Sarah who acted as our decorators. The Sarahs tackled their respective areas with fluttering, illuminated, draped, cultivated, amazing skill. Upper location manager Sarah encouraged guests to write their wishes on fluttering bits of gold-leafed paper that were tied by ribbons to the branches of orchard trees. She draped mismatched plastic tables with the mismatched ta-

blecloths we'd given her (Shhhh: They were used sheets from a secondhand store. And yes, we washed them!) and arranged greenery
from the surrounding forest around buffet tables. This Sarah over-
saw a crew of friends who arranged flowers from my aunt's garden
into a mismatched collection of vases to be set on the mismatched
tables covered in mismatched bedsheets. And she prepped for all of
this while living 1,500 miles away.

Lower location manager Sarah took care of decorating the reception area—my mother's meadow. She directed the building of
the geodesic dome. She hung what seemed like miles of Christmas
tree lights through trees and bushes and branches. She lit hundreds
(billions?) of tea candles in a hodgepodge of jars she'd spent months
collecting. She hung glittering hula hoops that were custom-crafted
as a gift from a friend and hooping compatriot. With a few boxes
of leftover supplies, lower location manager Sarah turned a rustic
meadow into a complete fantasy.

Go simple or find the crafty bitches

Offbeat Brides who go for outdoor locations often do so knowing
that it helps them get off easy with decorations. Offbeat reader
Bridget got married in a tulip field in Yokogoshi-machi, Japan, and
didn't need many decorations: thousands of tulips did the trick just
fine. Others get married on beaches or in the mountains or other
places where there is an abundance of natural beauty. I heard this
time and time again from brides: pick a beautiful location, and you
make it easy.

We also weren't the only ones to go for a simple theme. One au-
tumn bride reduced her theme simply to "gourds." A summer bride
described her theme as "the great outdoors" and made centerpieces
from "mismatched glass bowls filled with water, river rocks, and
floating candles, with loose flowers kind of tossed about."

If you're a naturally crafty bitch, you'll find yourself in your element when planning decorations. Offbeat reader Susan (she of the "wedding co-op" concept) is perhaps the consummate crafty bride. Susan first claimed that she deemphasized decor—"We didn't dye the toilet water to match our flowers or anything," she scoffed—but then she had to admit that the handcrafted paper flowers she made for her cupcake tree coordinated with the decoupaged gift bags she'd made for out-of-town guests. Sure, it might not be wedding-themed, color-coordinated toilet water, but if you have a natural inclination for the arts and aesthetics, you may find yourself coordinating visual elements in ways you never imagined.

If you're crafty, enjoy obsessing over your decorations. If you're not crafty, then look for a few people who are. There are mini–Martha Stewarts lurking everywhere, just waiting to show off what they can do with a foot of ribbon and two pieces of vellum paper.

24. PRE FUNK

Cloudy with a chance of showers, bachelorette parties & other excuses for penis cakes

I LOVE PLANNING AND HOSTING PARTIES, AND THE CLOSER OUR WEDDING got, the more wrapped up I got in my spreadsheets and checklists and the project management of the whole shebang. From a project-coordination role, all my resources were taken. I did not have time to plan any other sort of party, and neither did my friends, because they had all been roped into helping with the wedding.

Thankfully, one corner of our family had the time and desire to help us a bit. A month before the wedding, my father-in-law and his wife threw us a lovely shower in Montana. Because we'd been such coldhearted tightwads with our guest list (excluding dozens of old family friends who'd known Andreas for years), the Montana reception was a more traditional wedding event that everyone got to enjoy. My in-laws kept us from looking like the assholes we sort of were (sorry, everyone . . .) and got to throw us a shower that was a bit more their style than our freaky-deaky wedding.

As for the bachelorette party? Early on, a girlfriend suggested that we all go get our top layer of skin scrubbed off at the local Korean spa ("They're very thorough when they scrub you," she winked, pointing at her ass crack.), but by the time it got down to it, there was little time for pre-funks. There were no state troopers showing up with fuzzy handcuffs and citations for being a naughty bride. There were no rip-away pants.

I have to admit, I have a bit of a bias against the cutesy, precious sexuality of bachelor/bachelorette parties. I'd rather see my friends wearing a pair of rip-away pants than pay some random beefcake to waggle around in them. The other downer from my friends' points of view: I wouldn't be embarrassed by using a penis-shaped water bottle or by wearing my bra on the outside of my clothing. I have virtually no shame (I've been shushed in public for telling jokes that involve a vas deferens, analingus, and bloody pus), and it's an accomplishment to embarrass me or gross me out. My friends would have had to organize a bachelorette party that would be illegal in several states for me to blush even a little bit, and where's the fun in that?

Plus, there's that whole "one last hurrah" issue, with actions that would otherwise be against the rules being somewhat sanctioned at bachelor/bachelorette parties. Here's the thing: When it comes to Andreas and me, our rules are pretty lenient. There's not much Andreas could do at a bachelor party that would really offend me—unless he did it without taking pictures to show me afterward. And what rules we did have weren't going to change after the wedding.

Philosophy and boob grabbing

I'm not quite sure how I feel about the whole "Do all your bad stuff the night before getting hitched, cuz then your life ends!" modality. If you or your fiancé like eating penis cakes, drinking with your buddies, going to strip clubs, or wearing Day-Glo wigs, then I hope you're marrying someone who's going to slap on a wig, head to the strip club, and eat a penis cake with you on every anniversary.

I spoke to a lot of other folks who shared this attitude, some for the same "too busy" and "not my scene" reasons, and others for more ideological ones. Offbeat reader Lisa Marie didn't want her husband going to a strip club but explained, "We both have had a lot of friends that were/are strippers, and my beef isn't with the girls—it's with the horrible way they're treated by the strip clubs."

Offbeat reader Phyllis had a more old-fashioned reasoning: "Yes, I'm apparently a prude by today's standards, so we did have the 'no strippers, please' discussion. I guess that officially makes me no fun, but I was really pleased that his friends respected my wishes and didn't force the issue. Or, if they did secretly take him to a strip club, they're good enough friends to be kick-ass liars . . . and in a weird way, I have to respect that, too!"

Some saw this fetishized sexual behavior as not only offensive but indicative. "There's something sad about a culture that encourages men to believe that marriage is something you get roped into, and that you have to have a final night of lust and sex before you give in to the horrible clutches of marriage," observed Offbeat Bride reader Stacy.

Most often, I heard ways that Offbeatfolks used the parties as an excuse to do their own thing: bachelorette parties that are mellow cabin weekends canoeing with girlfriends, bachelor parties where dudes scrabbled around in train tunnels with flashlights.

But just when I'm ready to write off the whole traditional pre-funk thing, I hear stories of people having genuinely wonderful experiences at their showers and bachelorette parties. Phyllis explained that meeting the women of her extended family made her feel "welcomed and part of something bigger." Her bachelorette party included talking "about everything from religion to philosophy to life plans." Phyllis continued, "At one point, when the conversation got a little heavy, my friend Sarah leaned in to note the turn things had taken and ask me if it was okay for my bachelorette party. I said it was perfect and I wouldn't have it any other way. Oh, and she grabbed my boobs."

Showers seem to have a genuine place for young couples who haven't been living together—functioning almost as a housewarming. If you're having a big wedding (or if you have a big family), showers are also a nice way for extended family to meet in a quieter, more intimate space than your wedding is bound to be. And I'm super-jealous of Susan's craftsy shower, where she and all her girl-friends gathered to make felt flowers before her wedding and where the rule with gifts was "handcrafted only."

And if you need an excuse for penis cake, bachelorette parties are great. If you enjoy it, I would encourage you to eat penis cake all the time. Why reserve it for special occasions?

part four

The Trifecta of Wedding Conflict:
Loved Ones, Ceremony & Sanity

25. CONFLICT MEDIATION

Using therapy-speak to smooth things over

THERE IS, OF COURSE, THE DARK SIDE TO WEDDINGS—ESPECIALLY WHEN you have friends help you with everything. The "It takes a village" technique I mentioned in Chapter 17 isn't always a smooth ride. You get a lot of tasks generously taken off your plate, but you need to work overtime to keep all your helpers happy. Managing a volunteer staff is delicate work, and at times I felt like I was tiptoeing on Saltines trying to make sure everyone felt loved and appreciated.

As part of our wedding preparations, we needed to clear some campsites for guests in the forest of my mother's property. My mom lives a half-hour ferry ride from Seattle, so it's a relatively quick trip to the country. We put the call out to our group of friends: Did anyone want to take a day trip out to the woods to scope out the space and do a little light brushwork under the trees, raking campsites and trimming back bushes? We invited both location manager Sarahs and as many outdoorsy guyfriends as we could, and then we headed out to the forest.

Trying not to seem bossy, I'd been intentionally vague and told the location managers to just poke around and get a feel for the spaces, envisioning what they wanted where and how things might look. There was an awkward moment when, twenty minutes after arriving, one of the location managers got flustered and confused and found a reason to turn around and immediately head back into the city.

In talking things over after the fact, I learned that she felt unprepared and disoriented, and that she wished she'd had a bit more direction and guidance ahead of time about what

my expectations were—instead of my just saying, "Here's the
space . . . now brainstorm!"

Zoinks! In my effort to avoid bridal bossiness, I'd left her out in
the cold, totally confused and somewhat upset and . . . ack! Damn.

Everything turned out fine, eventually. We talked through the
issue, realized how the miscommunication arose, and both apolo-
gized. Everything got resolved.

But this wasn't a conversation that would have happened if I'd
been paying a professional to decorate. The vendor would have
shown up, I would have bossed them around, they would have done
their shit, and I would have paid them. If you have the budget, hiring vendors can save you a lot of interpersonal strife.

Offbeat reader Melissa had a snafu with her wedding photos
taken by a friend, and explained, "It really strained the relationship, and I sometimes wish we'd hired someone instead." Friends
can help you create a deeply personal wedding, but they have
feelings that can get ruffled—and your friends' feelings are important. Not that you should abuse a paid wedding vendor, but
you're probably not wondering whether you're being too bossy
when telling your hired caterer exactly what to cook. As Offbeat
Bride reader Jen so simply put it, "If you aren't paying people, you
have to be nicer to them."

Therapy-speak and scary scrutiny

My family's native tongue is therapy-speak, and although sometimes that can be a pain ("Ugh, do we have to talk about boundaries
again?!"), the somewhat contrived emotional articulation came in
handy for dealing with wedding-planning conflicts.

I learned to focus on what's known as "I statements," instead of
"you statements." For example, instead of saying, "You're making

me feel like shit!" you can try something like, "When you told me you didn't approve of the pink fishnet stockings under my wedding dress, I felt like you don't support my vision of this event." Offbeat reader Jen told me she also used this same technique, explaining, "It makes you sound all new-agey, but it makes other people feel less threatened." And less threatened is a good thing. Being able to talk about your feelings with your friends and family is always a good thing—during weddings, even more so.

Do what you can to "own your issues" and be self-deprecating. Introduce a conflict by saying, "I hope you can forgive me for being so stressed and freaked out about this, buuuuuut . . . " When you start the conversation by acknowledging that you're horribly flawed and in a tough spot, you can gain a little traction. This isn't blaming your wedding for everything or using your bridal status to excuse bad behavior—"I'm the bride, so I'm allowed to be a total nightmare about this!"—it's just acknowledging that, with all the weight of wedding planning, you might be a little emotionally compromised.

Here's the good news: people tend to be forgiving when you're planning a wedding. I found that it was remarkably easy to weasel a day off from work for wedding logistics, and the world seemed in many ways endlessly patient with me as I scrambled around getting my ducks in a row. People are willing to be patient with you, but don't ask them to put up with your anger or nastiness. Be kind to those around you during your wedding. You can never, ever thank people enough for their help or say enough times how appreciative you are of their patience as you stumble through the process of wedding planning.

Or, as Phyllis winked at me, "You can tell yourself the wedding is all about you, but the truth is, you're outnumbered and you're under the most scrutiny of your entire life. Be nice."

TIP: COPY 'N' PASTE CONFLICT RESOLUTION
(a.k.a. How to say "fuck off" and "I love you" and "this conversation is over" all at the same time)

Try versions of these Offbeat Bride–tested statements in YOUR conflicts:

» It means so much to me that you're so interested in my wedding planning. That said, I hope you'll be able to respect that my partner and I are putting a lot of thought into having the wedding reflect our unique relationship and values. I hope you can place your trust in our ability to find what we feel works best for us.

» Oh my goodness—it's so flattering that you felt you could come and talk to me about your thoughts on my wedding. I love hearing all the different ideas that we get from friends and family— I think you'll be excited to see what we come up with.

» I'm so sorry to hear that you're upset about my decision to [fill in the blank] at my upcoming wedding. I hope you understand that this was a decision my partner and I took very seriously, that we made after putting a lot of thought into how we could best make our wedding a reflection of our relationship. While I wish I could change how you feel, I respect that we all have different opinions about weddings . . . and I hope you know that this disagreement doesn't change how much I love you! I'm so looking forward to seeing you [at our wedding / some other time / whatever].

» Wow, thanks so much for sharing your ideas with me. It really makes me feel like you're as excited about this as we are! My partner and I believe really strongly in working together to shape a wedding that's a reflection of who we are, and I'll definitely be keeping your ideas in mind during our planning discussions.

» Thanks so much for all your suggestions about our wedding. Although we've decided to take our plans in a different direction, I just want you to know that we put a lot of thought into our decision and your input was so incredibly valuable to us. Thanks so much again . . . and we can't wait to have you there celebrating with us.

26. CEREMONY WITHOUT SANCTIMONY

Building tradition from the ground up

TRADITIONAL WEDDINGS MAKE WRITING CEREMONIES MAD LIBS–STYLE easy: "Do you promise to [verb], [verb], and [verb] [pronoun]? For [general adjective] or [general adjective], for [monetary adjective] or [monetary adjective], in [bad noun] and in [good noun]?"

Hey, it works. Ain't no arguing with that. But we wanted something completely our own, and of course the deviation made things endlessly more complex. Building our ceremony from the ground up was one of the more challenging aspects of the wedding-planning process.

Andreas and I are basically pragmatic agnostics: we have faith when we need it and beliefs when we want them, but they're pretty quietly integrated into the rest of our lives, and we don't practice them publicly. Neither of us is really into ceremony or spirituality on display. "She who knows the most, waves her crystals and DNA activations around the least," I say. By this logic, the couple that is the most committed feels the least need to prance around and crow about how committed they are—this questionable leap in logic isn't exactly accurate, but it goes a long way toward explaining why we approached the ceremony with such hesitation.

I grew up surrounded by ceremony. As a recovering Catholic, my mother still had a deep fondness of ritual and services. She and my father tried to indoctrinate me with an appreciation for the ceremonial via a hippie Sunday school called SEARCH, which stood for Seeking Enlightenment and Reaching Children's Hearts. Every week we would gather in a yurt and sing this never-ending song called "Somos el Barco" about how we were the boat, we were the sea, I lived in you, you lived in me.

When I got a little older, my mother started organizing coming-of-age ceremonies for my friends who'd just gotten their first periods. As is typical for things my mother suggests, I thought the idea was stupid, but my friends loved it . . . so I participated by making cakes covered with bloody frosting that read, "It's not gross, It's a gift from the goddess!"

My rebellious streak pushed me toward impatience with ceremony. The pretense and sanctimoniousness grated on my nerves. *Shut up about it already. We get it!* I'm just not into performative spirituality, and so public ceremonies have always lived somewhere near the bottom of my pet-peeve shit list, somewhere between misplaced apostrophes and people who can't walk their talk: I get impatient, irritable, and look for my escape hatch. I wish there were a ceremonial emergency exit behind every altar.

And yet there we were, designing our own ceremony—our own piece of sanctimoniousness all about us! Egotistical and sanctimonious: fucking perfect. Just what I've always wanted to be. Understandably, our first decision was to keep it short. We would keep our blowhard sermonizing to a minimum. Ten minutes, max.

Our second decision was to enlist an ally: an internet-ordained Universal Life minister, my godmother. Suzanne's sensibilities were close enough to ours that we knew she wouldn't make us uncomfortable. Although she tends toward my mother's more earth-based religions, she was willing and able to work with us to create exactly the sort of ceremony we wanted.

Andreas and I talked together about what we wanted. A welcome, maybe a reading, an exchange of vows, and then hurrah: the ceremonial French kissing. After reading on a friend's blog about the Jewish tradition of yichud, we were inspired to schedule a few minutes to ourselves after the ceremony to escape the chaos of the wedding.

Once we had this general structure in mind, we went for a couple of walks around Seattle's Greenlake with our minister, my godmother. We talked about the things we'd thought over, and Suzanne reflected back her perspectives. It was pretty collaborative.

We might have been extra lucky on this issue: our families were the epitome of respectfulness in letting us build the ceremony we wanted. My parents stayed relatively out of it, perhaps because they trusted our process with my godmother, the woman who had introduced them to each other thirty-five years earlier. Perhaps she was doing reconnaissance for them and they were happy with what she reported back. I don't know, but I like the idea of late-night walkie-talkie chats: "Yes, they decided to go with a mention of 'the forest around them,' that is a 'Roger' on at least one semi-earth-based religious reference." Andreas's parents, meanwhile, stayed out of the religion discussion completely—perhaps because my godmother reported back to them, too.

Seal the deal with vows

Once we'd gotten the structure of the ceremony planned, it was time to write our vows. Vows are difficult to write—and I say this as someone who writes for a living! There are those who believe that using traditional vows is part of binding your relationship to a ceremony that goes back generations upon generations, and then there are those who see their vows as a chance to express themselves personally. We were in the latter camp.

I also had a lot of help. I looked everywhere for inspiration. Because I'm a geek, by "everywhere," I mostly mean "everywhere online." Some of my biggest inspiration came from a blog post written by my friend Derek, a fellow geek who was getting married a week before me:

> Here's the thing about wedding ceremonies: They suck. I mean, all of them. They're either so traditional as to be painful ("honor and obey" would have made everyone in our audience laugh out loud) or so new-agey you'd hardly know a wedding was going on.
>
> So Heather and I rolled our own. We each wrote our vows and we collaborated on the entire ceremony. As a writer, it was a challenge I'd never even considered. What would a meaningful, emotional, sincere, yet irreverent wedding ceremony sound like?
>
> But there was one part that I was particularly proud of. When it came time for the rings, this is what I wrote for our officiant, my uncle Harry:
>
> "This is the point in the ceremony when I usually talk about the wedding bands being a perfect circle, having no beginning and no end. But we all know that these rings do have a beginning. Rock is dug up from the earth. Metal is liquefied in a furnace at a thousand degrees. Hot metal is poured into a mold, cooled, and then painstakingly polished. Something beautiful is made from raw elements.
>
> "Love is like that. It's hot, dirty work. It comes from humble beginnings, made by imperfect beings. It's the process of making something beautiful where there was once nothing at all."
>
> Harry said he liked it so much he might use it in other ceremonies.

Offbeat reader Bridget, a nondenominational wedding officiant, explained that, in her experience, couples tend to fall into one of three opinions about their vows:

1. They know what they want to say.
2. They don't know what they want to say, but they'll know it when they see it.
3. They don't care as long as it gets them married.

Figure out which of Bridget's groups you're in, and plan your vows accordingly. If you're in the first group, do some soul-searching and get writing. If you're in the second, get out there and start reading. If you're in the third, get an officiant you trust and let them say whatever they want.

Bridget explained, "Some of my clients' vows are irritatingly shallow; some of them are profoundly in depth; some of them are suffocating in their ardor. But all of them work for the couple who is saying them, because they are defining marriage for themselves, and vows are the place to articulate that."

Andreas and I wrote our vows together, but separately. We hiked to the top of Wildhorse Island in Montana, and then we sat back to back to do our writing. It was sort of nerve-racking when we turned around and read them aloud to each other, but what I thought was going to be a sappy moment really wasn't at all. We pragmatically looked over each other's words and then decided to use one ending for both of them to sort of bind them together.

Then we snuck off behind some rocks and did it to seal the deal.

27. SOMETHING BORROWED

Blending traditions, and why the seven steps,
handfasting & the blood of Christ
aren't mutually exclusive

IT'S EASY TO CONFUSE "UNTRADITIONAL" WITH "UNRELIGIOUS," BUT THE
two aren't mutually exclusive. You can be untraditionally religious
or part of an untraditional religion. Or you can just be like us and
blend the components you like from various religions.

Our wedding wasn't overtly religious, but it certainly had spiritual components, including my father-in-law ringing my father's
Buddhist meditation bell. (He's Lutheran, but didn't seem to mind.)
Deep breaths were encouraged and generalized, non-deity universal
forces were acknowledged.

My feelings about religious traditions in weddings are pretty
much the same as my feelings about the rest of wedding planning: if
it honestly and genuinely reflects the couple getting married, then
awesome. If it's something you're doing to keep family members
happy, or to impress someone . . . don't do it. Obviously, your faith
(or total lack thereof) may be a reflection of or reaction to your
family's values. But a wedding is one of the big public events of your
lifetime. Don't waste it on someone else's message.

I love Offbeat Bride reader Maria's perspective. Although she
grew up Catholic, she chose not to have a Catholic ceremony. She
said this was in part because she actually takes Catholicism quite
seriously. "In a Catholic ceremony, the bride and groom take communion. Before that, they must confess, and for the confession to
be valid, they must be sure they don't want to commit those sins
again. They might eventually do so, of course, but, for the confes-

sion to be valid, they must honestly feel right then that they do not want to commit them again. And I'm talking about sins like using birth control and not going to church on Sundays. All of my Catholic friends confessed while knowing that they wouldn't change these things, thus making their confessions invalid and committing at the time of their weddings one of their religion's worst sins: taking communion while in a state of sin. In my opinion, celebrating your marriage while committing one of the biggest sins in your religion is very wrong."

In other words, don't go invoking God and then inviting his/her/its wrath upon you. The religious components of your ceremony should mean something to you and your marriage. Maybe that meaning is a respect of your lineage and a desire to reflect it. That's cool if you plan to respect and honor that lineage through your marriage. If it's just for appearances? Well, you've got your conscience to deal with there. Plus an angry deity.

Then again, for some people there's no agonizing involved. One bride summed it up this way: "Jesus and his imaginary friend were not invited to our wedding." No waffling there. A dedicated atheist agreed, "I couldn't imagine going through a Christian ceremony. 'Blah blah blah, God, blah blah amen, eye roll' would be offensive to people who actually believe in the words I'd have been paying lip service to."

For those who choose to include religious elements in an untraditional way, it can be a rough road. Offbeat reader Amy knew she wanted a religious wedding—but not for the reasons you might expect. "Both my husband and I felt strongly that the government has no place decreeing the validity of relationships," she explained, "so it was important for us to have a wedding sanctioned by someone other than the state."

So, she wanted a religious wedding. Complicating matters is the fact that she's Jewish and her husband is Catholic. They wanted both faiths present at the ceremony, which became the battle of the ages. Amy said, "The Catholics never gave us any problem. They were happy to recognize our union, never suggested I convert, and were generally very relaxed and supportive. The rabbis, on the other hand—ugh! We met with half a dozen, and I nearly always wound up leaving in tears. Even the very liberal rabbis insisted that my husband convert, or at least renounce his religion. And they all tried to make me feel like I was a terrible person for marrying out!"

After much hunting, they found a rabbi who would officiate, but Amy realized that if you've got an untraditional vision for your religious ceremony, "finding the right officiant can be as hard as finding the love of your life (or harder!)."

TIP: DECOLONIZE YOUR WEDDING!

CANADIAN OFFBEAT BRIDE READER ALEXIS WANTED TO ACKNOWLEDGE Indigenous territory in her wedding and has advice on how you can, too:

When my partner and I discussed the elements we'd like to see in our wedding ceremony, a land acknowledgment was one of the first things that came to mind.

A wedding land acknowledgment is an expressive gesture of reconciliation, respect, and goodwill. Many non-Indigenous Canadians (and Americans, Australians, etc.) are unaware of the legacy of colonization, or its stifling and pervasive presence today. Taking pause to reflect upon the land's special relationship with the First People who hold its stewardship is a way of raising awareness of their historical, legal, and rightful claim. It also presents an opportunity to thank the host First People for their hospitality toward you and your guests during this momentous occasion.

>>>

Neither of us has Indigenous ancestry, so my partner and I contacted an elder to approve our wording. An elder is typically a senior individual who is charged with the safekeeping and dissemination of traditional knowledge. Universities are a good place to find a contact from your local First People, if a band administration, tribal council, or similar organization is unavailable. In some situations, an elder or other person may wish to attend your ceremony themselves, in which case they can welcome attendees in person. If you're lucky enough to experience this, make sure you're aware of proper protocol and etiquette. A small honorarium, donation, or gift of some kind is often a polite way of giving thanks. You can check in with Indigenous or local government or educational institutions for more information.

Our ceremony took place in a provincial park that is under the jurisdiction of a First People. However, if your venue is on contested land, you may describe it in your acknowledgment as "unceded territory," which means that the land was never surrendered or otherwise relinquished to colonial power. Determining the status of the location in question is a chance to uncover and better understand a significant aspect of human history that's been hitherto swept under the rug.

Here is how we began our wedding land acknowledgment:

"Welcome, family and friends. Paul and Alexis would like to acknowledge that we are on the traditional territory of the Snuneymuxw First Nation, who have been stewards to this land since time immemorial, and we extend our thanks for this hospitality."

Although I write from a Canadian perspective, wherein land acknowledgments are becoming more commonplace, in this small action, you and your partner can contribute to a greater narrative of recognizing Indigenous rights that is gaining momentum all over the world. Taking the time to affirm ancestral territory during what may be one of the most solemn and joyous ceremonies of your life sends a bold message, and yet it's also a force for normalizing the dialogue surrounding how colonization continues to affect us all. This act of recognition is a sober yet hopeful statement of solidarity, regard, and community. What could be more appropriate in celebrating a marriage?

Vague-splaining your wedding

If you or your partner are from a religious family and you're planning a secular wedding, there's one piece of solid advice I can
give you: don't ask your family for advice about your wedding.
If they ask for details, be vague in your responses. Yes, you're
excited about the awesome secular ceremony you're designing
from scratch, but, as Offbeat Bride reader Melissa explained, "Not
broadcasting in advance how different [your wedding is] going to
be will help a lot. Otherwise, people get all twitchy and anxious
and prepare themselves to be offended and hate it." If religious
family members offer their assistance, either politely decline ("We
want you to just be able to sit back and enjoy the day!") or point
them toward safe tasks, like food, ushering, or other nonreligious
logistics.

Another way to appease religious types at a secular wedding is
to provide moments for them to practice their faith without it en-
croaching on your ceremony. Call it "vague spirituality." One easy
way to do this is by invoking a moment of silence during your
ceremony—atheists will use it as a chance to think about how
happy they are for you, while more religious types might offer a
silent prayer. Another way to do this is a ring-warming, where the
rings are passed among family members before being exchanged
by the couple. Again: religious folks will most likely pray over the
rings or wave sage bundles or whatever they want, while nonreligious types will just warm up the ring and pass it along.

Have two weddings, solve one problem

When dealing with pressures from family to have a religious wedding, there's always this fail-safe: you can have two weddings. I
mean, have as many as you want—but two is probably plenty to

keep you busy. The best reason to have two ceremonies is that it allows you the freedom to have one wedding dictated by cultural, family, or religious traditions and then another that's an expression of the shared vision between you and your partner. This works best if the religious/traditional members of your family feel strongly enough about their convictions that they're willing to pay for their version of your wedding. You pay for your own, and, because they're getting "their wedding," family members can leave you alone.

Offbeat reader Rebecca went for the two-weddings option. Her fiancé, Sandeep, is Indian American, and so his mother organized a relatively traditional Hindu ceremony, while Rebecca focused her attention on what she called her "American ceremony."

Two days after their Hindu wedding, Rebecca and Sandeep went on to have the wedding they envisioned—one that they felt reflected them as a couple and made no mention of religion or spirituality. By having the two ceremonies, Sandeep's extended family got the wedding they wanted, while Rebecca and Sandeep got their own.

Rebecca did mention that her side of the family, whom she describes as "born-again Christians," were left out of the customized wedding option. They could attend either the Hindu ceremony or the "American ceremony." She said her religious family "didn't faint during the American ceremony and, more importantly, didn't bitch about it afterward. I figured it was meaningful enough to make up for the lack of religious mention. If they're bitching in private, I'm cool with that . . . as long as they don't say anything to me."

Rebecca speaks wisely. While building your wedding, it's easy to wrap yourself into emotional pretzels thinking about others' expectations and reactions. My theory is that this is an event you are planning as a celebration of your partnership and as a reflection of your relationship. There will always be those who will criticize a wedding, just as there are those who bad-mouth certain relationships that don't adhere to their politics, ideologies, or faith. Just as you'd ignore those who nay-say the relationship you've committed yourself to, so, too, should you ignore those who grumble about the wedding ceremony you envision for yourself.

Make peace with the fact that there will be those who bitch no matter what you do. You might as well do what makes you happy, so at least when you hear it, you'll know that the event they're griping about was exactly the one you wanted.

There's no accounting for taste, after all.

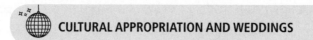

CULTURAL APPROPRIATION AND WEDDINGS

When a dominant culture takes a practice, tradition, theme, etc., from a marginalized culture, it could be a case of cultural appropriation, and should be thoughtfully considered—especially if you're sharing your wedding on social media.

The first step when considering borrowing a tradition from a culture other than your own is to really examine your reason for wanting to do so. What is your intention? Is there an authentic, personal tie to the culture?

The next step is to do your research. An anonymous Offbeat Bride wrote about her best practices when it came to ensuring her wedding would borrow respectfully: "In my experience, if you want to have some kind of tradition of another culture at your wedding, seek out someone who is familiar with it, and do your best to learn from them about it. Really listen, and then talk with them about what their cultural perspectives mean to you, and ask how (or whether) they feel you could honor your interest in that culture respectfully and in good taste. In my personal experience, people are more often than not interested in sharing their culture with those who approach them respectfully."

Last, check in with guests who might feel sensitive about your integrating cultural touches. If someone from the culture tells you they're not comfortable with what you're doing, it's not your place to argue.

28. WHOSE WEDDING IS THIS?

Battling over ownership of your nuptials

THE ONLY BUMP ON THE ROAD IN OUR CEREMONY PLAN CAME WHEN MY mother asked for something—in that way that German cops do when they want to search your backpack at six the morning after a music festival (not that I'd know about that). They say, "We're going to check your bags now, okay." Period. Despite the implication of a question, the last word is not followed by a verbal question mark.

My mother worded it like this: "I'd really like to sing the song that I sang at your father's and my wedding thirty years ago, okay."

I gave her a hug and told her we'd think about it. I called a few days later and explained that it wasn't going to work. We had already picked a processional vocalist, our friend Tania, who sings opera like a brick house. Tania has a voice that almost assaults you with its volume and clarity.

Tania was singing jazz. I wasn't sure how her huge-lunged broadcast of Etta James's "At Last" would fit with my mother strumming her acoustic guitar and crooning an old Judy Collins song called "Since You Asked." And I told my mother as much.

Naturally, my mother was hurt when I declined her offer/request. She quickly said (probably as much to herself as to me), "It's not a big deal—you've got plenty of other, much bigger things to think about right now." She was very gracious about it and didn't apply any pressure, although of course I felt the pressure anyway.

Such are the dynamics even the supposedly most mature of us can have with our parents, who reduce us to petulant fifteen-year-olds, huffing over a Grave Injustice we have just suffered at the hands of our totally irritating (and embarrassing!) family members.

TIP: EXPECT HURT FEELINGS

IT SEEMS TO BE PART OF PLANNING A WEDDING (AND PARTICULARLY part of planning a "from scratch" ceremony): someone's feelings will be hurt. I wish I had some magical piece of advice about how to deal with hurt family members, but I don't. Whatever you do, don't blame Bridezilla. Using that tired term as an excuse is basically like saying, "I go totally psychotic sometimes, and I'm not responsible for it because I'm wearing a white foofy dress and this is my special day."

There's no need to become a split-personality diva to deal with conflict. All you can do is try to deal with each situation with as much grace as possible. Take a deep breath, apologize to the hurt party, let them know that it wasn't your intention for them to feel this way, and then either stand your ground or find a way to compromise. Apologizing feels good, even if you're not compromising.

Sometimes when I talk to my mother, I can almost still feel my high school plastic retainer in my mouth. At this rate, it'll take me until somewhere in my fifties before I can talk to her without occasionally slipping into teenager mode.

If I'd been thinking more clearly, I would have used some of the conflict-resolution techniques I mentioned in Chapter 25, "Conflict Mediation." I could have used the "evolution versus rejection" technique you'll read about in Chapter 29, "Wrestling Down the Aisle." But let's be honest: this is real life, and perfectly tactful, articulated rejections take time to think up. I simply told my mother no and left her to her hurt feelings.

Ariel and the Ungrateful Wretches

But that's not where the story ends. Ultimately, I stumbled onto a great compromise. My mother got what she wanted when we realized that we had no recessional. We didn't want to walk out in silence (it seemed sort of creepy and awkward), and, because we weren't wiring the space for music, we realized that Mom and her guitar would fit perfectly. In some stubborn way, I felt like I was sticking to my guns: I let Mom get what she wanted (she sang), but I didn't totally let her get her way, because we exited at the end of the first verse.

That sounds awful of us, like we were running away from my mother's music—and it is awful of us. My mother has a beautiful voice, and our guests thoroughly enjoyed her lovely performance. But I was a brat growing up, and although all my hippie friends loved drums, I still can't stand them because they remind me of being awakened at 8 A.M. on Saturdays by my parents' djembes.

Therefore, in an awful way, it's probably perfectly in bratty character that I missed most of my mother's lovely performance while my friends enjoyed it. They're all much more appreciative than my mother's ungrateful wretch of a daughter. And, yes, that was what my parents used to call me when I was really being a brat: "Ariel, you ungrateful wretch!" If I ever start a band, I'm totally calling it Ariel and the Ungrateful Wretches. And I would not, of course, give any credit to my parents for the phrase.

Despite my initial resistance, my mother's idea to inject herself into the ceremony inspired us to give each of our four parents a role. Andreas's father rang in and closed the ceremony with a Tibetan bowl. My father read a poem. My outlaw mother acted as both our ring bearer and my maid of honor, holding my bouquet during the ring exchange.

Family dynamics turned up to eleven

Our family conflicts were infinitesimal compared with some of the epic battles that are waged over weddings. Mothers huff, "But that's not fair!" when they hear about underwater weddings. Family members sob over music choices or turn stone-faced at the suggestion of deity-free ceremonies. All too often these family members are women—mothers and sisters and aunts and grandmothers. Cousins, too. For many women, especially for more traditional women, the wedding is a matriarchal Mount Olympus—a time when family pride, feminine ego, maternal manipulation, and the dark side of woman-drama can reign supreme.

Basically, whatever your family dynamics were before the wedding, prepare yourself for more of the same but with a little added heat. Like a greenhouse of conflict—only on fire. There is truly an art to standing your ground with your family, and it takes an enormous amount of grace—or a complete lack of caring—to navigate these situations smoothly. Prepare yourself now for turf wars, even relatively small ones.

TIP: TRY "WHY?"

OFFBEAT READER DEREK WROTE A GREAT POST ONCE ABOUT USING THE word "why" instead of the word "no." He wrote it for graphic designers, but you can swap out the word "designer," and it offers beautiful wedding-planning advice for those dealing with pesky family members:

The next time you want to say "no," say this instead: "Why?" When you say "why" instead of "no," you open a conversation that can help inform both sides. We'd all much rather hear, "Why did you make this choice?" than "I don't like this." Don't get me wrong: You still need the ability to say "no." But in the end, being open to the "why" of things is the way to become a better designer [. . . er, bride! Groom! Other!]. Every request comes with a kernel of truth. If I can get the client [. . . er, family member! Friend! Other!] to verbalize the problem they're trying to solve, we can come up with a better solution together. I can talk them through the ripple-effects that come from any solution. When you say "why" instead of "no," you open a conversation that can help inform both sides.

Offbeat reader Leah developed a gently worded technique for dealing with pressure. "We did get questioned about some of our choices from friends and family. We found that the best way to handle the 'But why are you doing it that way?'–type questions was to say something along the lines of 'It [was/n't] the best choice for us.' It's nonconfrontational and doesn't make judgments about anyone else's choice, but also, I think, gently makes it clear that the topic is not open for discussion."

Naturally, money is a huge factor in considering all this. Some families will pay for weddings without exacting any control, but frequently if someone contributes resources to an event, they feel that they have some right to control things. They're a producer, while you and your fiancé are the directors. Sometimes this works just fine, but sometimes it can be an invitation for manipulative power dynamics.

We played it safe, splitting the cost in even thirds among our two families and us. My mother, because she was hosting the wedding, pitched in her few ideas. But, for the most part, we had control over the event.

It's not as though by accepting money you're dooming yourself to a power struggle. Offbeat reader Jen said, "If you need to accept money, sit down [with the benefactor] and really get clear: 'Is this a gift? Or do we need to do certain things in the wedding to make you comfortable with giving us this money?' Think of it this way: if it's a gift, it is supposed to be a loving, hands-off type of thing. No one tells you what to wear with your Christmas sweater that they got you, do they? If your donors can't agree with you, ask for it as a loan with no interest."

Offbeat reader Corrin made a great point when she told me, "My planning philosophy was that if I didn't feel strongly about something, I either went with someone else's idea or let it go completely. There's so much pressure for a bride to look at each thing as critical, when in fact not very much of it is. It's okay not to care about the tablecloths or what the table decorations look like. Let it go if it isn't important to you." Jen backed this up, saying, "If you can let it go and don't care, you're probably going to be better off."

Your mother-in-law desperately wants pink lilies at your wedding, and you don't know the difference between a gerbera and a tulip? Let your mother-in-law take care of the flowers! She'll do a beautiful job. If you don't care, hand the control over to someone who does. Loosen the reins, and ride that pink-lily pony all the way home.

 HOW TO DEAL WITH PRESSURE TO LOSE WEIGHT FOR YOUR WEDDING

Many Offbeat Bride readers deal with pressure from their mothers about losing weight for the wedding. I have two potential communication strategies for how to handle this situation, no matter who's applying the pressure:

THE QUICK BOUNDARY

The next time the issue comes up, simply tell your mother, "It means so much to me that you care so much about me. That said, I hope you can respect that I've put a lot of thought into this issue, and honor the fact that I've made a different decision than you might. Please trust my ability to make choices about my body that work best for me. I don't want to talk about this anymore."

If she presses the issue, make the line very clear: "Again, I really appreciate that this means so much to you, but I've told you where I stand on the issue. If you bring it up again, I'm going to have to end this conversation."

If she pushes it again, try this: reach out and hold her hand in yours (if that feels right), look into her eyes, and say, "I love you, and I'm done talking about this." Then get up, and walk the fuck away.

Lather, rinse, and repeat as the issue comes up. I know it feels harsh (. . . walk away?) but really all you're doing is articulating that (A) you love her, (B) you hear her, and (C) you're clear about where you stand on the issue and willing to draw very defined boundaries around talking about it.

>>>

THE LONGER DISCUSSION

Okay, so maybe you want to use this as an opportunity to have a longer discussion about the issue. That's awesome, if you've got the energy for it. (I'm not sure I would, if I were in the thick of wedding planning.) Here are the conversation tools I'd use:

First, recognize that your mother is coming from a place of concern—however misguided it may be. She wants you to look pretty and feel good and be healthy—all things you likely want too (even if you disagree with how to get there). Frame all conversations around recognizing this common ground.

Pick a few of your favorite self-identified plus-size brides from our site to show your mother. Show her clear examples of how beautiful and happy brides of ALL sizes look on their wedding days.

Talk about the feelings that come up for you when she talks about weight loss and your wedding. Does it make you feel like she doesn't support you? Does it bring up feelings of fear around her being disappointed in you? Avoid blame ("You make me feel sad!"), but articulate the emotions that come up after these conversations.

Share the process you've gone through to get to the place of body positivity. Tell her about what makes you feel confident and good in your body. Give her specific ideas about how she could contribute to those feelings.

29. WRESTLING DOWN THE AISLE

Examining that whole "Dad gives you away" concept

MANY WEDDING TRADITIONS STAND FOR THINGS THAT GIVE ME THE creeps, and the last thing I wanted to do was establish myself as the most recent incarnation of misogyny or female disempowerment. For example, why would I want my father to walk me down the aisle? The tradition was built from a time when a woman was considered her father's property and weddings were more of a familial business proposal than two people's choice to share a life together. I'm a hopeless daddy's girl, but casting ourselves in the roles of "owner" and "property" didn't feel like an especially powerful way to honor the father-daughter relationship that my father and I both hold in such high regard.

This break with tradition met with a little surprise from Andreas's family. During a family visit back to Dre's childhood home in Missoula, Montana, my future father-in-law and future sister-in-law cornered me, asking about the aisle. They were both dismayed that I wasn't walking with my father. Andreas's dad asked, "You're denying your father the opportunity to walk his only daughter—no, his only child—down the aisle?"

I blabbered on for a while about the history of the tradition (owner, property, chattel, cows, blah, blah, blah . . .), and the conversation ended with Andreas's sister patting her father reassuringly and saying, "Don't worry, I want you walking me down the aisle. I think the tradition is romantic." (A year later, my sister-in-law eloped, and her father was nowhere near the aisle of the New York courthouse where she said her vows. Oh, hypocrisy! You make fools of us all.)

Clearly, for many women (even the most progressive of us), the tradition has been stripped of its history and remains as a symbol of paternal love. Offbeat reader Brittany opted to be escorted by her father, explaining, "There was something that felt symbolic about my parents 'giving' me to my husband, not in the property sense so much as in the spiritual sense. I felt like it was their way of approving the union and telling me and my husband that now we comprise our own family."

Offbeat reader Lisa Marie echoes Brittany's sentiment; she also opted to be walked down the aisle. "I saw it as a joining of two families, although I think the idea of being 'given away' is antiquated. I'm sure there are plenty of women who like the tradition of having their fathers walk them down the aisle but have separated the tradition from the origin."

Perhaps I'm less evolved than that, because I just couldn't separate the tradition from the practice. In fact, I got skeeved out by what I couldn't help but think of as a romantic tradition with my father. Romance isn't really an aspect of our relationship. Friendship, trust, admiration, and pride, sure . . . but romance? Eh, not so much. There was a time when my father (formerly a professor, now a city bureaucrat) was leading tantric workshops. He offered to let me attend a workshop for free, which was very generous and sweet . . . but who wants to be in bed with a lover, thinking, Was it five breaths or four? What did my dad say? I love my father dearly, but Romance + Dad = Mmm, not really my cup of tea. I wouldn't take his tantric teachings into bed with me, thanks. Nor did I want him walking down the aisle with me, thanks again.

See, I wasn't marrying my dad; I was marrying Andreas. And I'd walk down the aisle with the man I was marrying. Besides, my relationship with my father wasn't changing with my marriage (it's not like I went from being supported by him to being

> **TIP:** SO, IS IT AN AISLE . . . OR
> A LONG, SKINNY MINEFIELD?
>
> To avoid family members' taking your aisle-walking decisions personally, try couching it as less of a rejection ("I don't want you to walk me down the aisle") and more of an evolution ("We want our entrance to symbolize the equality of our relationship"). For traditional types, it helps if you can explain your decision in a romantic way. I don't know why this helps, but it does. For example, if you choose to walk down the aisle with your partner, try using the metaphor of walking together toward your new life. It can also be helpful to offer the supposedly rejected family member a different role in the wedding. Instead of walking down the aisle, perhaps the father of the bride could do a reading, a candle lighting, or some other gesture that doesn't leave a bride feeling like her father has announced, "I own this here woman—but now she's *your* mouth to feed."

supported by my husband—I make my own cash), so why make a display of how once I had been with one man and now I was walking with another?

The bride's entrance is a tradition that gets tweaked a lot. Offbeat reader Susan walked down the aisle with her fiancé and recounted it as one of her favorite moments of her wedding. "I heard our music start, and Andrew and I stopped and said secret things to each other. That was so awesome. I know most people try to make the first moment they see each other at the start of the ceremony special, but, to me, it was just so wonderful being together and walking in as a couple. I loved being alone with him for a minute— it was so clearing. We were just holding hands and beaming at each other. We walked in together, and it was absolutely, no question, the happiest and most incredible moment of my life. When everyone saw us walk in holding hands, they started clapping and cheering, and I just felt so loved and happy."

Offbeat reader Echota elected to have her brothers walk her down the aisle, explaining that she wasn't close with her father and that her brothers "were the men in my life." Some brides decide that changing the ceremony wording from "Who gives this woman?" to "Who brings this woman?" addresses the issue.

One thing's for certain: this tradition seems to cause a lot of ripples for families. It's definitely one to be dealt with delicately, and I'm not sure whether I would recommend my explanation about chattel as the most effective technique if you elect to break with tradition.

For those raised with Jewish traditions, there are none of these father-giving-the-bride-away issues. Instead, both parents walk their daughter down the aisle. Offbeat reader Amy didn't see anything creepy about the tradition at all, explaining, "To me, it was a symbol of how two families (not just two individuals) were coming together."

Walking in with both parents is a tradition adopted by non-Jewish Offbeat Bride readers, too. Lisa recounted, "Getting married for the first time in my forties, I certainly didn't need to have anybody give me away. But because I'm so blessed that both my father and mother are still alive and in my life, I very much wanted to have them at my side. They're both big feminists, so they might have also balked at the traditional aspects of the ritual, but they were intrigued by this more egalitarian-seeming Jewish custom and were both very touched to be included."

Of course, there are those who subvert the aisle paradigm altogether. I know one bride who entered by being lowered down on a trapeze swing to the wedding march by Queen from the movie *Flash Gordon*.

Processional proclivities

Speaking of *Flash Gordon*, let's talk wedding music. Offbeat reader Tiffany thought she was having a safe, relatively traditional church wedding until she hit huge amounts of trouble over her choice of processional music. First she was told the church wouldn't allow recorded music, so she couldn't play a recording of her song of choice, "Moon River."

"It's not like I'm going to play 'Shout at the Devil,'" Tiffany har-rumphed. She found a string quartet to play the music live. But the fun wasn't over yet.

"I called my mom and told her the news," Tiffany remembers, reporting that the response was silence. "Turns out she had always imagined me walking down to Canon in D, the second–most popular song played at ceremonies. It's predictable, it's boring, it's the theme song for a lightbulb company—no joke! This is something she obviously felt strongly about but never shared with me. She was pretty upset—like, crying upset. Ultimately, I decided since Canon in D was so important to her, they could play it as she and the rest of the family come in to be seated." Whew. Safe compromise.

Sometimes even the stereotypical can be dangerous. Offbeat reader Amy initially wanted Wagner's classic "Wedding March" to be played at her wedding, but her rabbi refused, pointing out that Wagner's anti-Semitism made it offensive to play his music at her wedding—even if it wasn't a traditional Jewish ceremony.

Offbeat reader Rebecca also opted for something other than Wagner, laughing that she "scrapped the 'Here Comes the Bride' processional, even though my inner twelve-year-old thought that it wouldn't be a wedding without it. I stuffed her in a closet with her mouth taped shut and chose another classical piece, and it still felt like a wedding! Imagine that."

30. STAYING SANE

How to keep your proverbial shit together

So, STILL THINK YOU'RE EXEMPT FROM BRIDAL ANXIETY? HAVE YOU read my story and thought, Oh, but that child of hippies was so damn uptight with her used mugs and dirt dance floor? Make your peace with the fact that you are not going to escape a few moments of full-frontal freak-out. Even the studiously laid back can find themselves on a tooth-grinding roller coaster of anxiety when planning a wedding. Seriously, it happens to everyone.

The weight of bucking cultural traditions takes a lot of energy and brainpower—and usually all on top of a job and friends and family and remembering to flush the toilet. Even organizational whizzes find themselves clutching their printed, color-coded spreadsheets, five wedding planning apps running on their phones, hurtling toward a preset date with all too many expectations and the crushing weight of emotional gravity.

During the six months of our wedding planning, I was forced to develop several techniques for keeping my shit together. This isn't to say I didn't have a few shaky-handed crisis moments. Remember: it happens to everyone. One of my sample freak-outs went like this: *But I won't be able to talk to everyone! And people will be disappointed and feel ignored! And if I talk too much to friends, I'll be a bad daughter, and if I talk too much to family, I'll be a bad friend. Oh, woe! Woe is whiny me!*

I had a few techniques, however, that lessened the frequency of these whiny outbursts. Some of these techniques were specific to me and my peculiarities—my favorite involved getting baked and sitting on the couch in our sunny bay window, watching the rotating rainbows cast by the solar-powered rainbow machine given to me as a white-elephant gift. Friends called it my "hippie disco ball," and that thing gave me several hours of much-needed mental relaxation. I have no idea why.

Offbeat reader Amy had a different technique for dealing with wedding stress: aversion therapy. She was grinding through an honors thesis during her wedding preparation, and she laughed, "My advice for dealing with wedding anxiety is, have something besides the wedding to work on—something that's more important. Working on my thesis made the wedding seem like no big deal."

Amy has a point: a little perspective goes a long way with wedding planning. Ultimately, it's just a party. Deep breath. Step back.

I spoke to one bride who was recovering from cancer during her engagement. "It definitely changed my perspective about wedding planning," she said, which has to win some sort of prize for bridal understatement.

Making your peace with the fact that your wedding will not be some sort of perfect fantasy day also does wonders for bridal sanity. Accept the fact that things won't go exactly as you expect. Life, weddings, relationships, road trips, gardening, making out, haircuts: few of the fun things in life always go as expected. Let go of whatever dream world your wedding takes place in and remember that it's going to happen here on earth, where there are tantalizing unknowns around every corner.

Done is better than perfect

Offbeat reader Greta used this mantra throughout her wedding planning: *It doesn't have to be perfect.* She said, "There's no way everything's going to be perfect. It's a big, complicated, emotionally fraught party with a lot of unpredictable factors, and things are going to go wrong. Letting go of it being perfect made it possible to make decisions—difficult decisions, trivial decisions, any decisions—without tearing ourselves up about whether it was the exact right decision. And it let us enjoy the day itself, even when little things did go wrong. Besides, if everything goes perfectly according to a micromanaged plan, there's no room for surprises."

. . . Remember surprises? They can be good sometimes!

There also seems to be one constant about wedding anxiety: no matter how much time you give yourself to plan your wedding (six weeks, six months, six years), there will inevitably be a crunch near the end. Plan for it. Expect to have a couple of nightmares. And then prepare to be surprised when maybe it works out better than you expected.

I HAD AN ANXIETY ATTACK RIGHT BEFORE MY WEDDING: WHAT IT MEANT, WHAT IT DIDN'T, AND HOW TO COPE

Sometimes, wedding anxiety can involve more than a couple nightmares. Offbeat Bride reader Elli shared this insight about anxiety attacks and weddings:

I did not enjoy wedding planning, for the most part. All of the modern wedding "necessities" seemed totally unnecessary to me. I cut corners wherever possible, saved money at every opportunity, and rarely found myself stressed because I just didn't care about the details. I was getting married to the man I loved, and nothing could ruin that.

About five days before our wedding, however, everything changed. I had a run-of-the-mill stomachache, and a friend said good-naturedly, "Maybe you have the prewedding jitters!"

That's when I slowly started to freak out.

Is a wedding anxiety attack the same as cold feet?

I've suffered from anxiety my whole life. When I was five, I was terrified of the wind. At eight, I worried about the existence of God. At ten, I had my first panic attack and not a clue what was happening to me. I've had phases of compulsive disorder. I've struggled with sleep—worrying that I won't fall asleep, which causes me not to not fall asleep, which causes me

>>>

to worry all over again the next night. My anxiety is a classic case of the self-fulfilling prophecy.

That's the thing with anxious people. We worry about worrying. We worry about why we are worrying. We convince ourselves that the most dreaded thing we can think of is happening, no matter what logic tells us. When it came to my prewedding freak-out, I thought, What if this anxiety means I am having doubts? What if this is a bad sign? Normal people don't freak out before their wedding!

To make matters worse, my fiancé was back in Chicago finishing out the work week, while I had headed to my parents' house early to get things in order before the big day. I felt like an old-fashioned bride, sequestered in my parents' house, not able to see my betrothed until he lifted my veil the day of our wedding. Just the weekend before we were living our ordinary life together, and now suddenly everything seemed like such a strange and big deal. I suddenly wanted it all to be over with and to be on our honeymoon.

I wasn't anxious about standing up in front of everyone at the church. I wasn't anxious about being the center of attention, which is something I typically don't like. I wasn't anxious about getting married to my fiancé. I was anxious simply because I was anxious. Simply because my brain is wired in a way that I can't always control.

DOES HAVING A WEDDING ANXIETY ATTACK
MEAN YOUR MARRIAGE IS DOOMED?
In an attempt to stave off further anxiety, I decided to do what any good writer would do and research. I searched "I'm anxious before my wedding," "How to get through the wedding when you're anxious," "How to not be anxious for your wedding when you're an anxious person in general." Similar to how googling an illness automatically tells you that you have cancer, every search I made indicated that my marriage was doomed. "Prewedding jitters aren't a thing. They mean you aren't sure," one article said. "If you aren't excited about your wedding, you're probably not excited about your marriage," said another. My anxiety got more intense with every article. That awful little voice in my head was telling me, They are right, even though I knew they weren't. Wasn't there someone out there who suffered from anxiety and could relate to what I was going through?

So I did the only thing left for me to do: I cried to my parents. I broke down. It felt amazing. Finally, I got relief from the buildup of all my nervous energy.

Then my dad, who had been a witness to my peculiar breed of anxiety for twenty-nine years, said the most powerful thing: "This wedding is going to

>>>

happen no matter what, so there's no use fighting it." To normal people, that may seem like an extremely odd thing to say, but let me explain. Anxious people live with a perpetual monkey on their back. We feel responsible for, guilty about, and a prisoner to our thoughts. By telling me that this feeling I had wasn't going to ruin anything, my dad had freed me from the burden.

That night, I called my fiancé and told him about the last few anxious days. He wasn't even phased. (I would hope at that point he knew what he was getting himself into.) "It's a crazy week, isn't it?" he said. "I'll be there soon."

Our wedding ended up being beautiful and wonderful and miraculously anxiety-free. But I'll tell you what was even better. Leaving it all behind to go on the honeymoon and then returning to our simple, normal, happy life.

To any of you who suffer from generalized anxiety and are feeling off right now, let me reassure you: your anxiety isn't sending you any sort of hidden message. If you didn't want to get married, you would have been having nagging doubts for a while, not just this sudden burst in an otherwise great relationship. Let go of the burden and guilt. Know that you're not alone. And, most importantly, know that your wedding is going to happen, no matter how much you worry about it.

TIP: SANITY SELF-CARE

YOU MAY ALREADY KNOW WHAT HELPS YOU STAY SANEST (HOT TUB? masturbation? medication?), but here are a few general techniques that will help most anyone.

LESS CAFFEINE

I stopped drinking my morning wake-up cup about a month before the wedding. I was already in a state of chronic excitement, prone to spontaneous bursts of spastic dancing around the living room. The last thing I needed was chemically enhanced excitement, which in my world meant my strong cup of black tea every morning. Doing without it was difficult, mostly because I missed the ritual. I tried cups of milky spiced herbal tea, and it just wasn't the same.

I got screaming confirmation that the decaffeinated approach was a good choice after my first week. It was a relaxing Sunday morning, and I'd had a super-mellow weekend, so why not have a little cuppa with

>>>

breakfast? I spent the next four hours in a feverish panic, shuffling to-do lists and gasping. Suddenly I was way! way! behind! Nothing was at all ready! There wasn't enough time! There wasn't enough time!!!!

After I descended from Mount Freak-Out, I realized there was plenty of time, but that, gah! No more caffeine for me. It made a huge difference.

IMMUNE SYSTEM CARE

When I'm really stressed out, I have this utterly charming capacity for getting enormous cold sores on my lips. I knew that if I wasn't careful, I'd be smiling for my wedding portraits with a sore front and center.

If you have insurance, there's prescription antiviral medication that can help; but for those who don't have access to prescription medication, there is a great natural solution to help stave off cold sores: l-lysine. In the weeks leading up to my wedding, I took 1,600 milligrams of l-lysine daily as a preventive measure, hoping to stave off the semi-inevitable stress-induced, festering facial wound. It worked. Moral of the story? Whatever your immune deficiencies are (outbreaks, breakouts, nausea, rashes, etc.), do whatever you can to take extra, double, triple good care of yourself before the wedding.

ENOUGH SLEEP

Wedding planning really does affect your brain in weird ways; lots of brides report anxiety nightmares. I had one about there being no running water at our reception. Cutting caffeine is one way to help yourself get rest, but another helpful sanity-retainer I found was valerian tea. I can't abide sleep loss, so valerian was a lifesaver. Sleep-deprived psychosis is not my idea of a party, and a party is, after all, what weddings are supposed to be.

part five

The Wedding Itself

31. THANKS FOR COMING, HERE'S YOUR CAMPSITE!

And other creative guest accommodations

ANDREAS AND I BOTH COME FROM OUTDOORSY FAMILIES. WHILE SOME kids went to beach houses for their summers, my summer vacations were spent carrying my own weight, backpacking five miles out to a cove on the Washington coast. I learned how to dig latrines and poop in the sand and pack enough food for two families to eat for two weeks. Andreas, meanwhile, was curling up in an insulated sleeping bag in the snowy Montana mountains. His mother's vacation home is a rustic cabin with no electricity on a small island known for its wild horses. Despite the fact that we're city folk now, we both grew up in the outdoors, and so of course we would force this facet of ourselves on our out-of-town wedding guests.

So although many couples book blocks of hotel rooms for their guests, we spent a couple of spring weekends clearing out branches and ranking campsites in my mother's forest. We would put the call out to our friends: Who feels like going out to the island and getting dirty? We'll feed you and we'll love you forever. Plus, it's fun. We're not the only outdoorsy kids to have grown up and moved to the city—and our two "work parties" were half socializing and half lighthearted labor. One of our exquisitely fashionable friends put together a fantastic "rugged guy" coordinated outfit, matching his Carhartts to his argyle wool socks.

We were essentially building the hotel where many of our guests would spend a weekend, so it was fun to visualize the whole event—the New Yorkers might camp over here, and families with kids could have these spots, back a bit from the noise. Knowing our friends, some of them would be having existential, inebriated moments in these woods, so we wanted them to have cool shit to look at and a safe place to be.

The camping area was a forested grove of trees and ferns, relatively gorgeous on its own, but the ground was lumpy and the spaces for tents needed to be defined. I played the part of taskmaster at the work parties, with my mother helping us out with shovels, gloves, rakes, and some sage in a velveteen bag. She told our friends how to sprinkle a little sage at each place where the camps were created—you know, "to set the intention for the space and thank the forest for its gifts and graciousness."

When my mother starts talking like this, I tend to glaze over ("Okay, Mom: forest spirits, manifestations, blah blah blah . . . "), but I could probably stand to learn a lesson or two from my friends, who are inspired by and respectful of my mother's suburban-priestess leanings. And I'm agnostic enough to think, Who knows? Maybe that sage helped our wedding be the wonderful event it was.

My friends were all good at scattering their sage as my mother instructed, but they were less responsive when I waved my arms around and said, "You know what? We should clear all sticks out of the forest." I might as well have asked everyone to mow the lawn with fingernail clippers. My friends looked at me like I was crazy (I was just worrying about drunk friends poking their eyes out. Fine, maybe I was over-hostessing a little) and pretty much ignored me. I definitely had my bridal-control moments—not about monograms and flower arrangements but about sticks and dirt.

You can use one of these lovely deep holes!

By the time our wedding weekend rolled around, we had room for forty or so guests to camp, assuming that many local family and friends would head out when the sun went down. We'd booked up the bed-and-breakfast where the wedding ceremony was happening so that our closest family—my aunts, Dre's parents and their partners, and Dre's siblings—would have rooms.

We booked the largest suite at the bed-and-breakfast for ourselves. It was a smart choice for many reasons, even though we were sad not to be camping with our friends. It was sort of unfair: they got to hang out together all weekend, and we were a seven-minute forested walk away. In some ways, I would rather have been sleeping on dirt than in a nice bed.

Despite all the sage scattering, we woke up to rain the day before the wedding. The ground under the trees, however, appeared to be relatively dry as camping guests started trickling in for the weekend. My de facto best man, Tim, had been granted the title of senior camp counselor and was in charge of working with my mother and her girlfriend to get everyone settled into their campsites. Tim was basically our concierge, but, instead of bringing guests clean towels, he helped with tent poles and showed people where the facilities were. You can bet that most guests don't get "You can use a port-a-potty up the hill, or one of these lovely deep holes!" when they arrive at their wedding accommodations. But our friends and family are like us: they like pooping outside.

Our choices for accommodations were a good fit for our guests, but they certainly would not have been for many (or even most) wedding guests. I talked to a couple of Offbeat Brides who also camped at their weddings, but most booked hotel rooms and enjoyed the luxury. Especially for couples who live together, it can be nice to have a fancy, nonhome place to prepare for the wedding. One bride told me that she spent a good half hour playing with all the amenities when they got to their hotel, squealing, "Oooh, minibar! Check out the bathroom!" As for guests, many people book blocks of rooms and sometimes get discount arrangements at hotels.

Don't assume, however, that going this traditional hotel route will necessarily make your wedding planning any easier than making your guests fend for themselves in the woods. Some couples agonize over where the last-minute RSVPers are going to sleep.

As for me, clearing sticks and dealing with dirt sounds a hell of a lot easier.

TIP: LET GO AND LET GUESTS

OFFBEAT BRIDE READER STACY ADVISES THAT COUPLES "JUST GET A block of hotel rooms or make price-range suggestions, and let everyone figure it out on their own. Don't get involved! And if someone waits until the last minute to find a place to sleep—say it's great that they decided to come, and tell them you will see them at the wedding, and hang up the phone!"

Another reader, Corrin, remembers, "When I started planning, I felt this ridiculous need to take care of all of the guests. . . . It took me a while to let it go and realize that these folks are all grownups who manage to get through life without me the rest of the time, so I didn't have to get obsessive." Figure out where you're staying, and consider letting your guests fend for themselves. Make recommendations, but stay out of it.

32. THE NIGHT BEFORE

To rehearse or to recreate? That is the question

As our camping guests trickled in the night before our wedding, it became immediately apparent that this wasn't a "fancy rehearsal dinner" kind of night. Andreas and I had been together for so long that, apart from the odd cousin or two, our families knew each other pretty well. There wasn't much need to have a prewedding gathering where they could all meet and the groom's family could take their turn to show off how much money they spent.

We opted instead for a slightly wet potluck in the meadow around which most of our guests were camped. There was a smoky campfire for roasting weenies and s'mores. People sat on stumps or picnic benches or those cheap foldable fabric camping chairs, drinking and smoking various things. It was an eclectic mix of our guests—some family, some old raver friends, some professional colleagues, and even my oldest friend, a woman I'd known since we were six months old and our mothers decided to swap babysitting duties.

My mother, likely inspired by the diversity of the two dozen or so people there, pulled me aside.

"Can we do some sort of circle time?" she asked me. "It would be really fun if we could do that icebreaking exercise where everyone steps forward and introduces themselves, and then does a little movement to go with their name." Here she paused to waggle her arms around and cross her eyes, imitating the kind of free-form expressive movement someone might use to introduce themselves. "Then we all repeat the movement and say, 'Hi, person!' It would be a fun way for everyone to get to know each other!" she enthused.

You know that thing your mother does that's so embarrassing when you're twelve? My mother was doing it again. I gently nixed the icebreaker game, but I figured my mother had every right to get to know everyone staying on her property. A getting-to-know-you game I couldn't abide, but I could at least ask my guests to introduce themselves to my mother, their host for the weekend. We could stand in a circle and say our names, but, for god's sake, no arm waving.

And so around the circle we went—me head down with a blush and everyone else gamely going along. Because she had everyone gathered, my mother chose that time to give everyone a little introduction to how things worked when camping on her property. She pointed out where all the little paths were winding through the forest and where guests could find garden hoses to refill their water bottles. And then she educated everyone about humanure, reading from a little poetic essay she'd prepared:

This land uses simple compost toilets. Composting is an alchemical process where things are transformed from one form to another by microorganisms. In this system, sawdust, urine, TP, and poop—combined with plant material from the forest—are transformed into fertile, rich soil. The process begins immediately after you leave your droppings in the bucket and add some sawdust. It is amazing how the sawdust quickly absorbs all smell! After the bucket is full, it is dumped into a big tank, forest duff is added, and the process continues for a few more months. Eventually, the resulting compost has no sign or smell of toilet paper, poop, or harmful organisms; it is fertile soil.

This toilet-composting system is a beautiful example of a mutually beneficial relationship between the human world, the plant world, and the soils. After we ingest the food given us by Mother Earth, our waste is gathered, composted, and returned to her in

thanksgiving for the food. The earth is enriched by our humanure. No water is wasted. It is good for everyone and everything!

After an education like that, what else can you do but go to
bed? It was an early night for almost everyone. Many of our guests
had been traveling all day, and camping kind of encourages everyone to pace themselves—lights out at ten o'clock, when the Pacific
Northwest summer sun goes down! Well, except for the publishing
colleagues. Don't let the bookish exteriors fool you; they were still
eating at 10 P.M. when we went back up to the bed-and-breakfast,
and they apparently stayed up until 2 A.M. or so drinking and smoking. And that's with East Coast jet lag!

I was happy to go to bed early. We hadn't quite finished memo-
rizing our vows, and I had a sedative waiting for me. The night before their weddings, even offbeat couples often go for a modicum
of luxury . . . and for me, that's a quiet night of sleep in the woods.
With a Valium. I wanted to be well rested.

Andreas and I lay chastely in bed side by side, knees up with our
printed vows in front of us. We'd written them weeks before, atop
Grandma's peak on Wildhorse Island (see Chapter 26, "Ceremony
Without Sanctimony"), but we hadn't actually memorized them.
They were short, and we quizzed each other back and forth. A
couple of my lines were giving me a particularly hard time.

"I'm ready to stand beside you, united in love and mutual respect," I repeated to myself, thinking, *Who wrote this shit?!*

I had, of course. Wouldn't that mean it'd be easy for me to remember? But it was difficult to commit to memory. There might be
some armchair psychologists who would posit that this was a sub-
conscious effort on my brain's part not to commit. I saw it more as
my self-saboteur, chewing over the prospect of standing up in front
of more than a hundred of our friends and family, with cameras
snapping everywhere and history being made, and totally blanking

out on my lines. Or farting. It wasn't commitment fear (I was already in about as deep as you can get) but simple stage fright.

Lights were out, and we were asleep by 11:30 P.M. With the exception of some obnoxious sprinkler noises at dawn, Andreas and I slept straight through until 8 A.M. More than eight hours of sleep! Without the Valium, I might have made it five. I wanted a relaxed morning, and sedatives are one way to achieve that goal. I'm all for cognitive liberties. If you need to tweak your mind-set with a couple of cocktails or a ten-mile run or some other self-medication, do it.

Sometimes sleeping together is just sleeping together

Most of the Offbeat Brides I spoke to slept with their fiancés by their sides the night before their weddings, probably because most of us have lived with our partners for years. After all, because almost half of Americans cohabit with an unmarried romantic partner at some point, chances are pretty dang good that even more traditional brides have been living with their fiancés. And, when you live with someone, of course you want to sleep next to them. Offbeat reader Maria remembers, "We slept in the same bed we had for the last three-ish years. It would have been entirely unauthentic for us to pretend we hadn't been living (and sleeping) together just for the sake of some antiquated custom. And neither of us would have slept well."

Amusingly, as many cohabitating couples know, sometimes sleeping together just means sleeping together. Maria laughed, "Neither of us had the energy or inclination for sex—just some snuggling." There are others, though, who told great stories of sneaking home to their waterbed and having a last go at "wild unmarried sex." One bride reported that it helped her relax and sleep better. See? Sedatives come in many forms, including orgasms.

Whatever you need to sleep—you do that. If you sleep like a baby after singing show tunes in the shower, you do that. If you know that it takes a baggie of cannabis and a beer, well, you go find them. I'm not suggesting that anyone do anything they don't normally do. I'm just saying, treat yourself extra special the night before to make sure you sleep comfortably.

Treat yourself before you wreck yourself

. . . Because if you don't? There's a chance you might end up like poor Offbeat Bride reader Lisa, who spent the night before her wedding having a slumber party with her bridesmaids. Completely unmedicated.

"The minute my head hit the pillow, all the stress of the past few days (weeks!) caught up with me. I got a terrible spasm in my upper back—it was so bad that I woke up every time I changed position. I finally woke a bridesmaid, who gave me a bit of massage and more Advil. She drifted back off again, but I alternated between fitful sleep and trying to relax the spasm in a steaming hot shower. Just as I'd start nodding off, the thought that I must look my absolute best the next day would pop into my head, and I'd be awake again. Finally the sun started rising, and I decided to just get the hell out of bed." Only Lisa knows whether an orgasm and some muscle relaxants or other carefully selected relaxation technique could have saved her.

Many Offbeat Brides do opt for some sort of gathering the night before the wedding. I spoke to one bride who was having a super-casual ceremony, so she focused on the rehearsal dinner as the most formal part of the wedding. Others flip the equation, having a casual event to go with a high-production-value wedding. Offbeat reader Rebecca recounted, "I was fed up with formality and decreed that we would all go have pizza the day before the wedding while wearing jeans and just being casual. It was wonderful! It was only the bridal party and my maid of honor's mother, and it was so laid back. I'm glad we skipped the whole catered-affair thing, which would have been too much, I think. After all, just the day before the rehearsal dinner was our Hindu ceremony, and I was pretty tired of organized events by then anyway."

That said, no matter how tired you are, make sure you go over your vows one more time before falling asleep. Again, just trust me on this one.

33. WHO THE HELL ARE ALL THESE PEOPLE?

Getting to know your guests

ANDREAS AND I ARE, FIRST AND FOREMOST, THE OUTGROWTHS OF THE subcultures we've lived our lives in. So let's talk people: the professors, the hippies, the lesbian mothers, the ravers, the artists. The parents, the children. At our wedding we were surrounded by generations of unusual people: the fractal-shirt-wearing toddlers, the dot-com yuppies, the dedicated urbaphiles, the DJs and clubbers, the ambitious media types from New York and Los Angeles. Then there are our parents and their extended communities of aging hippies, academics, college deans, and Robert Bly warriors. Our wedding was a party where these generation-spanning weirdos, geeks, smarties, and outsiders could mingle, eat, and celebrate.

We started getting a feel for the variety of our wedding guests on the Friday before our wedding. As our out-of-town biological families settled in at the bed-and-breakfast, we watched the cars pouring in, carrying our out-of-town friends. There were the New Yorkers who'd flown in that morning, including a GQ editor who'd only been camping once in his life. Then there were the hippie ravers from Los Angeles, their tents all dusty from full-moon desert raves. Many of my former classmates from Columbia University traveled from afar, using my wedding as an excuse for a reunion. It was the best kind of "being used."

Andreas's cousin and her family showed up and unblinkingly integrated themselves into the scene, setting up their tent while their four-year-old daughter, Stella, cased out the trees.

It was a pretty eclectic crew back in the woods—mostly of our generation but everything from grimy urban hipsters to granola types in

199

bandanas, a chiropractor and several PhD students, a couple of editors, and even one high-energy pharmaceutical marketing executive.

Things only got more eclectic the next day. My high-school sweetheart came. ("You may have heard of me," he was overheard saying at the wedding. "Ariel sometimes writes about me on her blog.") Andreas's many cousins and mysterious uncles came. There were lots of lesbians, but none of our gay friends made it. ("Queens don't like camping," one told me. What's up with that!?) My mother brought two dates (her girlfriend and her boyfriend), just to make a point. We had a Hollywood contingent (a grip, costume designer, makeup artist, and cameraman) and New York media types, mixed in with long-haired thirtysomething students and up-to-the-second scenesters of various persuasions.

Our guests took the "wildly creative casual" dress code suggestion to heart, showing up in elaborate, amusing outfits. My parents, despite almost a decade of being divorced, accidentally wore coordinating outfits. Andreas's mother went wild with a splash of bright purple in her short, spiky hair. Andreas's four-year-old cousin wore a fantastic tutu with a sparkly tiara and magic wand but staunchly refused to put on panties. The sight of her bare bottom peeking through the layers of tulle meant she firmly filled the "Aww, aren't they just adorable?!" role that flower girls usually play.

Then there was our friend the designer, who'd made our wedding invites and who emblazoned her chest with multicolored metallic stickers that read, "ariel n andreas forever" across her ample bosom. A Seattle friend put on an enormous pair of purple wings and flitted around the wedding like a forest fairy.

Drawing a crowd

We only had a few gate-crashers. My mother had sneakily invited some neighbors to walk over for the ceremony, and my closest childhood friend brought her husband and baby, as invited, but then snuck in her mother and sister. These were crashers of the best kind—folks I wasn't sure would want to come, but who decided for themselves that they did and came anyway. After the fact, it was perfect. If you'd asked me about it while I was going through all my prewedding guest-list trauma, I probably would have spewed freak-out spittle all over your face.

We knew we had a widely varied group of people, and we urged them to get to know each other. One page of our eight-page program read:

> We also want this day to act as a celebration of the community of friends and family who have supported our relationship through the years. We are honored by your presence, and we hope you'll take the time to get to know your fellow guests—we're betting you'll find you've got more in common than just us!

I would say the final tally at our ceremony worked out to about 110 people, split in half between family (mostly Andreas's) and friends (which I used to pad out my small family of origin). Our extended circle of friends and coworkers showed up after dark for the reception, bumping the people count to closer to 125.

Although brides are constantly told that offbeat weddings will offend family members and freak people out, it seems like the more untraditional the wedding, the better the attendance. After all, who wants to go to another wedding where you can practically recite the ceremony from memory ("Ooh, here comes Corinthians!") and where you know exactly what comes next? People love a good show, and maybe it's even true that the traditional family members are looking forward to the righteous sensation of being offended. You know, like picking a scab, they have to go see what those degenerate kids are doing now.

Whereas many traditional brides are told to expect a 70 percent acceptance rate from guests, most of the Offbeat Brides I spoke to had more than 85 percent of their invitees show up—and several wedding crashers. One bride who had a campout wedding had some random backpacker on the periphery of her wedding weekend—he apparently had a great time and loved the music at the reception.

The ideal, of course, is to feel loved and supported by the people at your wedding. Whether that means tons of family, tons of friends, or just a few of your closest folks, you want to feel surrounded (embraced!) by love. Offbeat reader Corrin remembers, "We had just the right people at our wedding, and I do think they reflected the people in our everyday lives. It was big enough to be festive, and to make me take a breath and think, All these people love us! as I walked down the aisle."

That's the moment to aim for.

34. THE PAPARAZZI

Hiring your own stalker so you can live
the dream of being a celeb for a day

WE ALL HAVE OUR VAIN MOMENTS. EVEN THE GRUBBIEST AMONG US LIKE to look our grubby, glowing best. Our standards may be different, but we all want to look good, and, damnit, we want to commemorate how sassy-ass hot we looked at our weddings. So we hire our own paparazzi to follow us around for the day, photo documenting the event like a journalist or a celebrity stalker.

"Oh, don't mind me," the contemporary wedding photographer seems to say. "I'm just over here capturing a genuine moment of macro-focused sentimentality. The bride's finger? So lovely." The smile lines around the father of the bride's eyes. The ominous long shadow of a champagne flute. It can get quite serious in black and white, a newspaper-crisp presentation that this couple—they mattered! Today, they are the stars.

With the whole media/celebrity obsession thing we got going on, the cult of personality gets powerful reverence. In America, many smart, educated people who know much, much better still follow their favorite celebrities on social media. We grimace to each other and crease our brows at our own weakness for this level of mindless idol worship . . . but we keep doing it.

It makes sense, then, that so many of us indulge in fantasy-world weddings wherein we are the stars of the day. You are Cinderella in the pumpkin carriage (sometimes literally! Disney offers packaged Cinderella weddings, of course), and all the townspeople stand and watch as Tinkerbell flutters past, writing your names in the sky. You're the Oscar winner stepping out of the limo, skirt hitched up and flashbulbs reflecting off your pupils. You're the diplomat, the politician, the royalty, the famous heiress hounded in the parking lot.

God bless our wedding photographers for making these culture-whoring dreams a reality.

I knew our friends would take a million great photos (and they did!), but I'm a vain whore for the camera and needed a professional to capture the sheer vastness of my self-obsession. Oh, narcissism. How well you know the best angles to stand at. How to tip the chin and smile just right. After years of having pictures of posing celebrities stuffed down our eyeballs, we all know how to pose. And as for me? I was ready for my close-up.

Paying an experienced photographer was one of the wedding budget items that I refused to scrimp on. We spent one-fifth of our budget on our photographer and photos. Luckily, we have a friend who's a photographer, so we were able to keep our money in our little freakonomic group. (Think globally, spend your wedding budget locally?)

Our photographer had just gotten married herself and wanted to know all about which family shots we wanted and what we were looking for. I didn't really know where to start or what family pictures might be expected, so I went online to do a little research.

I found a horrifying list of recommended photos online. These suggestions spanned the usual family combinations and then got into precious and cloying cheeseball ideas, like "Close-up of groom's adorably nervous mug waiting for his other half" and "Dad whispering last-minute advice to groom." Eek! The whole contrived poses of stereotypical gender roles freaked me out. What kind of appropriately manly and useful advice is Dad whispering to the groom? Something like "She likes it in the ass, son"? We skipped photos like "Mom helping bride with one last detail, such as veil." During our wedding prep, my mother was probably dealing with buckets of humanure. I know that she certainly wasn't clucking around, help-ing me with my nonexistent veil. Boo on pictures that cram people into roles they're expected to play!

Our shots included things like "Groom pushing bride on dilap-idated blue plastic swing" and, later in the evening, "Bride rubbing fern frond on a nettle sting." Our photographer did take some shots of me getting ready, but they included the "Groom lacing bride up in corset"—no bridesmaids were present (my bridal bodyguard kept my distractions to a minimum), and I pretty much just got myself dressed. It wasn't an especially glamorous moment, so it's not an especially glamorous series of shots.

We did a fair number of family shots, standing around a big boulder on the edge of a grove of trees. We did as many of the various combinations as we remembered to do, which I think was enough. From there, it was your usual ceremony pictures, and then just the two of us on our yichud-inspired walk after the ceremony.

We'd talked over the plan for the wedding carefully with our photographer. Photographers always need to know the structure of a wedding so that they can plan their way around it, but, with offbeat weddings, you want to make extra sure your photographer knows when you're going to make guests hop on a trampoline or exactly when the fire spinner is going to enter the ceremony to do a burlesque routine.

In this day of digital cameras, smartphones, and an increasing number of Photoshop hobbyists, some couples opt to save money by letting their friends act as amateur photographers. Offbeat reader Branwyn skipped hiring a wedding photographer, explaining, "My husband and I are both introverts, both very private people. We have an independent streak a mile wide, and a strong DIY ethic. We had a $1,500 budget and could either have the wedding we wanted or a low- to mid-range photographer with absolutely noth-ing else. Put that way, the decision was easy. It's not that we lack appreciation for the art form of photography or don't think there's any skill involved. It's just not something we chose to prioritize."

Skipping a professional photographer is still relatively rare, even in the Offbeat Bride world. More often, I hear from lower-budget brides who wished they hadn't scrimped on their wedding photography. If you're a sentimentalist, it's worth prioritizing photography. My theory was that the food and decorations can be enjoyed for only a day—but I'm a huge picture whore and want photos around for my grandchildren to laugh at, so for me it was important to dedicate a sizable chunk of our budget to photography.

Too much paparazzi: Unplugged weddings

There you are at the altar, gazing into the eyes of your beloved, saying your vows. You turn to sneak a glance at your wedding guests, all your favorite beloved friends and family . . . and are greeted by a sea of faces staring at their LCD screens.

When your photos come back from your wedding photographer, all your guest shots include your favorite people staring at their favorite devices. People are smiling, but they're all staring at little screens.

Welcome to the era of the overdocumented twenty-first-century wedding, where, even if you've hired someone to take photos, every guest has a smartphone and is tweeting the whole event. They're there with you, but are they really present?

So you decide you want to have what's known as an unplugged wedding—maybe at least the ceremony. Encouraging your guests to put down their favorite devices can be a delicate dance . . . as one Offbeat Bride snapped, "If I was told I had to leave my phone at home, I'd likely stay with it." Yikes! As with any special request you make of your wedding guests, you need to be sensitive and respectful.

If you're unsure how to request unplugging in a way that won't piss off your guests, we're here to help. Below, I've got copy 'n' paste wording ideas for your officiant, wedding website, program—and even a sign you can post at the venue!

Before the wedding . . .

Talk to your photographer

Remember: wedding guests take photos because they want to be able to relive and share the experience of the day. If you're considering an unplugged wedding, you must commit to sharing photos with guests and make plans for how you're going to do so. Work with your wedding photographer to ensure you can make a small set of photos (even just five shots!) available digitally to guests within a couple days of the wedding. You can share them via e-mail, your wedding website, or social media—the method doesn't matter. Just make sure you've got it figured out with your photographer before your unplugged wedding.

Wording for wedsites & programs

If you're sharing wedding information online with guests via a wedding website, you can give them some perspectives before the wedding about why you're asking them to leave their devices off:

Unplugged wedding

We want you to be able to really enjoy our wedding day, feeling truly present and in the moment with us. We've hired an amazing wedding photographer named _____, who will be capturing the way the wedding looks—and we're inviting each of you to sit back, relax, and just enjoy how the wedding feels. We're respectfully asking that everyone consider leaving all cameras and cell phones off. Of course we will happy to share our wedding photos with you afterward!

You could include a short note in your programs:

We want you to be able to relax and have fun with us today! This in mind, we invite you to put down all your favorite devices and just be present in the moment with us. Please leave your camera in your bag (we've got photography covered!), and put your cell phone on mute (we promise they'll call back!).

We're happy to share our professional wedding photos later, but the greatest gift you can give us today is just being fully here with us in this sacred and special moment.

Offbeat Bride Aron is including this text in her program:

The bride and groom have asked that you share in their wedding fully and not through the lens of a camera or cell phone.

Offbeat Bride Audra included this text in her program:

We are honored that you are here today and present with us during the ceremony. Two photographers are covering the ceremony. We request that you refrain from photography during the entire ceremony. We promise that there will be plenty of images at your disposal!

At the wedding . . . enforcing unplugging

Appoint a member of your wedding party to help encourage other guests to put down their devices at the wedding. It doesn't have to be high drama: all they have to do is sidle up to their fellow guest and say quietly, "The bride and groom have asked me to respectfully suggest guests put down their electronics and just enjoy the day. Can I ask you to put your camera/phone away?" Whatever you do, don't rely on your photographer to be the heavy; it's not their job to make your guests behave. Plus, when the request to put away the camera or phone comes from a fellow guest, it's less likely to be seen as a grumpy encounter.

Wording ideas for officiants

The easiest way to remind your guests to power down their devices is to have your officiant make a brief announcement before the ceremony. A few ideas, ranging from the sacred to the silly:

Spiritual:

The couple respectfully requests that all guests honor the sanctity of this moment by turning off cell phones and cameras.

Emotional:

I invite you to be truly present at this special time. Please, turn off your cell phones and put down your cameras. The photographer will capture how this moment looks—I encourage you all to capture how it feels with your hearts, without the distraction of technology.

Ridiculous:

Ladies and gentlemen, prior to wedding take-off, all seat backs and tray tables must be in their upright and locked positions, all bags properly stowed, and all portable electronic devices turned off and stowed. This includes cell phones and cameras.

Thanks to Offbeat Bride reader Rockwell for this one:

As Shakespeare once said, please turn off your cell phones.

Offbeat reader Cat shared this anecdote:

At my best friend's wedding, the rabbi asked the bride to turn around and face the audience after her parents walked her to the altar. At this time he said, "Everyone, get the photo you really want now, because we ask that your cameras remain off for the remainder of the ceremony."

Printable sign for ceremony venue

Try this wording for a sign displayed near your guest book or in another prominent spot:

> Welcome to our unplugged wedding.
> We invite you to be fully present with us during the ceremony.
> Please turn off your cell phones and cameras.
> Thank you!

After the wedding . . . share your photos!

Make sure you share a few images with your guests within a couple days of the wedding—for a Saturday wedding, Monday or Tuesday is ideal. The wedding is still fresh in your guests' minds, and it's a great way to carry some of the wedding day afterglow into the workweek. As soon as all your wedding photos are available, make prints to include with each thank-you card. If possible, also make wedding photos available to guests online.

I'm certainly not saying that all weddings should be unplugged or that guests are doing anything wrong when they have their devices out. If it doesn't bother the couple, then it's not a problem. As with all things Offbeat Bride, ultimately this wedding decision comes down to what feels right to each couple.

That said, I do think that in this era of twenty-four-hour connectivity, where there's a smartphone in every pocket, a social media post in every encounter, and a digital hobbyist photographer in every family, it's important to carefully consider the issue.

35. HOLY FUCK, IT'S ACTUALLY HAPPENING

Months (or years!) of planning
lead up to two words: "I do"

OUR PHOTOS HAD BEEN TAKEN, THE GUESTS HAD BEEN HAPPILY PREPPED with pre-ceremonial cocktails, and the weather was fucking perfect. Just how I wanted: sunny but not too hot, the mountains peeking out over the trees, everyone on the bed-and-breakfast's patio, enjoying the view. The wedding, it seemed, was actually happening.

I tried to stop and look around and appreciate it. The little paper flags that upper location manager Sarah had encouraged folks to tie into the trees were amazing; there was just enough of a breeze to keep the golden ribbons in constant motion, and the gold-leafed paper was glinting gorgeously under the sun. People had written the sweetest things on them, too—blessings and good thoughts that I'll save until the paper crumbles.

But then, all too soon, it was time for Andreas and me to sneak off to the bridal cabin suite to prepare ourselves for the ceremony. We sat out on the back patio in the shade and collected ourselves. I drank water and ran through my vows again and again. (" . . . In return, I give you my vow that I will care for you, challenge you, and pat your head when you're feeling bad. . . . In return, I give you my vow that I will care for you, challenge you, and pat your head when you're feeling bad . . . ")

I sat next to Andreas and stared into my enormous bouquet (made from flowers growing in the gardens of the bed-and-breakfast) and noticed a tiny white spider on the oversize lily at the center. As I prepared to enter into the institution of marriage, I sat and stared at this impossibly small spider, daintily picking her way

> ## TIP: HOW TO AVOID WEDDING DAY MEMORY LOSS
>
> FORCE YOURSELF TO TAKE A COUPLE OF MOMENTS DURING YOUR wedding day to just stand aside, take a really deep breath, and appreciate it all for a moment. So many folks report having foggy memories of their wedding day, and it's no surprise—with all the stimulation and people and excitement, it's hard for your brain to slow down long enough to process and store any memories. If you make yourself step away for a moment or two, you'll give your mind the opportunity to imprint at least a few memories of your wedding day—these memories will be more valuable to you than any photograph or video. It's actually worth asking a trusted friend to remind you to do this several times during your wedding day, and to specifically build some "anti-memory-loss moments" into your day. These could be things like a wedding prep sacred snack, some scheduled pre-ceremony solitude, a ceremonial collective deep breath, or a post-ceremony walk.

through the center of the expansive lily, and my brain almost blew up. It was all so metaphorical! I was so overwhelmed!

We heard the Tibetan bell ring a few times to call everyone to sit down, and I listened to our guests being corralled onto the lawn, where they sat on blankets or perched in mismatched summer chairs. Then we heard my godmother addressing the crowd, and my father-in-law rang the bell three times to mark the start of the ceremony.

Holy fuck. It's actually happening.

Then our friend Tania began singing her a cappella, brick-house rendition of Etta James's "At Last." Tania worked the location perfectly, with her voice echoing off the hillside, pausing between lines to let people enjoy the resonance.

We started walking down the aisle (a path through the garden) to the lines "You smile / You smile / Oh, and then the spell was cast / And here we are in heaven / For you are mine at last." Our photographer was there, taking pictures as we strolled toward her. We reached our hoop altar just in time to take in the last refrain of Tania's song. People were sort of stupefied by her voice. I don't think it's customary to applaud at the end of a processional, but Tania earned it.

My godmother introduced Andreas and me—there was a gentle chuckle from the crowd when she described us as "two uniquely creative individuals"—and then she called my father up to read the poem I had asked him to write for the ceremony.

My father, as always, was articulate and emotional (apologizing for being a bit weepy after Tania's song), and then he delivered his poem. As any poet might be, he'd been a little peeved when I'd given him an "assignment"—to write a poem that involved circles and an island and love—but he did wonderfully.

Then, after a transition from my godmother, it was time for our vows. I was going first.

Holy fuck. This is actually happening.

I started in and was doing just fine. "Andreas, for almost seven years, you have been my most beloved companion and lover, the copilot of the world I inhabit . . . "

Then I blanked out. My godmother had told me that it was okay, preferable even, to take my time during my vows, so, when I couldn't remember what to say next, I quietly panicked inside my head (Holy fuck! This is actually happening! I'm forgetting my vows!), but on the outside I just stayed quiet, leaving a long pregnant pause.

I learned afterward that this pause was interpreted as a speech-defying moment of emotion on my behalf, which I guess it was—if by "emotion" you mean "confusion." Guests reported afterward that they thought I was trying to keep from crying, which is sort of funny to me, but, hey, I can get into the pageantry of it. I didn't intentionally mislead people, but, by taking my time, I inadvertently encouraged people to feel the event more fully, and that's a good thing. Or at least better than having them freak out for me because I clearly had no fucking clue which pledge came next.

After what was probably only five seconds but felt like a dragged-out minute or two, I skipped on to the next line of my vows and things continued smoothly. When I finished, Andreas kissed my hands (aww!) and began his vows.

When he was done (he didn't miss a word, unlike Forgetty Mc-Forgetfulson across the bouquet from him), he kissed my hands again and called his mother up to bring the rings. She brought them (cutely fretting about being all teary-eyed), and it worked out very smoothly. She handed us the rings and took my bouquet.

I was quite pleased with myself: at Seattle's Gay Pride Parade the weekend before our wedding, I'd picked up a sample pack of banana-flavored lube, and I'd greased the rings before the ceremony. They slipped right on.

Then our officiant proclaimed us married, and we went in for the long, tonguey kiss while everybody cheered.

Holy fuck. It's actually happening!

We stood and listened to the first stanza of my mother's sweet song ("What I'll give you, since you asked / Is all my time together / Take the ragged sunny days / The warm and rocky weather") and then exited the garden, stage left. As we headed out, I collected my bouquet from my outlaw mother, and my father and a few friends stood and showered us with rose petals and lavender blossoms. They smelled so sweet—but, man, that lavender got down in my duct-taped décolletage and was mighty uncomfortable. (Oh, yes, I duct-taped my breasts together. It's the best way to get the deepest cleavage. Plus, it introduces a hint of kink into the evening later on, as you get to rip it off.)

We headed off for our yichud-inspired walk, down the dirt road leading away from the bed-and-breakfast. Our photographer stalked us, although she broke paparazzi decorum when she started audibly sniffling and wailing, "I can't see through the viewfinder when I'm crying like this!"

As we rounded the corner of the dirt road, we were able to look back up at the bed-and-breakfast on the hill and see everyone still sitting on the lawn, listening to my mother sing. I tossed a wave over my shoulder, but I don't think anyone saw.

Holy fuck. It actually happened.

36. LET US FEED YOU

Yes, carnivores, it's a vegan buffet

OUR POST-CEREMONY WALK ENDED WITH OUR PICKING BLACKBERRIES off the heavy, thorny bushes that cover the Pacific Northwest. This was a nice, safe, first food to share as a married couple, because we could agree on it.

You see, Andreas and I eat different things. Raised a meat-and-potatoes boy, he became a vegan (no eggs, no dairy, no meat) in high school. With a few exceptions made for milk chocolate or the very rare European cheese, he hadn't eaten animal products for well over a decade. Meanwhile, I eat eggs, dairy, and seafood. My dream wedding menu would have included some northwest salmon, but Andreas was adamant that we have an all-vegan dinner at our wedding. I put up one tiny argument ("But I'm not vegan . . . "), but ultimately I sympathize with the fact that he was rarely in an environment where everything is vegan. If there's any event that should cater to his diet, it should be his wedding. Our wedding.

And, besides, good vegan food can be outrageously rich and flavorful, so I was happy to serve it. Plus, I'd watched Andreas maneuver his way through meat-laden family events for years. I think he got a little satisfaction out of forcing everyone to eat his food for a change—and show off just how gourmet his dietary restrictions could be.

We hired Erin, a friend who's a personal chef in Los Angeles, to cater the wedding. She's served huge crowds of hungry hippies and ravers and little old men and other picky eaters for many years, and she agreed to make her special tofu dish that Andreas adores. The caterer's fee? Plane tickets for Erin and her husband, Dallas, who's also a dear friend of ours. Conveniently, Dallas offered himself as kitchen bitch and bartender as part of the package deal. We lucked out!

With Andreas's vegan requests in order, Erin built us this menu:

APPETIZERS
Assortment of marinated olives
Cannellini bean dip with whole-wheat pita bread
Stuffed cherry tomatoes with spicy pesto filling

ENTRÉES
Stuffed portabella mushrooms with garlic basil filling
Stuffed zucchini with spicy tomato filling
Grilled tofu marinated in secret smoky sauce

SIDES
Couscous, garbanzo beans, carrots, and broccoli,
with a ginger vinaigrette
Greek country vegetables in a zesty tomato sauce

SALADS
Greek salad with cucumber, tomatoes,
and red onions in a balsamic vinaigrette
Green salad with baby greens and homemade dressing

DESSERT
Carrot cake, both rich vegan and sinfully nonvegan

No one missed the meat. And I certainly didn't miss the salmon.

Erin cooked in the industrial kitchen at the bed-and-breakfast, and, thanks to insider tips from her and other foodie friends, most of the ingredients for the meal were purchased at wholesale restaurant-supply spots, which kept our costs low.

Erin had settled into the kitchen, surrounded by a cloud of helpers. Family members scooped out tiny tomatoes and cut up vegetables and sliced pitas. The team of dishwashers was preassembled to
sweep through the wedding and clean the brightly colored plastic
picnic dishes we'd borrowed to serve on. There were a few harried
moments (as there usually are when food prep is involved), but
everything seemed to go according to plan.

When it finally came time to eat, I was in a state of relief. The
highest-pressure moments of the wedding were over: we had suc-
cessfully exchanged vows and signed the papers. Technically, we
were married. The rest was just food and fun.

Our amazing dinner was presented buffet style, the serving
dishes surrounded by fern fronds collected from the forest and
lovingly arranged by upper location manager Sarah. Guests piled
food on their plastic plates and filled their muglies with cocktails
and cheap wine. Less than half of our guests sat at the mismatched
tables we'd covered with the used bed sheets, and the rest sat on
blankets and sheets spread out on the lawn. Who sat where was
completely self-selected—although it was mostly family at the tables and friends on the grass.

Entertainment during dinner included some fantastic cello music, courtesy of high school–age family friends, and hula-hooping.
One of my lovely hooping friends brought several custom-made
wedding hoops as gifts, and several family members dared to take
them for a spin. You haven't really lived until you've seen your
mother-in-law hula-hoop at your wedding.

We trusted our caterer completely, so we didn't taste-test any
of our menu beforehand. We might have missed out. Many brides
I spoke to regaled me with amazing stories of "interviewing" caterers by trying their meals. Offbeat reader Elisabeth recounted,
"The tasting where we ate a whole dinner of our choice was the

best thing ever! We were totally stuffed and had to bring a bunch home—I remember that night having these lovely garlic farts from all the nice food. I was thinking that we could market 'nice farts' as a post-wedding favor."

Offbeat Bride readers almost unanimously opt for buffets these days. Offbeat reader Brittany explained, "The buffet was the way to go. Everyone got to eat as much or as little as they wanted of each item, and there was no counting up tallies of 'beef' or 'fish' on reply cards." And if there are only boxes for beef or fish, won't a vegan guest somewhere freak out? Much easier to do a buffet— or even food trucks—and let all the picky eaters figure it out for themselves.

Of course, vegan isn't the only kind of picky-eater food out there. Offbeat reader Amy was worried that her kosher rabbi would freak out about the oysters on the half shell that she just had to serve at her wedding. She gloated afterward, "Apparently, many of my guests had always been afraid to eat raw oysters, but they tried them at my wedding, and it changed their lives!"

It's not every wedding meal that can permanently alter guests' diets, but you never know: your iceberg lettuce–loving uncle might just discover that arugula is pretty damn tasty. We can't all change culinary lives, but we can try.

One sad truth remains, however: you won't eat much of the meal at your wedding. It's customary for someone to make up a plate for the bride, and I sat down and put some food in my mouth, but I was too excited and relieved and overstimulated and smiley to remember much about how it tasted. Stuffed portabella what? Grilled tofu marinated in who? Wedding glee made my brain forget what my mouth experienced.

TIP: BEST! LEFTOVERS! EVER!

A YEAR AFTER WE GOT MARRIED, I WENT TO A WEDDING WHERE THE caterers had included leftovers as part of their package. As the evening wound down, they started carefully loading the copious leftovers into to-go Tupperware containers. Most guests picked up a couple containers on their way home. It was a fantastic idea, and I wish we'd thought of something so clever. My mother ended up with obscene amounts of premium olives after our wedding, and I wish we could have shared some of that food. Another clever idea is to have someone pack you and your now-spouse two complete meals to eat the day *after* your wedding. You'll be calmer, less rushed, and infinitely more able to enjoy it.

37. TOASTED OR BURNT?

Slurred well-wishings and other
dangerous proclamations

AS DINNER STARTED WINDING DOWN BEHIND THE BED-AND-BREAKFAST, I took a moment to wander around and check out the front porch. There, I found a truly horrific scene—sunset. Or rather, almost sunset. It was the golden hour, that sliver of time before the sun sets. In my ideas about the wedding, I'd had a very clear picture in mind that we would all be doing toasts on the front porch at exactly this time, our guests' faces bathed in golden light befitting a 1970s album cover.

I went into a bit of a panic. I alerted upper location manager Sarah that we needed to get folks to the front patio now for toasts, before we lost the lovely light. She stood up to start to prepare people, but there ain't no stopping a crazed bride, and I decided almost immediately I was hauling everyone out front myself.

"Okay, everyone!" I yelled to the guests, who were finishing up their dinners on the back lawn and patio. "Now we're heading to the front lawn! The sunset is beautiful, so come on! Let's go! Grab your chairs if you want, but for god's sake, let's get to the front yard! Now!"

I was freaking out. The toasts need to get started quickly! Open the boxes of amazing champagne from Andreas's cousin! Pass the bottles out quickly! Dear god, hurry! The sun! It's setting! I kept gesturing to camp counselor / de facto best man, Tim, Go now! Start the toasts now! Hurry! The sun!

I decided I was so impatient that I didn't really care whether the champagne was poured, per se. Just grab a bottle, fuckers! The bottles of champagne made the rounds through the crowd. Quickly, people! The sun is setting! I'm sure my stress level was laid bare for everyone to see. Leave it to me to freak out over one thing and one thing only: the fucking sunset. Something I have zero control over.

And then? Ahhh. It all worked out.

As the sun crept toward the Olympic Mountains, Tim regaled our guests with the story of how Andreas and I met and fell in love, and everyone cheered and lifted their drinks. Thankfully, Tim did not go into as much detail as I have in this book, or the guests would probably still be standing around with their muglies half raised. No, Tim told a short and very sweet story about how, in the first months of our relationship, Andreas and I shouted, "I love you!" to each other outside a rave at Seattle's infamous Lish House.

It was a touching story, with one small caveat: neither Andreas nor I can remember the sweet event occurring. Then again, although many stereotypes about ravers are fabrications, memory loss is a complete reality. In many ways, it's appropriate that the story retold at the wedding of two aging ravers would involve declarations of love that we don't remember outside a party I can't quite place. How many people did I hug during my years of raving? I can't remember, but I know that I ended up marrying one of them, so what does it matter?

We were toasted by each of our parents in turn, and then my childhood friend stepped forward and led her own sweet tribute to me, looking around at the huge circle of freaks and friends and family and announcing that, for an only child, I had the biggest family she'd ever seen. I wasn't weepy on my wedding day, but her toast was the closest I got.

Andreas and I had a toast of our own, too. We stepped up on the stairs of the bed-and-breakfast and toasted all the people who helped with the wedding. We thanked them all over and over and over again and raised a glass to the dozens of people who'd helped us make the event happen. I heard about one couple who toasted the dating website where they'd met. That sounds so touching, in a twenty-first-century kind of way.

Couples toasting guests seems to be an emerging trend in offbeat weddings, and Offbeat Bride reader Stephanie isn't sure why more people don't do it. "I've rarely seen brides and grooms do a public thank-you—and I think it's really weird that it doesn't happen more often. When the couple doesn't toast their guests, it seems to add to the 'This wedding is about our parents, not us' attitude, or also the 'bride as distant participant who will only interact with you in the receiving line' thing."

Embrace the embarrassing

Toasting is another pragmatic tradition. Chances are good that your friends and family are just itching to tell the world about how much they like the two of you together and how they knew all along it was going to work. There's no need to have a best man do the first toast (or to have the first toast be led by a man at all), but it really is nice to give your guests the opportunity to toast you. It's one of those traditions with an actual reason.

Toasting also seems to be one of those traditions embraced by even the nontraditional, and, naturally, part of toasting is that moment when someone starts talking and you start to wonder, Oh shit, where is this going? Offbeat reader Corrin remembers, "My dad started his toast with a comment about how weddings are like funerals. There are so many bad places that he could have gone, but he pulled it off, got a laugh, and reminded us that while 'I love you,' is a good thing to say, it's also good to remember these words during moments of marital strife: 'I could be wrong.'" See? Even Offbeat Brides get sentimental and sweet bits of advice during toasts.

If you decide you don't want toasts, good luck with that! It's really difficult to keep people from toasting, so you're probably better off organizing toasts to your liking, rather than risking finding yourself surprised when it happens. Especially if your concern with toasts is that someone will say something embarrassing or inappropriate, it's in your best interest to carefully pick trusted toasters in advance, rather than leaving it open for the drunkest guest to stand up and tell the story about that one time when you got diarrhea at the grocery store, and how he knew then that you were destined for great things, and here you are!

Then again, if you're really worried about someone saying something embarrassing, I'd say loosen up a bit. Stories about diarrhea and being destined for greatness make great stories to tell the grandkids about your wedding.

38. THE SUGAR HIGH

Getting your friends & family
hooked on a dangerous drug: cake

I MAY HAVE BEEN A PUSHOVER FOR HAVING AN ALL-VEGAN DINNER BUF-
fet, but the one place I was not willing to compromise on food
was dessert. Goddamnit, I wanted a carrot cake, and carrot cake
must have cream-cheese frosting! I enjoy tofu. I like vegan food.
But when I'm having carrot cake, it needs cream cheese on top, and
that is not up for debate.

I suppose we were somewhat traditional by having cake at all.
When my parents got married in 1974, they were so against refined
sugar that, instead of cake, they had enormous wheels of cheese. I
have spoken to couples who opted for cookies, snow cones, pies,
cupcakes, and a million other non-cake desserts. One bride fretted a little about her cake alternative, joking, "Are people going
to throw their liquor-marinated berries in a phyllo basket at us because they wanted cake instead?"

Then there's Offbeat Bride reader K.T., who skipped the cake
and instead went for "a big beautiful pile of doughnuts, just stacked
on a tiered cake stand. When we did the cake cutting (doughnut
tearing?), we played *The Simpsons'* theme song, with Homer's voice
spliced in, saying 'Mmm, doughnuts.'"

The biggest reason to go for cake alternatives is that, well, some
people simply don't like cake. Offbeat reader Karin recounted, "We
went to a wedding expo at one point, and all the demo cakes were
dry. I couldn't believe it—this is supposed to convince me?" There's
also the hidden financial advantage: Some venues charge you a
cake-cutting fee, as much as a dollar per slice! Don't get me started

on how ridiculous this is, but it's an easy scam to avoid if you're, say, scooping ice cream instead.

Offbeat reader Jen is one of those cake haters. "The first time I got married, I told people that I was not cutting any stupid cake. And then my former mother-in-law brought a big, stupid cake. And I hate most cake. So I pulled out my ex-husband's costume sword and sliced the cake in half with a maniacal look on my face." She opted for truffles at her second wedding.

But, as for me, I adore carrot cake—and so cake it was. We were lucky enough to know a baker who also happens to have been my best friend in high school. When I called to tell Susannah we'd gotten engaged, her first response was an enthusiastic, "Oh my god—can I bake the cake?" Clearly, she's more a baker than a romantic.

We're probably lucky we had a patient friend working on the process, because it took a little figuring out. I insisted on the cream cheese–slathered carrot cake, but Andreas needed a vegan carrot cake.

Susannah decided to make two cakes—one for me, with eggs and creamy frosting, and one for him, with special, magical egg and dairy substitutes. In keeping with the circle theme, she wove the two separate cakes together into an eternity symbol—two circles that intersected and crossed. Eggy carrot cake slathered in cream cheese, intertwined with dense, rich, vegan carrot cake covered in . . . something white. I don't know what it was, but it was non-dairy and very sweet and tasty.

Our cakes were decorated very simply—a few leaves and a few dragonfly sugar cookies, which were my friend the baker's little nod to a dragonfly tattoo I have on my shoulder. I've heard from Offbeat Bride readers who decorated their cakes with actual rose petals or full flowers (make sure they're organic or homegrown—you don't want to risk poisoning your guests with pesticides!),

ribbons, sugared grapes, or berries (wash them far enough beforehand that they're dry when you put them on—otherwise they'll
bleed on your frosting).

When guests take tradition into their own hands

The toasts completed, we cut the cakes at dusk, with the sil-
houetted Olympic Mountains looming behind us. We clowned
around with the knives (knives are always fun!), posed for cakey
couple pictures, and then set to feeding each other. We had to
carefully orchestrate our bites of cake. I had a plate of vegan
cake to feed Andreas, and he had a plate of my sinful nonvegan
cake to feed me. It was like a big sugary metaphor of our relationship, bending over backward to respect each other's separate
decisions but sharing our life together. Who knew cake could be
so symbolic?

There was no smooshing of cake into each other's faces. That
new tradition might have been cute once, but all I can think is that
it's a weird, ritualized way of degrading each other in public.

Cake-smooshing is an extremely hot topic for Offbeat Brides.
One bride huffed, "I think it's at best an old, clichéd routine and at
worst, veiled hostility." Others contend that if feeding each other
is symbolic of kicking off a nurturing relationship, smooshing then
becomes symbolic of, well, humiliating each other.

Then there's perhaps the worst-case cake-smooshing scenario,
suffered by Offbeat Bride reader Jessica. She and her husband
opted to feed each other ("Gently," Jessica stressed) and to avoid
cake-smooshing. Then things got squirrelly. "My fourteen-year-old
cousin decided we were entirely too gentle. We simply weren't catering to her bellows of 'Smash it! Smash it! Smash it!'—which are
quite audible on the wedding video. And since we weren't showing

any signs of smashing, she took it upon herself to do it for us." And so, the cousin stepped forward and smooshed wedding cake into the face of the groom.

Isn't it great when guests decide to take wedding traditions into their own hands? You can try all you want—sometimes you just get sabotaged. With cake. Cake-otaged.

39. DUCK!

AFTER THE TOASTS WERE FINISHED, IT WAS TIME FOR ME TO DO, WELL, something with my bouquet. Except that I'm not at all into bouquet tosses. It's embarrassing to see women reluctantly herded into a group and then watch as they all step out of the way of a flying bundle of flowers. (Is this just my friends? I've never seen anyone dive for a bouquet.) Plus, bouquets are too pretty to throw around! You pay way too much money for this bunch of limited-lifespan flora, and then you go tossing that shit around? Hell no!

Furthermore, why is it only women vying to catch the bouquet? Is it because women are all conniving bitches looking for ways to manipulate their reluctant boyfriends into proposing? Because of course only women want to get married—everyone knows that all men have commitment problems, while women are just itching to tie the knot.

Offbeat reader Julia sums up many of my concerns: "Bouquet tosses have always been my LEAST FAVORITE part of weddings. To me, the traditional bouquet toss feels like women are just desperate to get married, the design doesn't accept LGBTQ+ couples well, and while I love my husband and am thrilled to be married to him, I feel like many people are just as happy without marriage. Why wish something on people they don't want?"

All these stereotypes make me cringe. I had no urge to toss a bouquet and play a further role in these misconceptions, so I hacked the toss into the gay marriage equality handoff that I talked about back in Chapter 14. To me, it felt like the best way to use

229

TIP: DO THE BOUQUET DANCE

ONE SENTIMENTAL WAY TO STRUCTURE THE BOUQUET HANDOFF IS TO have a bouquet dance, where you invite all the couples onto the dance floor and then ask couples who've been together less than one year to leave the floor, then five years, then ten, then fifteen, then twenty, then thirty, and on until you get to the last couple on the dance floor—the folks who've been together the longest.

traditions: you can honor the idea while using it to express your own ideologies. There's enough familiarity to prevent guests from drowning in confusion (think of these few traditions as life preservers tossed out to guests as they bob in a sea of midsummer night's wedding weirdness), but, by adapting the traditions for yourself, you take ownership of your own expressions of commitment.

Some brides do elect to toss their bouquets, but not in a traditional way. Offbeat reader Jen shot her bouquet from a cannon, with the "not-as-good man" (known in most weddings as the best man) announcing to guests that there was an 80 percent chance the cannon wouldn't work and a 10 percent chance they'd all die. Another bride divided her bouquet into pieces and distributed the pieces to guests with tongue-in-cheek fortunes.

Offbeat reader Amy recounted, "I announced at some point that I was going to throw my bouquet, and all of my friends followed me—boys and girls. I guess that says something about how I pick my friends, but I didn't even have to tell them I wanted this to be an egalitarian opportunity. . . . It was understood." As she stood before the group of young men and women, she "worried that everyone would just stand there and let the bouquet drop on the ground. But one of my best guy friends surprised me by lunging for the thing; he snapped it out of the air like it was a pop fly to center field!"

Offbeat reader Julia used this clever idea: "I had all my bridesmaids stand with me, and all guests gather in front of us. I gave a little speech, along the lines of 'Hello! I had to do things differently, so thank you all for standing for the bouquet toss. Obviously I love marriage, otherwise none of us would be here today. However, I feel that marriage is only one expression of love, and so, my wish for all of you today is: *may love come into your life.*' Then my bridesmaids and I all turned our backs to the guests. We had cut the ties on our bouquets in advance, so that when we all flung them above our shoulders, the flowers spread out and could be caught by many people!"

Then there was a bride named Katie who set her guests up for a traditional bouquet toss, and then after turning her back to them, pranked them by tossing a rubber chicken over her shoulder. Take that, tradition!

40. JUST SAY NO TO THE VILLAGE PEOPLE

The role of rhythm (or arrhythmia) in
the contemporary wedding ceremony

AFTER WE'D TAKEN CARE OF THE LAST OF OUR BASTARDIZED TRADITIONS (the sunset cake cutting, the twilight cake eating, the bouquet presenting), it was getting dark, and our wedding transitioned. My parents pulled out their hand drums and started up a promenade from the garden of the bed-and-breakfast to my mother's property, which was a five-minute walk down a gravel driveway that curved through a meadow and the forest.

Most of our guests made it down the hill, although a few chose that time to walk to their cars and head home. For those who followed the promenade, my parents led us down a forested path and into my mother's meadow, where lower location manager Sarah had created a twinkling forest fairyland.

There were candles everywhere, miles of Christmas tree lights, and hula hoops for playing. A techno-loving friend had donated his sound system for the evening, and we had our three out-of-town DJs scheduled to play. It was, for all intents and purposes, a small rave. But with family members.

Our first DJ, Megasoul, hooked up her dueling iPods (aww, remember those?) and played what we'd selected to be our first song, Me'Shell NdegeOcello's "Love Song #1." This was one way in which our wedding was perfectly traditional: the first dance was awkward and sort of weird as we hugged and slow-danced like a pair of sixth graders at a school function. People stood around watching us, and we both breathed a sigh of relief when it was over and the dance music came on.

TIP: THE JOYS AND PAINS
OF SKIPPING A DJ

SOME OFFBEAT COUPLES BUILD THEIR OWN PLAYLISTS FOR THEIR
weddings, skipping a DJ in lieu of hooking up their devices. It's a de-
cent option if you need to go low budget—but as with all matters of
technology and gadgetry, have a backup ready! Offbeat reader Susan
hit a major road bump at her reception when the device playing her
carefully prepared playlists crapped out. "It inexplicably stuck one-third
of the way through a Supremes song, on the first of our three dance
playlists. But our awesome friends put new stuff on, and I don't think
anyone else even noticed that the music had stopped for a minute. It
was a bummer not to have all of our favorite songs playing all night,
but, hey, it got us through the ceremony and dinner hour, at least."
Also, recognize that many human DJs play double duty, acting as an
MC who ushers the wedding from one moment to another. Spotify
can't do that.

I spoke to several brides who, being infinitely smarter than
us, had choreographed first dances. One did a foxtrot; another
pulled off a scandalous tango that culminated with her skirt being theatrically ripped off. Then again, some couples simply ar-
en't dancers ("I didn't want the wedding to be *Dance Party USA*,"
one introverted bride confided) and opt to do their one awkward
slow dance and then spend the rest of the reception talking to
people; some just skip the dance situation completely. Hell, if
you don't like dancing, don't do it. Like every other wedding
tradition, if it doesn't resonate with you, there's no point. Over
the years, I've seen everything from first drink, first karaoke, first
game (video games, board games, so many others!), first jump in a
bouncy castle, first group dance with all the guests, and even first
lightsaber duel!

That said, Andreas and I are dancers, and our friends needed no encouragement—but for the people who were a little less sure on their dancing feet, there were the hula hoops. Hula hoops might seem like a silly way to get people moving, but hey, whatever it takes. Offbeat reader Corrin agreed that sometimes desperate times call for desperate measures. "The Macarena and the chicken dance were strictly verboten, but we were open to some of the less offensive ones. I'm not generally a fan of the group dances, like the electric slide and whatnot, but I have to say, it was fun to see the slightly older folks get up and shake it when those songs came on."

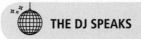 **THE DJ SPEAKS**

Our second DJ of the evening, Scott Haapala, may have played breakbeat for our reception . . . but he spent three years during college as a wedding rent-a-DJ. Scott picked up a few tips that he offered up for Offbeat Brides who go the traditional DJ route:

VISUAL OVERKILL
Do you really need disco lights and a laser at your wedding? Having rave lighting gear is going to be a confusing overkill if you're going to be playing a mix of pop, disco, country, rock, and old-school hip-hop.

MAKE SURE YOUR DJ KNOWS YOUR FAVORITE MUSIC
Ask how much they know about each genre you want, especially if you want one to be more heavily played than another. In my second month of DJing, I was once asked to play 90 percent country at a wedding, and I knew only about three country songs. During the wedding, I looked through my playlist and recognized the name Garth Brooks, and chose his song 'The Thunder Rolls.' Now, for those of us who don't know much about country music, this could appear to be a reasonable decision. Thirty seconds into the song, however, I was approached by the bride with all of the bridesmaids and told to 'turn this song off!' Evidently, the song is about a man who goes out and cheats on his wife, and she ends up shooting him in the end. Oops.

>>>

AND AS FOR FORCING PEOPLE TO DANCE?

A DJ can try to get on the microphone and call people out onto the dance floor, but that is only effective once an hour at most. Beyond that, it's up to the crowd and the amount of liquor that's being served.

Scott said that the only way to make sure everyone dances is to "have a group of guests who all like the same kind of music and a DJ who plays that style!" It sounds so simple.

⋆˚✦

Our DJs were not the types to put on "YMCA." Megasoul started things off accessibly with rare groove and soul. She played funky songs people knew, like Stevie Wonder and a then-young Justin Timberlake. I toddled around, alternating between dancing, talking, hooping, and people watching.

It can be a major challenge to make your musical tastes more family friendly. One bride with dark tendencies recounted, "Most of the songs I think of as romantic tend to be about death and unrequited love, for example, 'And if a double-decker bus / Crashes into us / To die by your side / Is such a heavenly way to die.' So we went through several song lists before we found something cheerfully romantic, noncheesy, and with a beat we could dance to."

Then again, why cater to mainstream tastes? For Offbeat Brides from underground music communities, introducing their families to the music they love is part of the joy. Offbeat reader Brittany had a wedding that was basically a small jam band festival.

She wanted to share the experience of these festivals with her family, explaining, "One thing I always loved about those music festivals was the feeling of being surrounded by friends you hadn't ever met before, and the total freedom to let loose and be totally comfortable with yourself. Our band played a bluegrass-rock style, with upright bass, mandolin, guitar, Dobro, drums, and trumpet. When they took the stage, all our friends immediately started dancing like they were in a bar—not in the typical wedding style. I had some older guests commenting on how great it was that they didn't need partners to dance. I had been a little worried that the style of band would alienate the older guests, but by the third or fourth song, nearly everyone was dancing!"

As is fitting for retired ravers, our music was very loud. The two Mackie speakers were cranking out one thousand watts of sound, and I was glad I'd sent personalized letters to all my mother's neighbors months in advance, letting them know about the wedding and asking in advance for their patience that night. I sympathize with the fact that not everyone wants to live next to my mother and her women's eco-retreat center, and she'd already experienced friction with her neighbor to the north. He'd called the authorities on her a few times, and we were really worried that he would get our wedding, well, busted. (It would actually have been fitting for the wedding of two people who first kissed at a semilegal warehouse party, but still. No cops at our wedding, please.)

Evidently, our letter to the neighbors worked, because as the music got louder and thumpier, we had absolutely no problems with noise complaints. We got in several hours of loud, hard music, and although our friends aren't big drinkers, it's safe to say that, as midnight approached, people got wasted. Some got sloppy, a few spiraled into psychedelic tailspins, and the dancing got wild. And our friend Brian, a creaky old desert raver from Los Angeles, DJed the last set of the evening.

That said, things also calmed down before it got too late. We turned the music off around 2:30 A.M. (switching to a simple boom box), as most folks were sort of transitioning into cuddle-around-the-campfire mode. I knew that would be the way things would work—our crew liked to party, but we also got tired a little earlier than we used to.

TIP: COGNITIVE LIBERTIES, A.K.A. HOW TO DEAL WITH PEOPLE WHO GET HIGH AT YOUR WEDDING

WHILE TRADITIONAL BRIDES MAY WORRY ABOUT UNCLE JOEY GETTING drunk and lecherous, some Offbeat Brides have, well, other concerns. Offbeat reader Debra recounted, "Most of our friends are stoners, and we had different groups of smoker friends coming together and knew that would be a big part of their bonding together. I requested ahead of time for people to please keep it discreet, and they did, for the most part. That was probably my biggest stress surrounding the wedding. I didn't want my conservative relatives to see my friends smoking and have there be drama. Most brides worry about flowers and food, but I was consumed with worry about this! I wish I hadn't fretted so much, though, as everyone was very discreet and respectful of my wishes."

We had similar concerns with our fun-loving friends, and I sent out a big e-mail to this subset of guests before the wedding, advising them to be careful. The e-mail began, "The wedding's coming right up, and I wanted to check in with all of you about one very important wedding topic: gettin' fucked up!" and continued to advise friends to "be aware of who's around you when you're preparing to smoke—step into a tent or wander into the woods a bit, and perhaps avoid shouting things like 'Oh my god I feel so great holy shit it's like a roller coaster here I go whoosh!' in places where you could be overheard."

Like Debra, we found that our friends who chose to partake were exceptionally discreet—way more discreet than your average lecherous old drunk. While a drunk might grope the wrong guests on the reception dance floor, our high friends just wanted to hug everyone and chew over their philosophies of love.

41. YOURS, MINE, OURS

The ins & outs of wedding sex

As our wedding day came to a close (or rather, as the day after our wedding day entered its first few early morning hours), my new husband and I found ourselves lounging around the campfire. It was 3 A.M., and the last of our guests were winding down from the day, curled around the last bottles of champagne and each other, talking and laughing. Most of these people were friends who'd worked all day on decorating, preparing food, directing parking, and generally running around all over the place, and so it was impressive to see how late we'd all stayed up.

One of the most delightful parts of our wedding was seeing how well our disparate groups of friends mixed together. At one point, I overheard lower location manager Sarah introducing herself to one of the out-of-town DJs, and the next time I glanced over, she was sitting on his lap and giggling.

Then there were the thirtysomethings, one from Los Angeles and one from Seattle, who both got ragingly inebriated and ended up dry-humping in the grass next to the dance floor as the rest of us tittered behind our hands and quietly applauded. Weeks later, when I asked my friends to recount their favorite moments at the wedding, one remembered lying in her tent with a leftover can of whipped cream, listening to the two dry-humpers getting to know each other in a tent a few trees over. That's how you know the wedding's been a success: Is there so much love in the air that it overtakes guests and throws them into wild sexual congress? Now that's a fucking wedding. Literally.

Wedding Crashers jokes aside, there certainly are plenty of folks who hook up at weddings. Marshall Miller joked in *Nerve* magazine, "Wedding hookups are the new black." One friend, a feminist activist and sexuality writer, told me that she's infamous for her wedding hookups and that in fact she met her current partner at a wedding.

"After all," she quipped, "I know the bride and groom are going to be too tired to get any that night. Who would want to fuck after such a long day? I figure it's my job to consummate the marriage, as tradition dictates. It's a responsibility I take very seriously."

Offbeat reader Elisabeth was pleased as punch when her best friend and her husband's brother hit it off at their wedding. Despite living in different cities, the friend and the brother still manage to spend some "alone time" together whenever he's in town. "We're getting better at not teasing them," Elisabeth laughed.

Offbeat reader Becca laughed over "the hookup strategy" at her wedding. "After the reception, many of the guests headed to a nearby bar. We stuck around for some drinks, some shots, some laughs, and, when my husband and I were ready to call it a night, the best man pulled me aside. He asked me to stay for a couple of minutes and talk to one of the attractive single female guests while he went to the bathroom. He wanted me to keep her busy so that she wouldn't leave while he was gone! That's right—after I told him that we were going to head back to our hotel for the night, the best man asked me to be his wing woman!"

With a hint of pride, Becca told me, "Even when I'm busy being a bride, I have unfailing wing-woman skills. I was able to keep the girl occupied until the best man got back, and they left together. It turned out well for everyone involved—with the exception of the best man's hotel roommate, who had to sleep on the floor of someone else's room after he walked in on the best man and the girl getting it on."

There are also, of course, the post-wedding breakups. One bride joked that "the wedding seemed to precipitate a couple of marriages and a couple of divorces among the guests," so I guess we shouldn't have been too surprised when, shortly after our wedding, two of our closest friends broke up. I guess weddings can be inspiring on a lot of levels, including the "This totally isn't working" one. Weddings act as emotional catalysts for all sorts of things—romance, breakups, alcoholism—and all you can do is sit back and watch the stories unfold. Really, your guests owe you a little show after all you did for them. They get wedding favors, and you get the entertainment of watching an uncle pass out during karaoke or the excitement of watching people dry-hump in the bushes.

Consummating at 3 P.M. the next day

After an hour of cuddling around the campfire, us newlyweds decided we were finally ready to go to bed. This was when it was sort of sad that we weren't camping with the rest of our friends—we had to say goodnight and walk back up the hill under the stars. The walk was pure magic, curving through the trees and then through a field, with the stars twinkling overhead and the first light of dawn starting to creep over the horizon. (It's the payoff for wet Seattle winters: In the summer, the sky starts lightening at 4 A.M.)

Lest you think this walk is a romantic prelude to our consummating our marriage, guess again. Despite our circle-themed wedding being all about cycles, the fates did not conspire to have my personal cycle align ideally for wedding-night nookie. And honestly, after six years of sex, we both prefer to be awake and enjoying it when we're copulating. By the time we crawled into our conjugal bed a little after 4 A.M., we'd each had a twenty-hour day and were exhausted to the core. Who wants a bloody dead-fuck on their wedding night?

Offbeat reader Brittany laughed at the idea of having sex on her wedding night. "The band played till dawn! We were lucky to make it to bed at all!" Offbeat reader Jen had a similar experience, although she explained that although "we didn't get to bed until 7:30 A.M., we slept and then we consummated the marriage at, like, 3 P.M. the next day." That said, I did speak to many brides who said they made a point to leave their receptions early enough to enjoy their first night of married sex. One bride explained, "I know a lot of people don't [have wedding-night sex], but it seemed incredibly depressing not to. I think it helped that we left the reception whilst we still had energy."

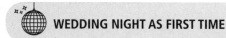 **WEDDING NIGHT AS FIRST TIME**

What about Offbeat Brides who are virgins on their wedding nights? There aren't many of you who go this route (*offbeat* offbeat!), but my advice is this: masturbate a lot ahead of time so you know how to tell your partner how to get you off. And this advice goes beyond sex.

When each partner takes responsibility for themselves (sexually and otherwise) it makes the times when you come together (ha!) that much more special. You know neither of you is there out of obligation or a sense of responsibility. You're both there because you want to be.

When you're empowered to take care of your own business as an individual, you're a stronger half of a partnership. Again, this isn't just sex. It's easier to work with other people when you take responsibility for taking care of your own shit. It's easier to be friends with people when you know your own boundaries. Having insight into yourself and what works for you (sexually or otherwise) puts you into a great position to really get the most from every situation.

part six

As the Dust Settles

42. BOOTY, PART 1: THE HONEYMOON

The conjugal fun, on the road

AH, THE HONEYMOON! A CHANCE TO RELAX AND UNWIND FROM THE wedding and to bask in doing nothing but, well, doing it. Luxurious Tahitian stilt cabins. Romantic mountain lodges. Chocolates on your pillow! Special moments between just the two of you. Or couch surfing across Europe for almost a month, which is what we ended up doing.

If pretty much everything went as planned with our wedding, pretty much nothing went quite as anticipated on the honeymoon. When we first made our plans, we'd decided to tap into a fantasy we'd had for years: we would go to a friend's vineyard in France and work for three weeks of the harvest, picking grapes off the vine in the Mediterranean sun. We would spend time with my pregnant godsister and her husband, who live in France and had been unable to make it to the wedding.

It was our breed of romance: yes, sunny French vineyards are hyper-poetic, but we'd be sharing rustic rooms with other harvesters and spending our days doing long, sweaty manual labor among the grapes. We'd spend evenings with French friends and family, drinking and eating and laughing. Not exactly the lap of luxury, but we were excited to be part of something so beautiful. The harvest! The vines! It was perfect!

Except for, well, it didn't turn out that way at all. In the weeks between our wedding and our honeymoon, we learned that, thanks to French labor laws, our vintner friend couldn't actually hire us to work in the fields. When we volunteered to work for free, he explained that even that wasn't allowed. France is famous for its bureaucracy, and the laws around wine and labor are some of the toughest. Our vintner friend would risk stiff fines from winery inspectors who snoop around during harvest times, looking for migrant workers. This snapped our honeymoon into focus: we'd hoped to spend the month as migrant laborers—and we'd just been denied our labor.

So, there went that vision out the quaintly shuttered window. My godsister helped us adapt relatively quickly. We started the trip off with a few days with her and her husband in the lavender fields of Provence, then a few days at the vineyard, sleeping in a little loaned tent. The tent, like our original honeymoon plans, met with a dramatic demise—it was crushed by a massive windstorm that knocked out power and blew trees over. Thankfully, we were not in the tent at the time. We were with the vineyard workers, drunk on outrageously good wine, sitting in the dark and clapping and singing folk songs.

In addition to the tent, my godsister also generously loaned us her tiny little hatchback. Thankfully, the hatchback did not meet with the same demise as the tent. We spent a week on a camping road trip of Provence, tooling around from Mediterranean beaches to the shores of Lac de Sainte-Croix to the towering canyon walls of the Gorges du Verdon. We camped in a gravel parking lot with a bunch of Germans and rented a refrigerator for our food. For a couple of kids raised backpacking in the Cascades and the Rockies, it was a bit of a shock.

I had an internet friend who was eager to put us up for a few days in Madrid. Some Los Angeles raver pals got us in touch with an expat in Barcelona who showed us the best vegan cooperative restaurants in the city. We also made it to Paris, where an expat friend from Seattle hosted us for Frisbee games and showed us the secret dirty things sculpted into the exterior of the Notre Dame

Cathedral. We went wherever we had a couch or a piece of floor to sleep on, and we did whatever the couch owners felt like doing.

So, although our wedding was obsessively planned, our honeymoon was a stumbling, spontaneous comedy of errors. Despite this difference, the two were actually pretty much the same: we turned to our extended community of friends and family and pieced together a great experience. One was preplanned, the other free-flowing. Both were awesome.

Was it Tahiti? Was it feather beds? Most definitely not. But was it every bit as offbeat as our wedding? Yes, and then some.

One thing we did differently was that we waited a while before heading out on our honeymoon. Because we were originally trying to time our trip with the grape harvest, we'd booked our tickets for almost a month after our wedding day. Ultimately, we needn't have waited, because we couldn't work the harvest anyway . . . but it was nice to have a few weeks to tie up all the loose ends from our wedding and get prepared for our almost-monthlong honeymoon. It would have been difficult, I think, to have prepared for a huge party and a monthlong vacation at the same time.

Bunny costumes in love hotels

Although some Offbeat Brides go for more romantic honeymoons, sometimes they are romantic in unexpected ways. Offbeat reader Bridget spent her honeymoon traveling around Japan, checking in each night at a different "love hotel." She explained the concept to me: "Since space is at a premium and Japanese families still live with three generations under one roof, love hotels—impeccably clean and spacious themed rooms rented during the day in two-hour blocks—can be found in every city. Though they're pretty expensive during the day, the night rentals are super-cheap. We slept in rotating circus beds, bathed in giant golden clams, sang in the buff on our own private karaoke stage, disco-danced before mirrored walls lit with colored racing amusement-park lights, and were startled by a surprise glow-in-the-dark panoramic mural of the New York skyline once the lights went out!" Her only sadness about her honeymoon? "I still regret not purchasing one of the many costumes (nurse, samurai, bunny!) available for sexy role play from the vending machine next to the bed."

Seriously, if you have the opportunity to get a bunny costume on your honeymoon, do it.

Although low-key honeymoons can be perfect for some brides, there's also a reason lots of folks go on big, luxurious vacations: you are freaking exhausted after your wedding. One bride who opted for a weeklong camping-trip honeymoon recounted, "I was so exhausted from the wedding that I was really craving a relaxing trip and a nice hotel, and we didn't have that. I didn't understand why people go on honeymoons until we actually had the wedding—and then it was too late to plan a big honeymoon."

And then there are those who skip the honeymoon completely. As Offbeat Bride reader Leah said, "Having paid for the wedding ourselves, a big vacation wasn't really in the (credit) cards for us."

43. BOOTY, PART 2: THE GIFTS

Wading through the blenders, toasters & acres of thank-you cards

OH, THE BOOTY. I AM A WICKED MATERIALIST, DESPITE MY "LIVE SIMPLY that others may simply live" upbringing. There's no point in denying that I was excited about all our wedding gifts. Of course, most of our gifts were of the time-and-energy sort—the majority of our friends skipped the candlesticks and gave us their skills and help on our wedding day. These are not gifts that come with bows on top, but, in some ways, our wedding was a big communal gift, wrapped in our friends' and family members' hands and hearts. And, hell, we would have toasted with Two-Buck Chuck if one of Dre's cousins hadn't given us cases of fantastic champagne.

That said, there were more standard gifts as well. Some of them arrived in the mail before the wedding, but most got stacked up on a table at the event itself. A few gifts immediately revealed themselves—the bright pink bag from Babeland, Seattle's women-run sex shop, contrasted nicely with all the lavender floral gift wrap.

Other gifts, even once unwrapped, were more than a little confusing. A friend approached me at one point during the wedding and gestured over to the gift table, next to which a large wooden structure had appeared.

"Is that a gong rack?" my friend asked. A gong—wait, what?! I glanced over at the table and saw a beautiful handcrafted wooden something. We have two woodworkers in the extended family, and it was clear that one of them had made us something quite lovely. But was it really a gong rack? We didn't own a gong. It was the most mysterious gift on (or rather, next to) the table.

Days later, as we opened cards, we figured out that it wasn't a gong rack—it was a gorgeous quilt rack. Aha! We didn't have a quilt any more than we had a gong, but the next gift we opened was a beautiful gold-threaded sari from Andreas's cousin, the Hollywood costume designer. It happened to exactly match the red of our bedroom walls, and Andreas and I excitedly rushed into the bedroom, set the quilt rack up at the foot of our bed, tacked the sari to the ceiling, and created a remarkably lovely impromptu bed canopy. Obviously, neither of these gifts was on our registry, but in terms of daily (and nightly!) enjoyment, they might have been some of the best booty we received.

Although many brides wrestle with people who refuse to shop on the registry, most have to admit that, often, the best gifts are surprises. The handmade wind chimes, the bottles of champagne for your first anniversary, the paintings and other bits of family art. These are just a few of the happy deviations from registry that I heard about. Granted, I also heard about some really, really bad gifts, but I'll be gentle and leave those out.

Guests sticking to the registry didn't work out as well as we'd hoped—through some sort of technical glitch, we received not one, not two, but three blenders. One was exchanged for an insane H. R. Giger–like lamp, while the other was traded in for some of the coolest kitchen gadgets ever, including an avocado slicer. We also got two gorgeous wooden salad bowls from two different guests. No problem: one is used for salad, and the other is a countertop fruit bowl.

We got one gift that appeared to be the result of a wrinkle in the fabric of time, clearly destined for a recently married friend of mine. The gift was the most gorgeous representation of the theme of our friend's wedding, and I could only imagine that a rift in the space-time continuum resulted in the gift's appearance at our wedding instead of our friends'. To correct this anomaly of physics, it was my honor to pass the wonderful gift on to our friends as a way of thanking them for everything they did to help us with our wedding. I refuse to think there's anything wrong with regifting, and I can only hope the gift giver would agree. Etiquette dictates not telling them, so I didn't . . . but I really wish I could.

There were, of course, the two biggest gifts: each of our fathers rewarded us for making it legal by presenting two matched checks to help us with a down payment for a conjugal home. These gifts were almost more than gifts—they were kick starts for our new phase of, well, adulthood. After all, as newlyweds, the next thing on the agenda must be home buying, right? Thanks to our fathers, it was.

Get to the thank-you cards a.s.a.p.

In a plot twist of meta-gifting, one of the most useful gifts we received was a set of thank-you cards from lower location manager Sarah. Once the ripped paper and pink tissue had settled, we got right down to working on our thank-yous. Of course I had a spreadsheet for who had given us what, with addresses at the ready so that we could tear through our thank-yous and make sure every last person got their appropriate appreciation.

Naturally, we managed to fuck up a few. My biggest embarrassment was failing to thank my mother. She called me a year after the wedding (a full year!) and whimpered that it really hurt her feelings to see everyone else's thank-you cards when she hadn't gotten one. D'oh. Because her gift to us was hosting the whole event, it was a major oversight. We forgot to thank one of the people who made the whole damn thing possible! Oh, lord. I sent her not one but two cards to make up for it, but I still feel guilty.

Learn from my mistake: Always make sure all parents are thanked profusely for everything they did for the wedding. Don't make the mistake of trusting your stupid spreadsheet like I did. Do your parents' thank-you cards first.

TIP: UNGRATEFUL HORRORS

OFFBEAT BRIDE READER BRITNEY ALSO GOT LARGE CHECKS AS WED-ding gifts, and she brings up a great point: "I wanted to send out all the thank-yous for money before we deposited the checks, so that was good motivation to get them done quickly." This is impeccable advice. For monetary gifts, make sure the thank-yous are sent before you go to the bank and deposit the checks.

44. A ROSE BY ANY OTHER NAME

The conundrum of picking a last name

POOR ARIEL MEADOW FETZ. SHE NEVER STOOD A CHANCE, REALLY.
First and foremost, she was shot down by my second-generation
gender egalitarianism and the fact that I had a career built on my
given name. I also had to face up to Andreas's staunch, academic
feminism. Ariel Meadow Fetz was aborted, and the anti-choicers
didn't even get a chance to wave around bloody signs and protest.

"Mrs. Fetz" had a window of opportunity for a while, though.
Growing up, I'd always been one of those girls who practiced
writing her future married name. Ariel Meadow Beck, I wrote in
bubbled cursive in seventh grade, which later gave way to Ariel
Meadow Himmelstein, Ariel Meadow Harrison, Ariel Meadow
Lemire, Ariel Meadow Dunbar. By the time I got around to Ariel
Meadow Nordstrom at age seventeen, I was already starting to have
second thoughts. I sort of liked my birth name.

And, by the time I met Andreas at twenty-two, I had one fleeting
adolescent reflex of learning his name and thinking, Ariel Meadow
F—uck this shit. I'm Ariel Meadow Stallings. Regardless of who he
might be. Offbeat reader Leah said, "A rose by any other name may
smell as sweet, but me by another name? I can't imagine it!"

Another Offbeat Bride reader, Marjorie, also kept her name,
explaining that using her husband's last name simply wasn't an option: "We're feminists, but the fun kind. Not the type who sing
dirgey folk songs and talk about our 'personhood,' the type who
really do try to be fair to each other while maintaining a sense of
humor and respect for difference."

Then again, six years later, when Andreas and I got engaged, I did play around with various ideas. Should we hyphenate? I knew lots of hyphenated kids growing up, and I always felt concern for them and their mouthfuls of twelve-syllable names. Maybe, I thought, we could combine our names. What about "Fetzlings"? It sounded completely ridiculous, like a distant relative of the Tribbles from *Star Trek*.

Then there was my odd idea of swapping first names. One morning I got a funny phone call from a telemarketer. "Is this the Andreas household?" the woman asked, suggesting that they'd gotten Andreas's first and last names flipped. Then I thought, How great would it be to take your spouse's first name as your last name? He would be Andreas Tillman Ariel, and I would be Ariel Meadow Andreas. It made a strange, deranged sense. There was a bit of ownership there.

Even that quickly discarded solution, however, wouldn't solve the ultimate offbeat bride-and-future-parent's dilemma: What about the kids? Strangely, Andreas and I are without models in this arena: despite the fact that both our mothers are feminists, we both have our fathers' last names. Our solution was to give our son, Tavi, born in 2009, both our last names. So he's got two last names, with no hyphen. It's a mouthful but it works.

Some Offbeat Brides don't keep their names

The assumption about Offbeat Brides is that of course we'll keep our names, and we'll be proud of it! Like most assumptions, it's frequently wrong. Sometimes, brides told me, politics be damned, their husband's last name just sounds better. Offbeat reader Jen remembers, "The first time I got married, I took my husband's last name . . . because, to tell the truth, he just had a cooler last name than the one I grew up with." A reader named Stacy had similar sentiments, saying, "Honestly, I don't really care. I was never a big fan of my last name, and I wasn't sad to see it go."

This laissez-faire attitude is surprisingly common when it comes to last names. Amy told me that changing her name was no big deal, because, "I have a dozen names—pet names, nicknames, internet handles, and I am known by different names in different countries." Offbeat reader Lisa Marie had a similar attitude, saying that she chose to take her husband's name in part because "my name never mattered much to me—I'm not even very attached to my first name and would be fine changing that as well. Call me what you will; I know who I am."

Other new brides see the choice not as a political issue but as one of family choice. Offbeat reader Amy might not have cared so much about her last name, but she wanted to show "we were a family and not just some cohabiting group of strangers." Another reader put it in a sort of sports paradigm, explaining that she wanted her family to have a "team name."

Some couples address the "team name" conundrum by compromising on a new common last (or even middle) name. After long political discussions, Offbeat Bride reader Maria and her husband planned to legally adopt a new shared middle name. "Except," she remembers, "we never actually did it. Inertia overcame us, and neither of us has changed our name one bit." She does, however, take solace in being able to explain to people who ask that "neither of us changed our name." She told me the answer pleases her because, as she said, "it implicitly questions the assumption that only women would change their name upon marriage."

The increasingly popular option of both spouses taking a new common name is a great idea—unless one or both partners have professional recognition associated with their given names. Offbeat reader Susan recounted, "Some good friends of ours chose a whole new last name, which I think is such a great, meet-in-the-middle option . . . but I'm a writer and have published under my own name for years. In a practical (and professional) sense, it would be more or less starting over from scratch to suddenly reappear as Susan Anythingelse. My husband has made films and published under his last name, too, so it was completely impractical for us to both change to something else and both lose all name recognition in our fields."

Based on my observations, about half the brides I hear from opt to keep their own names, many for the same reasons I did, which is to say the reasons you'd expect—but sometimes reasons you wouldn't. Offbeat reader Leah laughed, "My husband wasn't interested in changing his name, and hell if I would if he wasn't! My name isn't a character I've been playing for thirty-two years; it's me."

That said, women who keep their names need to be prepared for the family members who refuse to acknowledge it. You can get your panties in a bunch, or you can take reader Phyllis's approach: "Many of our more old-fashioned family members assume I have my husband's last name. I only know that because of the cards that come in the mail for 'Mrs. Him.' I think it's cute! Even if it's a check, the bank doesn't seem to care—so why should I? At least they're thinking of me."

Then again, women who take their husband's name must also acknowledge that they'll get grief for opting for the more traditional option. Amy told me, "Definitely the hardest thing about changing my name was facing down the feminist police, who sometimes assume I'm a slave to men just because I don't really care what my last name is. But I know I'm still a radical feminist, and that's what matters in the end."

One reader summarized the issue when she said, "No matter what you do, you will get grief from someone who did the opposite. It is a choice that everyone faces when they get married, and everyone has a lifetime of experience that shapes that choice.

A very good friend (who calls herself a feminist) told me, upon finding out that I changed my name, that it was the twent-first century, and I was allowed to keep my last name if I wanted to—as if I wasn't aware that it was an option! Sometimes I feel a little defensive about changing my name, as I imagine the name-keepers feel as well. I have a very equitable relationship with my husband, and I'd hate to think that people assume otherwise just because I changed my name."

I'm happy that I chose to keep my birth name. That said, despite all my efforts, Ariel Meadow Fetz lives on. She's a phantom floating around our house, drifting from room to room. I can't see her, but I know she's here: she gets ass-loads of junk mail.

45. POSTWEDDIN' DEPRESSION

How to cope once the tiara is put into storage

FOR THOSE WHO ARE A LITTLE HESITANT TO ADOPT THE BRIDENTITY TO begin with, the transition out of wedding mode tends to be a little easier . . . but there's still some letdown, even if you lead a fulfilling life packed with adventure and excitement. Offbeat reader Irene confessed to feeling "relieved, but empty at the same time. I was surprised I felt that way; wishing I could have my wedding day back. I remember thinking, 'I love my marriage . . . but I miss my wedding.'"

The Offbeat Brides I spoke to who reported post-wedding slumps mostly blamed hangovers and physical exhaustion, combined with a readiness to get back to their lives. Offbeat reader Mary cut her honeymoon short after a wave of post-wedding exhaustion hit her. "We were traveling all along the East Coast, and a point came when we just felt like going home. We ended up canceling some of our plans and driving home two days early. It was like the high we were on from the wedding and the excitement of being husband and wife finally just crashed down on us, and we were ready to go back to normal life."

There's also just a totally understandable transition period. One Offbeat Bride reader recounted, "We came back from our honeymoon on a Friday or Saturday, and I remember walking around almost in a daze. No big responsibilities! No calls to make! It took a while to feel normal again."

Some people, however, find themselves having some dark thoughts. Some even admit to being scathingly jealous of newly engaged couples, resentful that they might somehow have a better wedding. This is a dangerous path to walk down, and if you sense these feelings coming up, it's advisable that you turn your attention away from the engaged couple (who've done nothing wrong) and weddings as a whole, and instead focus yourself on planning a weekend road trip with a group of friends, founding a nonprofit, picking up a new sport, or getting yourself invested in some other new, healthy, productive endeavor. Weddings are not competitions, and if, in your post-wedded slump, you find yourself slipping into the mind frame of trying to compare your wedding to others (past or future), do whatever you can to recalibrate your emotions. Seriously. You'll be doing yourself and women everywhere a favor.

Then again, mostly it's just a relief when the wedding is over. I may be an attention whore, but it was a huge release to have the pressure of planning a wedding off my project plate.

This sentiment has been echoed again and again by Offbeat Bride readers. One recounted, "It was nice to have the world slow down again! I was really happy to get back to regular life and didn't miss the wedding planning at all. I had just finished school, and so my focus shifted to finding a job and getting my career going."

My theory is that many nontraditional brides skip the stereotypical post-wedding slump because many of us live action-packed lives and have lots of other ways to get attention and validation. One bride who's active in theater laughed, "I feel like I'm the center of attention quite enough, thank you." Another chimed in, "I enjoyed the attention of the wedding but quickly found other ways of getting attention—I've been a ham all my life."

TIP: *REALLY* MISS WEDDINGS? HELP YOUR FRIENDS!

THERE ARE SOME BRIDES WHO REALLY CAN'T LET GO OF WEDDINGS, and this is a good thing for their friends. Offbeat reader Maria explained it this way:

>>>

After spending entirely too much time learning about wedding traditions (real and as imagined by the wedding-industrial complex), wedding-budgeting techniques, alternatives to weddings, alternatives to wedding traditions—and bombarding myself and my fiancé with all possible options—I returned to "civilian life" with a wonderful husband, a subtly altered relationship, fantastic memories, and an overabundance of wedding knowledge. Want to save money on photographs? I know just the right keyword combinations to use on Craigslist to find a talented up-and-comer. Want to do your own flowers? Not only have I done so, I can point you at resources to learn how to do it yourself, and I know where you can find flowers untainted by pesticides or unfair labor conditions. Not sure you want to have flowers? I can point you to all sorts of alternate traditions, including carrying prayer books and using photographs as centerpieces. Not sure you want to have a wedding? I can validate your decision with otherwise useless trivia about how the white wedding has been created and marketed over the past century.

In other words, those who can no longer do weddings must teach weddings. Or write books about them. . . .

46. GETTING WIFED

The answer to the question,
"So, how's married life?"

HOW HAVE THINGS CHANGED NOW THAT YOU'RE MARRIED? YOU GET cheaper car insurance; it's easier for authority figures to understand the nature of your relationship. Basically, those changes reflect all the reasons we chose to get married. We wanted to get insurance and finances—we got it. We wanted to have a party—we had one. The ripples kept spreading after the event; the circle kept getting bigger. Family members were introduced. Our community was solid. The reception-night hook-ups tried each other on for a while.

Ideally, there's a match between a couple's motivations for marrying and the resulting post-wedding changes. Getting engaged should signify that you and your partner's ideas about marriage are aligned, your expectations are matched. Perhaps you both want to get married because, for the two of you, that means you'll never leave the house alone again. Perhaps the two of you got married because, in your world, married couples can have kinkier, wilder, more trusting sex.

If these expectations are shared, things can be delightful. You got married because you wanted to share your love of building hamster tubes all over your house? Awesome! Then again, unmatched expectations can be resentments waiting to happen, hiding behind assumptions and waiting for a nice tragic moment to hop out. If your expectations were something like "Marriage will improve my partner," you might be in for a big surprise. If both parties believe this to be true, they might be able to manifest it and both improve as people and make their assumptions a reality. But signing a piece of paper doesn't magically change people. Each of us has to make a choice to shift, and saying "I do" doesn't fix anything.

I suppose the key is to just make sure you and your partner agree on your expectations. I read an advice column once about a woman who let her husband stay out late during their engagement but snarked on the side that, well, once they got married, she sure as hell wasn't going to let him do that kind of stuff.

Can you imagine if she'd actually verbalized that to him? "Well, dear, I think that one of my expectations is that after we get married, I'm going to turn into a selfish, controlling person who doesn't like you spending time with your friends because it threatens me." I can't speak for the fiancé of this fabled woman (who may not really even exist or might be inside everyone), but I certainly wouldn't buy into that deal willingly.

Then again, there are some people who would buy into that just fine. It could work for them just right—maybe that guy's hungry for someone to tell him what to do, and he's just itching to get spanked later and play with power dynamics. If so, *rock!* That works out perfectly.

. . . At least initially. People change, after all, and divorce rates are remarkably high, even among self-aware, communicative people who go to therapy a lot and who think they know better than to fall into relationship traps. Even among queer folks. Even among people with open relationships. Even among people who have H. P. Lovecraft–themed wedding vows. Let us not forget ourselves and grow overconfident in our arbitrary status of "committed." Take no day together for granted.

The things that change and the things that stay the same

As much as I pay lip service to how "nothing changes after getting married," it's not completely true. Nothing changed in our relationship, but there were many changes in how people treated us. I was pulled over for speeding once, and when the officer saw that the car was registered in someone else's name, he gave me the eye.

"Who's Andreas Fetz?" he squinted at me.

"My husband," I answered. "I kept my name."

Now, if my answer had been that the car was borrowed from "my boyfriend," I think this cop would have given me grief. He looked like the type. Did my boyfriend know I'd taken his car? How long had I known this supposed boyfriend? Was this a guy I'd fucked out behind a bar the night before and then "borrowed" his car as he lay sleeping? We skipped all those questions with my answer. It was my husband's car. Of course I had permission to drive it. I didn't get the ticket. Who knows whether it really was because I'm married, but I have my suspicions.

As a married couple, our finances became a bit more shared. We kept separate checking accounts, but the money was perhaps a little more fluid between them. Then again, after so many years of living together, things were already pretty fluid.

Sadly, being married has also meant that I'm assumed to be complicit in the creepy, fucked-up gender dynamics that much of America seems to so enjoy. I was explaining to an insurance agent over the phone that my husband had lost a piece of paperwork, and she laughed conspiratorially and said, "Husbands are good at that kind of thing, aren't they?" Why, yes, they are! Just like wives are good at being passive-aggressive bitches who stay home and cook for the menfolk while secretly running the world via manipulation and conniving plots! That husband of mine, he just loves sports—but I prefer the soaps, myself!

Insert epic eye roll.

Offbeat reader Catherine described these projections as "being wifed." She explained that, after her wedding, "People stopped looking at me and put me in their 'wife box.' Frankly, I don't like people who have little categories like that. It says a lot about a person that they have rigid, stereotypical ideas about how other people should live their lives and are perfectly comfortable blurting out their offensive notions to a near-stranger."

I think most of us offbeat wives work with our spouses to redefine the institution of marriage. We work hard to question every role we're handed, every assumption that gets served up, day after day. It's exhausting sometimes, of course. Just as, in some ways, it'd be much easier to just have the damn template wedding, in many ways, it would be easier to live the more normal married life. The one where you walk through it without intention, without critical thought. Why is he holding the door open for you? Why are the Christmas cards addressed to "Mr. & Mrs. Him"? Why do people always ask the new wife about when the baby is coming—and never the husband?

It takes two, damn it

Hold on. That last one was just an example, but I have to rant for a moment. I know, I know, of course everyone wants to know when there's a baby coming. Happy couples of baby-making ages and social contract are positioned in the perfect culturally accepted procreation position. Here's the thing, though: people only asked me. Never ever Andreas.

Hey, world: making a baby takes two people. I am not somehow in charge of the decision just because I got the fallopian tubes. When I got asked (and trust me, I got asked a lot), my answer was always, "Ask Andreas." Come on, people! Let's be egalitarian with the procreative harassment! Harass the owner of the vas deferens too!

Then there's the assumption that, now that we're married, we'll only spend time with each other.

I realize that, even among offbeat types, many people get married and stop hanging out with other people. I do not understand this. I know that it's instinctual to pair-bond, but geez, does that mean you can't hang out with anyone else? That your spouse suddenly has to fill the roles of lover, roommate, confidant, business partner, friend, and everything else? Ack, the pressure. I'm so glad that Andreas and I have friends whom we hang out with separately. Why would I want to be there while he's playing foosball until 6 A.M.? Boring! Why would he want to be there while I'm smoking and gossiping with my gay boyfriend? Ugh, how tedious!

We do not function as a unit. We're two people in a relationship, not one person with two heads. Marriage was not some sort of elective conjoined twin surgery.

EPILOGUE

The wedding that never ends

AND SO, THIS IS WHERE THE PARTICULAR BOOK ENDS. BUT OF COURSE, life just kept on happening. In fact, our wedding was so much fun that we decided to do it every year for almost a decade.

Okay, okay, not really—but sort of. I sure as hell couldn't deal with all the spreadsheets and conflict mediation and humanure essays year after year, but we did have an annual campout in the meadow on my mom's property every summer for almost a decade after our wedding. We called it Meadowfabulous, and it wasn't really an anniversary party . . . it was more like we condensed the wedding down to our favorite parts: camping, dancing, forests, freaks.

The fact that we wanted to keep doing it every year suggests that if our goal was to throw a wedding that was mostly just a fun party, we succeeded. Whew! Plus, the summer campout felt like a way to renew our vows to our community of beloved friends and family over and over, so they knew how much we loved them.

What came next? Well, in the years after my 2004 wedding, I went on to buy a home, build a business, and have a child. Then in 2015, my life fell apart and I got to rebuild myself from the ground up. . . . It was awful and oddly wonderful, but that particular shit-show is a different story for a different book.

Wherever your aisle may take you next, here's hoping that it kicks ass.

ACKNOWLEDGMENTS

First and foremost, I am indebted to BoldFace Books, an imaginary publishing house that existed at Columbia University's Graduate School of Journalism for about ten days in 2004—just long enough for some Columbia Publishing Course students to come up with the initial idea that ultimately became the book in your hands.

My wedding (and therefore *Offbeat Bride*) would never have been possible without the hours, days, weeks, and months of help from family and friends. Hopefully this book is the 288-page thank-you card each of them deserves for all their hard work. A very special thanks also to my family and friends for allowing me to write about them.

Endless love and appreciation also go to the bridal lab rats who acted as my initial book research pool in 2005, and then the thousands of offbeatbride.com readers who have shared their stories online with me in years since. My contributors have always managed to amaze and inspire me with their voices and insight. Some of their names were changed for this book, but none of their ideas were watered down.

Thanks also to my crew of literati associates—to Terra Chalberg, for her tough love when I needed it; Michelle Goodman, for her commiseration and support; my current editor, Laura, at Seal Press who believed in me when I desperately needed to feel like I had someone in my corner.

Enormous gratitude to the Offbeat Empire LLC staff who continue to do the daily work of keeping offbeatbride.com updated and awesome for all the newly engaged beloveds who swing by our corner of the internet. And a huge shout-out to Caroline Diezyn, the longtime copyeditor at the Offbeat Empire, whose work contributed greatly to this third edition of the book.

Most importantly, thanks to all my cherished readers. In the years since *Offbeat Bride* was first published by Seal Press, 50 million of you have been a part of my work via the Offbeat Empire's websites and the three editions of this book. You have gifted me with the ability to support my family doing the work I love. If you are reading these words, then you are right here close with me in my heart. Thank you.

ABOUT THE AUTHOR

JENNY JIMENEZ

ARIEL MEADOW STALLINGS LIKES to poke at the soft places of overlap between culture, identity, relationships, and personal development. She got her start in the mid-1990s editing a rave magazine, graduated from the Columbia Publishing Course in 2001, and then spent most of the '00s in the corporate trenches as a copywriter for the *Seattle Times*, Microsoft, and Amazon. Since 2007, she has focused her work on managing her bootstrapped digital media company, the Offbeat Empire LLC. She lives in Seattle with her son, and if she's not reading or writing books, chances are good that she's dancing or happy-crying.